Gender Identity and Gender Relations Redefined

Stephanie Bernhard

Gender Identity and Gender Relations Redefined

Muller's and Grafton's Female Countertradition to Hard-Boiled Detective Fiction

 J.B. METZLER

Stephanie Bernhard
American Studies
Universität Mainz
Mainz, Germany

Zugleich Inauguraldissertation zur Erlangung des Akademischen Grades eines Dr. phil., vorgelegt dem Fachbereich 05—Philosophie und Philologie der Johannes Gutenberg-Universität Mainz.
Referent: apl. Prof. Dr. Manfred Siebald
Korreferentin: Univ.- Prof. Dr. Mita Banerjee
Tag des Prüfungskolloquiums: 05.02.2024

ISBN 978-3-662-69866-2   ISBN 978-3-662-69867-9 (eBook)
https://doi.org/10.1007/978-3-662-69867-9

© The Editor(s) (if applicable) and The Author(s), under exclusive license to Springer-Verlag GmbH, DE, part of Springer Nature 2024

This work is subject to copyright. All rights are solely and exclusively licensed by the Publisher, whether the whole or part of the material is concerned, specifically the rights of translation, reprinting, reuse of illustrations, recitation, broadcasting, reproduction on microfilms or in any other physical way, and transmission or information storage and retrieval, electronic adaptation, computer software, or by similar or dissimilar methodology now known or hereafter developed.
The use of general descriptive names, registered names, trademarks, service marks, etc. in this publication does not imply, even in the absence of a specific statement, that such names are exempt from the relevant protective laws and regulations and therefore free for general use.
The publisher, the authors and the editors are safe to assume that the advice and information in this book are believed to be true and accurate at the date of publication. Neither the publisher nor the authors or the editors give a warranty, expressed or implied, with respect to the material contained herein or for any errors or omissions that may have been made. The publisher remains neutral with regard to jurisdictional claims in published maps and institutional affiliations.

This J.B. Metzler imprint is published by the registered company Springer-Verlag GmbH, DE, part of Springer Nature.
The registered company address is: Heidelberger Platz 3, 14197 Berlin, Germany

If disposing of this product, please recycle the paper.

Contents

1 **Introduction** 1
2 **Characteristics of Detective Fiction from Its Inception to the 1920s** 11
3 **The Golden Age of Detective Fiction in England** 15
4 **American Hard-Boiled Detective Fiction** 21
    4.1 Emergence of the New Formula 21
    4.2 Main Characteristics of the Hard-Boiled Style 23
        4.2.1 The New Type of Detective in an Innovative Setting 23
        4.2.2 Emerging Significance of Female Characters 26
    4.3 Dashiell Hammett 29
    4.4 Raymond Chandler 31
        4.4.1 *The Big Sleep* 33
            4.4.1.1 The Prototypical Hard-Boiled Detective 33
            4.4.1.2 The Deceptive *Femme Fatale* 37
    4.5 Further Developments 43
5 **Female Hard-Boiled Detective Fiction** 47
    5.1 Changing Gender Conception in Real Life 47
    5.2 A Variety of Female Detectives in the Late Twentieth Century 55
    5.3 Sara Paretsky 59
    5.4 Marcia Muller 62
        5.4.1 *Edwin of the Iron Shoes* 63

		5.4.1.1	The Innovative Female Private Investigator	63
		5.4.1.2	The Stubborn Male Main Character	71
		5.4.1.3	A Variety of Minor Characters	79
	5.4.2	*The Dangerous Hour*		83
		5.4.2.1	The Mature Female Detective	83
		5.4.2.2	Rewarding Partnership and Marriage	92
	5.4.3	*The Color of Fear*		95
		5.4.3.1	The Female Detective and Her Private and Professional Partner	95
		5.4.3.2	Remaining Gender Conflicts	98
5.5	Sue Grafton			100
	5.5.1	*"A" Is for Alibi*		102
		5.5.1.1	The Self-Sufficient Woman Detective	102
		5.5.1.2	The Deceptive *Homme Fatal*	107
		5.5.1.3	Diverse Male Side Characters	113
	5.5.2	*"O" Is for Outlaw*		114
		5.5.2.1	The Nonconformist Detective	114
		5.5.2.2	Her Failed Marriage	120
		5.5.2.3	Further Troubled and Unequal Relations	123
	5.5.3	*"Y" Is for Yesterday*		125
		5.5.3.1	The Imperturbable Detective	125
		5.5.3.2	The Male Ripper	130
		5.5.3.3	Various Lifestyles of Modern Women	133
5.6	Muller's and Grafton's Innovations Compared to Their Forerunners			135
	5.6.1	Characteristics of the Female Detectives		135
	5.6.2	Various Lifestyles and Qualities of Female and Male Characters		140
	5.6.3	Social Concerns Beyond Gender		143

6 Conclusion ... 145

Works Cited ... 155

Introduction

Detective fiction addresses the human concern that the social order, which enables our society to function, might be disturbed. The works present criminal offences that violate shared norms and values and endanger social cohesion. These crimes lead to suspenseful riddles with surprising turns that require talented detectives who decipher clues and solve the puzzles. This plot construction allows readers to gain insights into the dark sides of life and to participate in the restoration of order from the comfort of home. Detective fiction raises the hope that injustice is just a temporary condition and that good finally triumphs over evil.

Within this framework of the criminal act and its detection, the genre is versatile, and it constantly changes, taking inspiration, for its modified characters and themes, from contemporary life. Thus, detective fiction is a source of information on social situations at different times, and it has always been popular. However, although practitioners such as Edgar Allan Poe (1809–1849), Arthur Conan Doyle (1859–1930), Agatha Christie (1890–1976), Dorothy L. Sayers (1893–1957), Dashiell Hammett (1894–1961), and Raymond Chandler (1888–1959) had been widely read, the canon of American literature did not include their works up to a certain point in time.

This canon was brought into being at the end of the eighteenth century and is a corpus of literary texts considered valuable to American culture because they are the outcome of historically and culturally fluctuating interpretations. Up until the 1960s, the literary canon was restricted concerning the literary genres allowed, as well as with respect to the authors' backgrounds. Scholars viewed popular literature negatively, just like works written by women or ethnic minorities. In the late 1960s, this view began to change, and critics demanded an adequate

© The Author(s), under exclusive license to Springer-Verlag GmbH, DE, part of Springer Nature 2024
S. Bernhard, *Gender Identity and Gender Relations Redefined*,
https://doi.org/10.1007/978-3-662-69867-9_1

consideration of America's literary diversity and cultural plurality in the country's literary canon. Harold Bloom finally realized this with *The Western Canon* in 1994, in which he discusses English language authors he considers as central to the canon (cf. Bloom).

Concerning the popular genre of detective fiction, scholars finally revalued its literary standing and realized, not only because numerous writers of successful mysteries have been academics, that "[t]he link between scholarship and detective fiction has long been established" (cf. Winks, Foreword ix). Jerome H. Delamater and Ruth Prigozy, in their *Theory and Practice of Classic Detective Fiction*, rightly emphasize the significance of the works as objects of theoretical study. They claim that exploring the nature of the genre, its audience, and its relationship to other literary forms has become almost as important as the writing of detective fiction itself (cf. 1).

This becomes visible in Dorothy L. Sayers's introduction to *Great Short Stories of Detection, Mystery and Horror*, in which she argues that the rules of the detective form are similar to the highly estimated Aristotelian patterns (cf. 37). Similarly, Robin W. Winks emphasizes the sophisticated methods of analysis that writers of detective fiction use, such as "[d]eductive logic, inductive reasoning, close textual analysis, the interrogation of evidence, the search for incongruities, patterns, and causal relationships." Winks asserts that the methods listed above are exactly those that scholars employ in the fields of literary criticism, philosophy, philology, and history (cf. Foreword ix).

John G. Cawelti argues further that the methodical procedure of the genre, namely intentionally deceiving the reader by playing with complex hints and keeping the truth hidden, influenced major American modernist and postmodernist writers, such as Vladimir Nabokov (1899–1977) and William Faulkner (1897–1962) and thus, it can be considered an aspect of serious literature (cf. "Canonization" 6–13).

Apart from its methods, the themes of detective fiction are of general interest. The works often deal more with various psychological and social issues, which readers can relate to, than with the actual crime solving. Howard Haycraft claims that hard-boiled detective novels, for instance, are "character studies of close to top rank in their own right" (171). Therefore, when looking at recent accounts and the number of reprints of classical detective novels, it is obvious that these texts are now part of cultural memory.

Today, it is not only unthinkable to consider American literature without popular genres such as detective fiction, but also without various works by women and writers of color. After these former minority groups had been granted more rights, in the late 1960s, critics of the canon referred to a new liberal American

1 Introduction

self-conception based on sexual and racial pluralism, and meanwhile the canon includes a great number of female and ethnic minority writers, also including the combination of the two attributes, for instance, Toni Morrison (1931–2019).

Despite this progress, female authorship does not guarantee an increased gender awareness, let alone a pioneering approach. In addition, as scholar Maggie Humm rightly claims, "[w]omen-centered detective fiction is not in and of itself progressive" (cf. 237). And indeed, even if there were female protagonists from the 1920s onwards, the authors did not yet present them as liberated women, as British author Agatha Christie's domestic amateur detective Miss Marple proves.

Finally, following the valorization of women in real life, achieved by the feminist movement, an increasing number of female authors consciously introduced independent women detectives, which was a great advancement. Until the beginning of the twentieth century, both sexes[1] were rather stereotyped, and women were merely victims or minor additions to the male heroes. With American hard-boiled detective novels from the 1920s onwards, presenting tough male heroes, female characters gained in importance, but they were portrayed in a negative manner, posing potential threats to the detectives. Since the 1980s, with the emergence of American female hard-boiled detective fiction, the protagonists have even been professionals who are tough and successful in their work.

In this context, Cawelti rightly argues that "[s]ome of the more significant recent developments in writing by women and minorities have emerged from the detective story tradition." He further claims that "the detective story has become a genre in which writers explore new social values and definitions and push against the traditional boundaries of gender and race to play imaginatively with new kinds of social character and human relations." Thus, the detective genre contains a quest "for greater equality among different regional, ethnic, and gender groups" (cf. "Canonization" 5–13).

For all these reasons, both the detective genre and its practitioners, female as well as male, now receive serious treatment from literary scholars. In the context of this study, which focuses on gender identity and gender relations in hard-boiled works, it would lead too far to mention the scientific discourses of Poe, Conan Doyle, and the English writers of the Golden Age of detective fiction.[2] Still, it is

---

[1] This dissertation does not consider the category of a third sex since it was only legally recognized after the analyzed novels had been written.

[2] It is worth mentioning that, in honor of the 125th anniversary of Christie's birthday, contemporary mystery writers elaborated on how she influenced their own writing (cf. Martin Doyle's "Agatha Christie: Genius or Hack? Crime Writers Pass Judgement and Pick Favorites."*The Irish Times*. 16 September, 2015). In addition, for recent revaluations of

noteworthy that Manfred Siebald explored the life, values, and progressive social commentaries on gender roles in the works of Dorothy L. Sayers in 2017.

There are many surveys of American detective fiction and the development of the genre in general, most currently by John G. Cawelti, Julian Symons, and Ulrich Suerbaum. Concerning American hard-boiled detective fiction, there are numerous appreciations of Hammett's and Chandler's works. Hans-Martin Braun and Robert I. Edenbaum wrote analyses of Hammett's novels in the 1970s, and Richard Layman and Frank MacShane concerned themselves with Hammett's life. Philip Durham reviewed Chandler's novels in the 1960s, and Scott Christianson analyzed his hard-boiled sentimentality in the 1990s. The hard-boiled formula of the 1920s and 1930s was analyzed again more broadly by Sean McCann in 2000 and by Leonard Cassuto in 2009.

In addition to reviews of works by male writers, the reevaluation of female detective fiction began in the 1980s, starting mainly with Carolyn Heilbrun's work on gender and detective fiction and Kathleen Gregory Klein's and Maureen T. Reddy's opposing views on the progressiveness of female hard-boiled detectives. Susan J. Leonardi specifically dealt with academic amateur detectives, and Patricia Craig and Mary Cadogan concentrated on feminist hard-boiled detectives in particular. Winter S. Elliott analyzed Muller's approach in a collection of essays edited by Alexander N. Howe and Christine A. Jackson in 2008. Scott Christianson discussed Grafton's feminist hard-boiled detectives, and Priscilla L. Walton looked at gender reversal in Grafton's works in 1995. Natalie Hevener Kaufman and Carol McGinnis Kay explored the world of Grafton's protagonist in 2000. Lastly, William R. Klink analyzed female hard-boiled detective novels and traced the influences of female authors back to male authors in the genre in 2014. Where expedient, this study will give a more elaborate literary discussion and critical appreciation of these contributions.

While many scholars have concentrated on the three female hard-boiled authors Marcia Muller, Sue Grafton, and Sara Paretsky as a group, the present study explores and compares only Muller's and Grafton's works in detail. While they differ from each other, they differ more from feminist authors such as Paretsky.

The present study is a literary one, and it employs a historical approach in that it tries to understand the texts in their temporal and spatial contexts. It does not only consider gender relations in the light of the unequal treatment of women by men, but it analyzes the depiction of women as well as men in the literary

---

Dorothy L. Sayers, see Victoria Stewart's work *Crime Writing in Interwar Britain: Fact and Fiction in the Golden Age*.

1 Introduction 5

texts, and traces how gender is socially constructed and evaluated in everyday life. Hence, the approach is in the tradition of gender studies, an interdisciplinary academic field that analyzes gender identity and gender relations. This includes women's studies, men's studies, lesbian and gay studies, as well as queer studies. In order to specify the method at hand, the following outline will explain the connection between these disciplines.

Women's studies, an academic field devoted to the analysis of the lives of women, relies on the theories and convictions of feminism as an object of scientific research. Feminism is a rather heterogenous social movement that includes various political activities and socio-critical studies. It is based on the belief that the social, political, economic, and symbolic discrimination of women in a patriarchal society reveals a systematic and ideological denial of gender equality. Feminism fights this unequal treatment of women and aims at improving their participation in all spheres of life (cf. Funk 71).

After the Seneca Falls Convention in the United States in 1848, the feminist cause was pursued in the late nineteenth and early twentieth centuries. It can be divided into four waves. First-wave feminism fought for women's right to vote, and second-wave feminism aimed at legal and social equality in general, having its peak in the 1960s and 1970s (cf. 49). From the 1990s onwards, active feminism lost some of its momentum. Third-wave feminism mainly concentrated on gender equality in business and politics as well as on the double burden of employment and domestic responsibilities (cf. Iannello 70–77). Since around 2010, fourth-wave feminism has reacted to the fact that, in the 2000s, economic enhancements for women have slowed. Moreover, it considers women's challenges in modern society, such as media-induced sexual harassment (cf. Chamberlain 111–115).

Recently, feminism has opened up new areas of activity, such as eco-feminism, which analyzes structural parallels between the ruthless exploitation of nature and the suppression of women (cf. Funk 52–53). Another current approach is intersectionality. It explores how different aspects of a person's social identity, for instance, gender, class, and race, but also new categories such as religion, disability, and age, create discrimination (cf. 55–56).

The second component of gender studies is men's studies, an academic field that originated in the 1980s. It analyzes what it means to be a man in modern society. The late emergence of a theory of male existence resulted from the fact that men were long viewed as the norm, while women were considered as the second sex. Over the years, however, men feared social discrimination and a loss of importance. Men's studies, as a result, focuses on the male gender identity, societal expectations of masculinity and male sexuality, and topics such as male health (cf. 56–61).

The formation of gender studies, a more recent instrument for the analysis of gender identity and gender relations, combines women's and men's studies. While women's studies rather one-sidedly concentrates on patriarchal structures that suppress women and on the consequences of this hierarchy, and men's studies basically does the opposite, gender studies analyzes the construction of gender in general and explores the social conditions that allow for certain gender roles. The focus is on the relationships between the social players, which is to say individuals, groups, and institutions, that reveal gender relations in everyday life (cf. 22–23). Moreover, the approach systematically develops the aforementioned disciplines further, including postmodernist concepts aiming at the deconstruction of traditional gender structures.

In the course of the twentieth century, Ferdinand de Saussure (1857–1913), Jean Baudrillard (1929–2007) and Jacques Derrida (1930–2004) constituted that there is a gulf between reality and representation and that a sign does not unambiguously correspond with the idea that it signifies (cf. 79–85). Such thoughts can be applied to gender. Poststructuralist feminist Judith Butler (*1956) argues that representations of reality, such as gender, and concepts such as femininity and masculinity, are socially and culturally constructed. Her work *Gender Trouble: Feminism and the Subversion of Identity*, published in 1990, is considered the constituent document of gender studies since it demands a reinterpretation of the interrelatedness of sex and gender and a methodology which questions such traditional convictions (cf. Funk 87).

In her approach, Butler disagrees with the assumption of gender essentialism that gender is a structural feature that attributes constant and invariable properties to all women and men. Notions of femininity, as feminist theorist Elizabeth Grosz stated in 1995, concern psychological characteristics, such as nurturance, empathy, support, modesty, and non-competitiveness. They can also imply social practices such as intuitiveness, emotional response, concern, and commitment to the family or to helping others in general (cf. 47–48). Male values of behavior, in contrast, are supposed to be assertion and toughness, and men are thought to focus on competition, material success, and self-realization (cf. Hofstede 6).

To Butler, generalizing female and male characteristics as if they were ahistorical is inadequate. She rather follows the constructivist assumption that gender is a subordinate and symbolic category that may change (cf. Funk 7–10). Butler aims at breaking the supposed link between sex and gender since, to her, the coherence of these categories is not natural, but performative. As a consequence,

1 Introduction

she uses gender as an independent category and detaches certain characteristics from the biological sex (85–93).

Butler even goes one step further in denying not only the connection between sex and gender, but also between sex and sexuality. Just as she claims that sex does not necessarily imply a certain gender, she negates that a specific sex determines sexual desires. Sexuality, to her, is just as performative and socially as well as culturally constructed as gender. Thus, sexual desire can be flexible, which is the fundamental idea of gay and lesbian studies. These fields of study originated in the USA in the 1970s and 1980s and offered homosexual approaches as alternative concepts to the supposedly heterosexual norm.

Queer studies extends this perspective and claims that any sexual as well as gender identity is performative and can be resisted. In her famous work *Undoing Gender*, published in 2004, Butler does not only discuss clear-cut relations between female and male, but she claims that sex is no less socially constructed than gender and sexuality. This idea was one of the foundations of queer theory. It is associated with such topics as intersex, gender ambiguity, and gender-corrective surgery, as well as cross-dressing (cf. Jenny L. Davis 4). For instance, the theory exemplifies gender's performative nature, using the example of drag queens and drag kings, people who use clothing and makeup to imitate and often exaggerate gender roles of the other sex. They create a confusion of the categories sex, gender, and sexuality, with the purpose of delineating any form of sexual categorization as means of suppression. Thus, gender identity dissolves into individual identity (cf. Funk 93–96).

This study relies on gender studies as a method of analysis for detective fiction, and it focuses on the depiction of female as well as male characters and their identities. Moreover, since it unveils sexism in male works and studies female works with a female framework, it makes use of Elaine Showalter's feminist critique and gynocriticism (cf. "Elaine Showalter"). The study's aim is to analyze the relations among social players and to understand the construction of gender, along with gender-specific social marginalization, in its social and historical context. Concerning the terminology, the study will refer to the categories of female and male, covering the biological sex, as "sex," and to the concepts of femininity and masculinity as "gender." The attributes introduced by Grosz and Hofstede will serve as the features traditionally associated with them. Homosexuality as well as queer dialogues will only play minor roles, but if there are characters who show such characteristics, the study will refer to them.

In detail, this study will analyze to what extent, on closer inspection, American hard-boiled detective fiction by and about professional women reinvents the formula and the gender perceptions of their male forerunners. It will be examined if the female authors replace the tough and stereotyped male detectives by female ones and fundamentally debase men in the way male writers debased women, or if the works alter the norms and ideologies of the male original. This would imply an adjustment in the depiction of female as well as male characteristics and roles toward a less stereotyped, but more authentic presentation.

The novels discussed in detail, treated in chronological order, are Raymond Chandler's *The Big Sleep* (1939), which will serve as a prototype for comparison with Marcia Muller's *Edwin of the Iron Shoes* (1977), *The Dangerous Hour* (2004), and *The Color of Fear* (2017) as well as Sue Grafton's *"A" Is for Alibi* (1982), *"O" Is for Outlaw* (1999), and *"Y" Is for Yesterday* (2017). The study will assess the prototypical male hard-boiled protagonist and the two female hard-boiled detectives and compare them in terms of their habits, social environments, attitudes, and their methods of detection. It will also analyze other female and male characters, especially concerning their lifestyles and their attitudes toward the opposite sex. If there are professional as well as private relations between women and men, they will be in the focus since they reveal the extent of practiced gender equality.

The selection of works within each series of Muller and Grafton includes early novels, later ones, and the latest ones, or rather, because of Grafton's recent death in 2017, her last work. This allows this study to finally determine her detective's development. All the selected novels focus on gender relations and offer a variety of female and male characters with different characteristics and lifestyles so that the development of gender issues over the years can be traced.

This literary analysis of course needs some context. Therefore, in a first step, an outline of the history of detective fiction and its main authors and characteristics up to the 1920s will present the standards of the genre, which are necessary for analyzing contemporary works. It will consider any existing female characters and their presentations. Due to the fact that the genre was mainly developed and refined in the USA and Great Britain, these two countries will be in the focus.

The following chapter will present the features of the Golden Age of detective fiction in England in the 1920s and 1930s. It will introduce the most prominent authors of the hard-boiled subgenre, along with their detectives. Since there are female detectives among them, the focus will be on the question to what extent women-centered works express progressive thoughts about gender roles.

In a third step, there will be an outline and a contextualization of the main characteristics of the American hard-boiled formula from the 1920s onwards. The discussion of a selected hard-boiled novel will illustrate the theoretical foundations, and its depiction of the male detective and the female minor characters as well as the relationships between women and men, will provide a

1 Introduction

basis for the assessment of differences in male and female hard-boiled works in this aspect. Subsequently, further developments within the subgenre will be delineated, including the depiction of female characters.

The main part of the study, following a presentation of the achievements of the feminist movement, will give an outline of the occurrence of female amateur detectives from the 1960s. Their works paved the way for female hard-boiled detectives by the 1980s. After an introduction to their method, selected works by Marcia Muller and Sue Grafton will be analyzed in terms of the characteristics and the developments of the female detectives, their relations to male characters, and the portrayal of female and male characters in general. The following summary will relate these female detectives to each other and finally compare them with their male predecessors. The conclusion will ultimately answer the central question and offer perspectives for further research.

Characteristics of Detective Fiction from Its Inception to the 1920s

The male hard-boiled private eye novel from the 1920s onwards as well as its female modification, emerging in the 1980s, are in the tradition of detective fiction in general, which came into being in America in the nineteenth century. Detective fiction is a unique genre that is distinct from crime fiction (cf. Symons 9). Although literature about crimes and murders can be found in early American literary history abundantly,[1] it was not mainly concerned with the clarification of evidence and cannot be equated with detective fiction. While crime fiction mainly concentrates on the crime itself and on the villain, detective fiction focuses on the rational problem-solving accomplished by a detective (cf. Hornung 181).

Moreover, up to the nineteenth century, crime was mostly solved by obliged confession. Exposure of a crime by a detective was a new method, based on the era of the Enlightenment and its focus on rational thinking (cf. Kaufman and McGinnis Kay 284). Most scholars agree that until well into the nineteenth century, there was no fiction in which a crime prompted an exciting riddle to be solved by a detective.[2] The American writer, poet, and literary critic Edgar Allan Poe (1809–1849) first developed this concept and hence, the invention and the rise of detective fiction are mostly accredited to him.

---

[1] Early literature, such as seventeenth-century New England execution sermons, shows that there has always been a general interest in reading and writing about criminals and crimes. The breaking of laws and subsequent consequences, for both offenders and their communities, have always been a matter of public concern (cf. Whitney 170).

[2] There is some historical research eager in its search for early puzzles and rational deduction in the very beginnings of recorded history, such as in Greek myths (cf. Symons 24).

© The Author(s), under exclusive license to Springer-Verlag GmbH, DE, part of Springer Nature 2024
S. Bernhard, *Gender Identity and Gender Relations Redefined*,
https://doi.org/10.1007/978-3-662-69867-9_2

Poe invented a noble, educated amateur detective, C. Auguste Dupin, and made him the protagonist of three stories written in the 1840s. His short story "The Murders in the Rue Morgue" is widely considered the first genuine detective story (cf. Panek 24). Poe's tales are narratives of the process of investigation, or tales of ratiocination, since he attached importance to the intellectual capacity of the detective and to precise observation.[3] He made Dupin observe situations critically and employ his rational faculties, in addition to his efficient intuition. The detective is clearly at the core of Poe's works. Apart from him, there is his companion, as well as the villain and some minor characters. Women are not in the center of attention. They are usually victims and their perspectives are not made subjects of discussion. In "The Murders in the Rue Morgue," for example, Madame L'Espanaye and her daughter have been killed and only trigger the case (cf. 126).

Apart from the conception of the character of the detective, Poe employed several characteristics which contemporary detective fiction, female as well as male, still makes use of. Stephen Rachman hints at "the metropolitan setting,... the vain, befuddled law enforcement official, the wronged suspect, the confession, [and] the cleverly convoluted solution." Therefore, according to Rachman, Poe has "given the form its initial shape [and] created its first great detective" (17). In addition, Poe offered his readers a fictional representation of the world by setting the action in a modern environment. He dealt with, at the time, newly emerging issues relating to modern cities such as police institutions.[4]

Many successive writers adopted the characteristics Poe developed for the detective story. Hence, his writing does not only exist as literature, but also as a point of reference for contemporary writers and literary critics. In reviewing Poe's influence on detective fiction, T. J. Binyon claims that "[i]n the century and a half since Dupin first appeared in print, the detective story has changed very little in essence." He explains that it has become more complex and possibly more sophisticated, but it is true "it has avoided all the vagaries of literary fashion, and the principles laid down in Poe's works are still as valid as they were then" (132).

---

[3] The story "The Purloined Letter" from 1844, for instance, deals with people who overlook evidence, namely a letter. The narrator points at the consequences of inaccurate speculation by highlighting their resulting failure. He illustrates that the most unlikely solution might at times be the correct one and that therefore, detailed observation is crucial (cf. Poe, "The Purloined Letter" 354–356).

[4] "The Murders in the Rue Morgue," for instance, is set in the urban every-day life of the metropolis Paris, one of the first cities to establish institutions of policing (cf. Poe, "The Murders in the Rue Morgue" 121; Panek 26).

2 Characteristics of Detective Fiction from Its Inception ...

After Poe, in America, some female writers from the 1860s onwards integrated his method into their tales about women's experiences. Catherine Ross Nickerson calls this subgenre "domestic detective fiction" because it combines elements of sensationalist papers, popular nonfiction crime stories, and the domestic novel. It also uses Gothic elements that became popular with Harriet Beecher Stowe (1811–1896), Louisa May Alcott (1832–1888), and Charlotte Brontë (1816–1855). Nickerson names Metta Victoria Fuller Victor (1831–1885), Pauline Hopkins (1859–1930), Anna Katherine Green (1846–1935), and Mary Roberts Rinehart (1876–1958) as major writers of this subgenre of domestic detective fiction (cf. 29). They portrayed female detectives, mostly spinsters but still within a domestic sphere. Thus, their works were not progressive concerning the depiction of women.

At around the same time, in Great Britain, there were the sensation writers. William Wilkie Collins (1824–1889) was the most famous author of this group, combining romantic tales with realistic criminal biographies and already hinting at the unequal position of married women in law at the time (cf. Panek 48).

After them, Scottish physician and writer Arthur Conan Doyle (1859–1930) created Sherlock Holmes, arguably the most famous of all fictional detectives. Holmes occurred in four novels and fifty-six short stories, which were written between 1887 and 1927. His stories appeared in popular illustrated magazines, became immensely successful, and marked the beginning of the detective story as a continuing popular literary form (cf. Panek 79).

The character of Holmes is famous for his intellectual mastery. He draws large conclusions from the smallest observations. Moreover, he is skilled in many fields such as literature and philosophy (cf. 82). Holmes operates in the closed social community of upper-middle-class English villages and Conan Doyle only focused on few characters in his works. The stories are mostly narrated by Holmes's friend, assistant, and biographer, Dr. John H. Watson, and concentrate on Holmes, Watson, the client, and the culprit. The focus is on detection. Women are rarely in the focus of the novels, and if they are, they usually serve the function to give further information on the cases. In "A Scandal in Bohemia," however, there is Irene Adler, a woman who outwits Holmes. The detective appreciates her skills, but Irene seems to be an exception among women at the time, and so the text does not make a progressive statement about women in general (cf. 37).

It is obvious that Conan Doyle was influenced by the style of Poe's detective Dupin since he borrowed the narrative technique and continued Dupin's method of logical reasoning and of interpreting clues.[5] However, Conan Doyle did not

---

[5] For a detailed analysis of Poe's influence on Conan Doyle, see Panek 80–83.

deal with public topics as much as Poe did. He offered occasional connections to scientific criminology, which was developing at the time (cf. Panek 88), but he mainly stuck to the plot and to the aim of providing clever and moral entertainment. The fact that the detective restores the order that has temporarily been challenged by a crime makes the novels comforting for the reader. When Conan Doyle quit writing Holmes stories, dozens of British people were inspired by his creation and became writers of detective fiction.

Most of them presented male detectives, but two of them, James Redding Ware (1832–1909), writing under the pseudonym Andrew Forrester, and William Stephens Hayward (1835–1870), created one female detective each. However, the worldviews of the characters were not in the focus and they both switched to male detectives after that (cf. Klein, *The Woman Detective* 29). Further female detectives were designed by Matthias MacDonnell Bodkin (1850–1933) and Catherine Louisa Pirkis (1841–1910). Their detectives were either young women, who solved cases while searching for a husband, or old spinsters. Hence, they did not reform traditional gender roles (cf. Klein 72–73).

In America, Anna Katherine Green (1846–1935) created two female detectives: Amelia Butterworth, an unmarried woman detective, and Violet Strange, a professional and quite independent detective, but in the end, she did not manage to challenge patriarchal supremacy (cf. Klein 75–78). None of these authors is famous today since they were overshadowed by Conan Doyle and the Golden Age writers before and after (cf. Panek 96).

3. The Golden Age of Detective Fiction in England

Various writers of the Golden Age of detective fiction[1] in England in the 1920s and 1930s took up Conan Doyle's form as a model, developed it further, and popularized it. They worked together closely and defined their goals and the fiction they wrote mainly in regular meetings of the so-called Detection Club. The club was formed—initiated by Anthony Berkeley (1893–1971)—in 1930 by a group of British mystery writers, including, amongst others, Agatha Christie (1890–1976), Dorothy L. Sayers (1893–1957), Margery Allingham (1904–1966), Ronald Knox (1888–1957), Gilbert Keith Chesterton (1874–1936), Freeman Wills Crofts (1879–1957), and R. Austin Freeman (1862–1943). They shared ideas, wrote some collaborative works, and established rules for writing detective novels that were supposed to enable the reader to detect the guilty figures. For example, the criminal must be someone mentioned in the early parts of the story, but must not be anyone whose thoughts the reader has been allowed to follow (cf. Welton, first rule).

Willard Huntington Wright (1888–1939), who wrote under the pseudonym S. S. Van Dine and was one of few popular American authors that participated in the definable Golden Age movement at the time, also created a code of practice for writing detective fiction. He called it a "credo for the detective story" in his "Twenty Rules for Writing Detective Stories" in 1928. He declared, for instance,

---

[1] The term "Golden Age" was coined by Howard Haycraft in *Murder for Pleasure* as an appreciation of the improvement in style, the increased plausibility, and the emphasis on character achieved by writers at the time (cf. 158).

that all clues must be plainly stated so that the reader has the same chance to solve the case as the detective, who must find the culprit by logical deduction. Furthermore, he set the rule that there must be no coincidence and no love interest in the novels. He also defined the nature of the detective, since the different authors usually created their detectives on an individual basis so that they slightly differed from the others in their attitudes and skills.[2] The detective must not, for instance, turn out to be the culprit (cf. Van Dine 5–6).

In sum, the Golden Age writers mostly adhered to the basic features of the detective novel that had been developed by Poe and Conan Doyle. They did so in order not to disappoint readers' expectations. Nonetheless, they offered a refined style and became very self-confident. Along with creating a distinguished detective, they shifted the focus away from the crime and toward a portrayal of the manners of people and place. Some also added an individual tone to their novels by including serious considerations of moral, ethical, psychological, and social issues. By this, they made the genre attract a greater mass and a new kind of readers in the educated members of the middle class. The "Golden Ages of publishing and advertisement," as Panek calls the time (120), intensified the appeal of the genre. The British writers Agatha Christie, Dorothy L. Sayers and Margery Allingham mainly coined the genre,[3] and their approaches will be briefly outlined in the following.

Agatha Christie is now considered one of the most important figures of the Golden Age of the genre, although she was not as well appreciated in her own time. Back then, the fiction of her contemporaries Dorothy L. Sayers and Margery Allingham was perceived to be more demanding and trendsetting. Christie wrote seventy detective novels, one hundred and fifty short stories, and some drama. In the course of her writing career, she created several detectives, amongst whom her amateur detectives Hercule Poirot and Miss Marple are the most popular. They both are notable for their logic, justice, and morality (cf. Suerbaum 75–90).

---

[2] They did so because the most important identification mark of each author is the detective. Being the major voice in the novel, the detective figure testifies to the individual thoughts of the author, and the public's judgment of the novels chiefly focuses on the detective who links the different works of a series (cf. Suerbaum 103).

[3] Ngaio Marsh (1895–1982) was also an influential writer during the Golden Age. Originally from New Zealand, she lived for some years in England where most of her novels, featuring British detective Roderick Alleyn, are set. Less popular British Golden Age writers were Michael Innes (1906–1993) and Philip MacDonald (1900–1980). John Dickson Carr (1906–1977) and Ellery Queen (1905–1982) were American, but wrote in the style of the British Golden Age writers.

Poirot is a retired Belgian police officer who is a neat, wise, and experienced detective, also skilled in psychology. Miss Marple is an aged spinster with a good sense of humor, who often helps the police to solve difficult cases. Christie's works are clearly influenced by her upper-middle-class background and she wrote mysteries that were not concerned with sensitive issues outside the idyllic life in the countryside (cf. Fitzgibbon 40). She did not mention any current political crises, but the works create a comfortable world.[4]

Christie did not concentrate on just a few characters, but she depicted a whole community and introduced its members in an elaborate manner. This includes their moral attitudes, standing in the community, and relationships with each other. Hence, her aim was not only to detect the culprit and to reveal the sequence of events, but also to uncover what is really going on in the characters' minds. Thus, her works are novels of deduction, but they also deal with the motives of the criminals and their partly secret alliances with other characters.

This concentration on characters' inner lives allowed Christie to design complex detective stories, with everybody being suspicious at a certain point. Moreover, she created complex plots and gave the reader each piece of information at the right moment to build up the story. For these achievements, amongst others, Christie was given several awards (cf. Fitzgibbon 23). The fact that films and television series present her most famous characters Poirot and Miss Marple still today shows that her works are timeless and continue to appeal to contemporary readers.

Dorothy Leigh Sayers, better known as Dorothy L. Sayers, was a scholarly woman and also an essayist and literary critic. She, more than most of her contemporaries, depicted the social reality of the time in a particularly detailed manner, often concentrating on academic and religious issues. Sayers created Lord Peter Wimsey, an aristocratic amateur detective and the protagonist of ten novels and several short stories published from 1923 onwards. He is urbane, elegant, and educated in many fields such as history, music, chemistry, and gastronomy (cf. Symons 110). With this character, Sayers raised the detective story to the level of the novel of manners. Her works are high-quality riddles of detection and inform the readers about the aristocratic social life in England between the two World Wars and about people's concerns at the time, such as the relationship between science and faith or gender roles.

---

[4] Especially when she wrote her later works, *The Body in the Library*, for example, which was published in 1942, Christie did not make references to the precarious political and military situation (cf. Christie).

Some of the ideas expressed by Sayers's characters, especially by Harriet Deborah Vane, a mystery writer, are in line with progressive thinking. In *Gaudy Night*, the oppression of women at the time is a plot element and Harriet advocates women's education (cf. 169). Moreover, the protagonist repeatedly criticizes the fact that promising scholarly careers are extinguished by marriage (cf. 169–170), and so the ideal of the independent and working woman is presented. However, Harriet finally realizes that marriage with the right person is an enrichment, returns Lord Peter Wimsey's love (cf. 496), and marries him (cf. *Busman's Honeymoon* 6–7).

Nevertheless, as Manfred Siebald claims, Sayers combined a detective riddle with progressive commentaries on gender roles, albeit in a moderate way. He highlights that she advocated the equality of women and men as they are both humans, and she characterized people and their abilities in an individual, rather than in a class-related manner. According to Siebald, Sayers showed that each person, regardless of the sex, has individual preferences and skills and demanded that they should be allowed to exercise them (cf. 137–141). Such progressive thinking was unusual in the 1930s.

Margery Allingham wrote eighteen novels and more than twenty short stories, mostly featuring private detective Albert Campion. He is a Cambridge man and collector of fine arts. He sometimes appears more as an adventurer than a detective, and he successfully manages to operate in the nobility, on the one hand, and in the world of the criminal class, on the other. An important female character in the Campion series is elegant Lady Amanda Fitton, an aircraft designer with unusual mechanical skills (cf. Allingham 80), whom he ultimately marries. In her, Allingham clearly portrayed an extraordinary woman. While her early novels were rather light-hearted parodies with an adventurous detective, some of her later novels are serious character studies featuring a much more responsible investigator (cf. Panek 128).

In general, the Golden Age of detective fiction was mainly an era of women writers.[5] The creation of detective fiction gave them the chance to distance themselves from the supposedly typically female love romance at the end of the

---

[5] Among men, Ronald Knox and Gilbert Keith Chesterton were both famous writers as well as scholars. Knox created detective Miles Bredon and he used detective fiction to convey conservative, humanist values such as the significance of faith, family, and the Western tradition. He was commissioned, in 1929, to write the introduction to the anthology *Best Detective Stories of the Year* (1928). Chesterton is especially famous for his sophisticated Father Brown mysteries that portray complex situations. The novels of these two authors rather underlined traditional values and did not offer any space for the exploration of women's perceptions of the world.

3 The Golden Age of Detective Fiction in England

Victorian era and liberated them in terms of form. Although most of the female writers did not offer progressive feminist thoughts or a typically feminine perspective of the world, they did portray some extraordinary and skilled women, and they hinted at social ills impacting women's status in a male-ordered world. The implementation of such thoughts into an alternative lifestyle for women, however, first took place in detective novels of the 1980s. The Golden Age of the detective novel ended when some of the aforementioned authors stopped writing detective fiction and others turned to the thriller or placed emphasis on much more serious social issues after 1939 (cf. Panek 142).

ID# American Hard-Boiled Detective Fiction

4.1 Emergence of the New Formula

Few American authors, after Poe, contributed to detective fiction until the 1920s—the most prominent were Mary Roberts Rinehart, S. S. Van Dine, Ellery Queen, and John Dickson Carr. All the same, they did not create their own formula, but they mainly imitated and developed the conventions and the elegant style of the British writers. With the emergence of hard-boiled[1] detective fiction in the late 1920s, however, American writers created an innovative and fundamentally different subgenre. The founders of this style, most prominently Dashiell Hammett and Raymond Chandler, considered the traditional British form outdated and contrived and sought to create a new and more realistic style of detective fiction in contrast to the idealizing British one.[2] With this in mind, they broke with the gentility of the British authors and replaced their ordered world with a relentless account of urban American society and its crimes. Therefore, the hard-boiled detective could no longer be a wealthy amateur, but an ordinary, professional investigator who speaks the American vernacular and who works for a living.

---

[1] The term was reputedly coined by Dashiell Hammett in *Red Harvest* when Dinah Brand, the girlfriend of a local gangster, describes the protagonist, Continental Op, as a "fat, middle[-]aged, hard[-]boiled, pig[-]headed guy" to show his lack of emotional connection (cf. 107).

[2] Considering literary history, this is a reverse development. In contrast to early American authors such as Nathaniel Hawthorne (1804–1864), who wrote romances as a form of opposition to nineteenth-century British factual Victorian novels—for example Charles Dickens's (1812–1870) critical commentaries on poverty and crime—the American hard-boiled writers then aimed for an alternative and more realistic concept than the idealized British one.

© The Author(s), under exclusive license to Springer-Verlag GmbH, DE, part of Springer Nature 2024
S. Bernhard, *Gender Identity and Gender Relations Redefined*,
https://doi.org/10.1007/978-3-662-69867-9_4

In this manner, the hard-boiled authors created a clearly American subgenre that was received with great public interest. In retrospect, their fiction achieved a popularity that British Golden Age fiction never attained. An evident reason for the success of this hard-boiled style can be located in conditions of the time. The works were written and published at a time of great national insecurity and social disorder, their authors were inspired by this reality, and many readers had a great interest in the realistic depiction of prevailing social conditions in fiction.

The First World War created many economic and social problems for the United States, such as the unemployment of returning veterans and violent riots. The Progressive Movement, which lasted through the 1920s, partly brought about an improvement of conditions. Among other concerns, it tried to limit corruption and to prevent that economic power was held by a few untrustworthy magnates, since the public observed large corporations and business monopolies increasingly critically and wanted to see them disappear. However, their abolishment and the elimination of the discontent of many people was only partly achieved. The following economic boom of the 1920s, in which life in the United States was generally marked by prosperity and cultural progressivism, did not cover the whole society and had its downsides such as Prohibition and resulting smuggling and gang crime. As a consequence of organized crime, detective departments were newly created and urban police institutions slowly began to professionalize in the 1920s (cf. Prüfer 12–14).

The economic upswing eventually turned out negatively and led to inflation in the late 1920s, resulting in the Stock Market Crash of October 1929. A crisis in the American economy followed, increasing the unemployment rate. This was devastating for people's self-respect. Many struggled to meet their basic needs. These circumstances led to the Great Depression and to resentment of the masses. President Franklin D. Roosevelt (1882–1945) established the New Deal, a series of programs to counter the crisis, in 1933, but it took several years to end the problems and the social discontent.

Detective fiction at the time examined these prevailing social ills and offered unprecedented insights into the newly emerging detective departments, and it showed the police's poorly conceived, and sometimes corrupt, techniques. Above all, detective fiction portrayed a hero who fought corruption and crime. This was comforting for the readers (cf. 15–16).

Therefore, by the late 1920s, as Sean McCann phrases it, "the hard-boiled style ruled the pulp universe" (46) since hard-boiled detectives first appeared in pulp magazines that were descended from late-nineteenth-century dime novels.[3] In the following decades, the hard-boiled detectives became even more popular and some of them, such as Hammett's Sam Spade or Chandler's Philip Marlowe, were adapted for television and radio (cf. Cawelti, *Adventure* 139).

4.2 Main Characteristics of the Hard-Boiled Style

4.2.1 The New Type of Detective in an Innovative Setting

American authors of hard-boiled detective fiction do not portray a safe and isolated place any longer, and they go beyond the illustration of a single crime committed by a gentleman-like thief. Rather, crime is omnipresent and brutal. The milieus in which the novels are set are more than mere scenery for a murder. The places of crime are representative urban cities, mostly in the American West. The prevailing atmosphere in this modern urban environment is one of pessimism.

Thereby, hard-boiled authors establish new standards for realism and depict the pervasive corruption of society. The world is no longer quiet and picturesque like, for example, in Christie's novels, but the urban space is rapidly changing and disordered. Crime does not come as a surprise that temporarily disturbs beauty, but it is related to the existing violence and the misery of the Depression years.

In his famous theoretical essay "The Simple Art of Murder," Raymond Chandler describes how, just below the surface, the urban world is full of criminals and their conspiracies:

---

[3] Paperbound books which were mostly bought at newsstands. They started out as poor imitations of British fiction, but when they were in demand, publishers such as Beadle, Smith & Street, and Tousey employed numberless authors who introduced a large public to the concept of the detective and his adventures in the late nineteenth century. The detective story became part of a regular branch of cheap fiction in America and it featured all kinds of different, mostly private, detectives from the fireman to the preacher detective. Dime novels contributed to the shaping of the hard-boiled story since their detective continued in altered form (cf. Panek 145). Shortly before the first dime novel business collapsed, publishers initiated the pulp magazine. They printed on cheap paper, attracted people´s attention by creating colorful and sensational covers and printed advertisements. Each issue offered a complete novel, parts of serial novels, and short stories. From 1915 onwards, with the first detective pulp magazine, *Detective Story Monthly*, published by Smith & Street, the former dime novel series were replaced and pulp detective magazines were in demand (cf. 148–149).

The realist in murder writes of a world in which gangsters can rule nations and almost rule cities, in which hotels and apartment houses and celebrated restaurants are owned by men who made their money out of brothels, in which a screen star can be the fingerman for a mob, and the nice man down the hall is a boss of the numbers racket; a world where a judge with a cellar full of bootleg liquor can send a man to jail for having a pint in his pocket, where the mayor of your town may have condoned murder as an instrument of moneymaking, where no man can walk down a dark street in safety because law and order are things we talk about but refrain from practicing.... (58)

As the quote underlines, "[t]he prevailing corruption of American society, shown in the power of gangsters and their acceptance by many who were socially respectable, [and] the collapse of any respected code" (Symons 135) are prevailing aspects of the hard-boiled sleuth's daily life. In this context, Jochen Schmidt argues that Californian society, where many hard-boiled novels are set, is suitable because the contrast between rich and poor, out of which most conflicts arise, was more serious here than elsewhere in America in the 1920s (cf. 50).

Consequently, the hard-boiled detective has to do more than mere puzzle-solving in this environment, and he is faced with all its downsides. In the beginning of a novel, he is usually given a mission that seems easy at first sight, but it finally turns out to be complex. John G. Cawelti describes how an apparently harmless case often turns out to be a dangerous affair: "Everything changes its meaning: the initial mission turns out to be a smoke screen for another, more devious plot; the supposed victim turns out to be a villain; the lover ends up as the murderess and the faithful friend as a rotten betrayer;... and all the seemingly respectable and successful people turn out to be members of the gang" (146).

The American hard-boiled detective is a tough and ordinary man who comes from the lower middle class. Unlike earlier detectives, he is a professional who is driven by the necessities of his job. He is constantly moving and will not hesitate to make use of his muscular strength or of his gun. Hence, he is part of the dishonorable society and employs his familiarity with the corrupt underworld in order to reveal crimes. McCann explains that hard-boiled fiction — more than the detective's intelligence — "foreground[s] the detective's craft knowledge, his physical strength and skill" (46). Thus, according to Jan-Christoph Prüfer, the "crucial step in the Americanization of the detective as a fictional hero [is] taking the hero away from the bookshelves and putting him into the streets" (78).

It has been claimed that, in these streets, "Hercule Poirot would promptly be tossed into the river wearing concrete booties" (Kaufman and McGinnis Kay 288). The American hard-boiled detective, in contrast, is capable of coping in this surrounding. Due to his origin, his language is not nearly as exalted as that

4.2 Main Characteristics of the Hard-Boiled Style

of the British investigator. Moreover, he is no longer concerned about a dignified appearance, but he drinks, smokes, and acts violently. This allows him to navigate through the underworld easily.

Despite this, he is different from the rest of the corrupt society because he is a skilled and dedicated worker who is honorable and has a sense of morality. Cawelti argues that "the hard-boiled detective is a traditional man of virtue in an amoral and corrupt world. His toughness and cynicism form a protective coloration protecting the essence of his character, which is honorable and noble" (*Adventure* 152). The hard-boiled detective ultimately adheres to strict moral lines.

Richard Slotkin underlines this idea by defining the hard-boiled protagonist as a combination of outlaw and actual detective. He "has seen the underside of American democracy and capitalism and can tell the difference between law and justice, and he knows that society lives more by law than by justice. Yet he also embodies the politics of the police detective, the belief that we need order, some kind of code to live by" (99). Due to the combination of these two natures, the hard-boiled detective seems to act like the other outlaws at times, but he finally solves the cases in a righteous manner.

This ambivalent character of the detective is what Slotkin considers the main attraction of the hard-boiled novel. He argues that "[w]e are in love with authority, we know that on the one hand we need authority and hard lines of value, and on the other that authority is often corrupt and misdirected and that those hard lines of value are often blurry. The detective allows us to enjoy both of these features simultaneously, to play imaginatively at being both policeman and outlaw" (99–100).

Being more efficient than the police is, the detective is on unfriendly terms with them and works as a loner.[4] A lone man who tries to create meaning is not an innovative idea in America literary history.[5] What is more, according to Suerbaum, the detective's solo run reflects one of America's fundamental myths, namely that of a lonely, common man who is unprepared and not particularly privileged, but who manages to act as a respectable hero in a corrupt world when

---

[4] This contest between the hero and the police is as old as Poe.

[5] The lone individual who tries to create meaning in a complex world has been a dominant feature of American literature ever since. Transcendentalists, such as Ralph Waldo Emerson (1803–1882) and Henry David Thoreau (1817–1862), described the blessings of solitude and self-reliance in nineteenth-century literature. Many other American literary works of the twentieth century dealt with life in a world without guidance, and writers such as Stephen Crane (1871–1900) and Ernest Hemingway (1899–1961) showed the resulting alienation experienced by the individual.

legal institutions fail (cf. 129). Likewise, one has to consider that the hard-boiled novel developed alongside the cowboy story. This genre as well as World War I and its military combats might have had an influence on the construction of the detective as a lone fighter. John Scaggs views the hard-boiled subgenre as a translation of the romanticism of the lone Western frontier hero into a modern setting (cf. 57).

However, unlike the cowboy, who rides on horseback into the sunset after his completed mission, the detective will have to face the corrupt world repeatedly because despite his efforts, he cannot restore full order. This would be unrealistic in consideration of the disordered surrounding. Instead, he uncovers deceitful characters and solves single cases. However, according to Suerbaum, there is a "basic success ideology" (157). Even if the detective only restores a small amount of order in a corrupt world in which there is much more crime than just the murder he has solved, his victory is symbolic and raises hope.

Consequently, as McCann describes, "[t]he detective, who speaks the vernacular of the working-class city, is also its champion. Navigating the furthest corners of the metropolis, he ranges across its social and geographical terrain, tying the disparate features of the urban landscape into a legible map" (47). In doing so, the detective is regularly exposed to physical dangers, and he has to face moral and sexual challenges.

4.2.2 Emerging Significance of Female Characters

Women play an important role in American hard-boiled detective fiction. Because of their presence, the detective has to face sexual enticements, and he has emotional and sexual intercourse with some of them. Cawelti argues that "[t]he function of the woman in the hard-boiled formula then is not simply that of appropriate sexual consort to the dashing hero; she also poses certain basic challenges to the detective's physical and psychological security." He concludes that sex is "an object of pleasure, yet it also has a disturbing tendency to become a temptation, a trap, and a betrayal" (*Adventure* 153).

Hence, although women play a major role, Leonard Cassuto rightly points out that the style and worldview of the hard-boiled novels are "archetypically male" (4) in that they mostly reduce women to their sexual attractiveness. Moreover, the female characters in the novels are stereotyped as being dangerous and wanting to take advantage of men. They often turn out to be murderers or members of

4.2 Main Characteristics of the Hard-Boiled Style

the criminal gang and pose fatal threats to the detective. Apart from this typical so-called *femme fatale*,[6] the seductive and ominous female character of the hard-boiled novels, a minor female character is, in some novels, the detective's secretary. However, she is not a desirable woman or, to speak in Cawelti's terms, an appropriate sexual consort for the detective, but rather a respectful and undemanding support.[7] Hence, women in hard-boiled novels are either both tempting and dangerous young women or undesirable and obedient figures.

The increased importance of women in hard-boiled detective fiction can be ascribed to the fact that American women more and more called attention to themselves and their rights in the second half of the nineteenth and the early twentieth century. This movement is referred to as first-wave feminism. Up to that point, women were supposed to follow a lifestyle that implied the Victorian idea of the domestic woman who is solely dedicated to her family and home. Moreover, women were not allowed to own property, had no legal rights to their own children, no right to vote, and no access to education, skilled work or independent social status. In addition, they were prevented from taking part in discussions about politics and power (cf. Bouchier 11–12).

Nevertheless, many women were active in churches and charity associations, and in the anti-slavery movement. It did not take long until those women realized that the same restrictions applied to them as to slaves. When women, despite their activities in the abolitionist cause, were excluded from participation in the World Anti-Slavery Convention in London in 1840, they started spreading the idea of liberation and feminism in their female networks. They referred to the promises of freedom and equality made by the Declaration of Independence and the US Constitution. After the first concrete demands for woman's suffrage had been voiced in the 1830s, the American women's movement was officially launched at a convention at Seneca Falls in 1848. Apart from women's right to vote, it called for reforms such as better access to education and professions, and property rights for married women (cf. 10–11).

The more time passed, the more women yearned for voting rights. When freed male slaves were allowed to vote in 1866, women ultimately struggled for

---

[6] French phrase for "ominous woman" which was coined in the nineteenth century (cf. Mizejewski 19).

[7] For example, in Hammett's *The Maltese Falcon*, Spade treats his secretary, Effie Perine, on cordial terms, and their rapport is intimate. She is the only woman allowed to ask him about private affairs (cf. 25–27), and he holds her opinion and her arguments in high regard (cf. 39). He does not feel threatened by her because she represents an older image of femininity and respects male authority. She is not independent, but she still lives with her mother (cf. 166).

female suffrage. Hence, the National Woman Suffrage Association was founded by Susan B. Anthony (1820–1906) and Elizabeth Cady Stanton (1815–1902) in New York City in 1869. It fought for women's enfranchisement and for more rights for women in all fields of life such as changes in property, marriage, and family laws. Amongst other activities, parades for women's rights were held in many states.

Although they had achieved minor changes by the end of the nineteenth century, there were still hardly any states in which women had full voting rights. The 19th Amendment, which was meant to enfranchise women, was introduced into Congress in 1878, but it was rejected and continued to be rejected until 1920. After Stanton's and Anthony's death, a new organization (National American Woman Suffrage Association) continued their work, and in 1920, the 19th Amendment was finally ratified (cf. 12). With this achievement, the first wave of feminism is generally considered to have ended although the guarantee of full equality was work for future feminists.

In the following years, feminists remained active in women's causes and women were given more rights in their working environments. In 1923, a small Women's Party led by activist Alice Paul (1885–1977) wrote and first introduced the Equal Rights Amendment in Congress, seeking to end the legal distinction between women and men in terms of employment (cf. 18). From then on, also caused by the growing urbanization and the emergence of a new middle class, especially in large cities, more and more women entered the work force.

Women being part of the work force and therefore socially and financially independent caused a new perception of gender roles and a change in women's self-perception. Having managed to gain more rights, women wanted to demonstrate their newly-won importance and realize their new freedoms. As a result, for example, the divorce rate started to increase (cf. 14–15). One has to consider that this modern way of life only affected a minority, while many, especially middle-aged, working-class women still led domestic lives (cf. 17). Mostly young women enjoyed their newly won freedom.

The 1920s, also called Roaring Twenties, were a liberal period influenced by social and political turbulence and multicultural exchange that followed the end of World War I. The so-called flappers appeared, young women who rejected traditional values and acceptable behavior by being emotionally hard and sexually provocative. They wore short skirts and used cosmetics in order to underline their sex appeal, and they wore their hair bobbed. They no longer wanted to look like the traditional woman; they behaved like men in that they drank and smoked in public. Overall, they wanted to demonstrate that life could be exciting for women.

From that point in time, many—mostly young and privileged—women no longer stayed at home and some refused to get married. They rather took part in all kinds of social activities such as beauty and sports events.[8] In 1925, the World Exposition of Women's Progress opened in Chicago and represented one hundred occupations in which women engaged, as well as their accomplishments in the arts, literature, science, and industry. This exhibition was, on the one hand, intended to raise funds to help support women's organizations, and on the other it served as a source for young women seeking information on careers (cf. 14–15).

All in all, at the time when American hard-boiled detective novels emerged, women emphatically called attention to themselves and could no longer be ignored, also because they became competitors in men's traditional workplaces. Thus, the negative description of modern women in detective fiction of the time is, in part, a response to the emergence of new women's roles and probably results from the fear of men that independent women could destabilize the social order and threaten them in their personal lives (cf. Cassuto 116). At least in their fiction, male authors maintained traditional role patterns.

4.3 Dashiell Hammett

The story widely considered the first American hard-boiled detective story is "The False Burton Combs" by Carroll John Daly (1889–1958). First published in *Black Mask*[9] in 1922, it introduced Daly's famous detective Race Williams. Despite Daly's great reputation at the time, later writers moved away from such characters as his brutal, violent, and hard-talking detective. His pattern is, for example, revived in Mickey Spillane's (1918–2006) works featuring Mike Hammer, which became famous in the 1950s (cf. Binyon 38–39).

Above all, it is the work of Dashiell Hammett that made the hard-boiled style popular. In 1923, a few months after the publication of Daly's story, Hammett published his first short story, "Arson Plus," in *Black Mask* under the pseudonym

---

[8] During the 1920s, for example, the Miss America contest was held every year. Moreover, women were allowed to compete in Olympic sports events by then (cf. Bouchier 17).

[9] The *Black Mask* magazine was not exclusively a detective story magazine in the beginning, and it was not the owners who made the magazine so important for the history of the detective story, but the editors and writers. The owners discovered writers such as Carroll John Daly, Dashiell Hammett, Raymond Chandler, and Joseph T. Shaw (1874–1952). The latter became the magazine's editor from 1926 until 1936. He advised writers and also rejected stories, and so he created a certain standard. The magazine became the most important means of distribution of the hard-boiled story (cf. Panek 149–150).

Peter Collinson, partly drawing on Daly's work. However, Hammett distanced himself from Daly's characteristics, such as his fantastic setting, melodramatic plotting, and simplistic characterization. He relied on a plausible world with a rational plot—which was partly inspired by his own early occupation as an operative with the Pinkerton National Detective Service in Baltimore—and complex characters. He also disagreed with Daly's overly violent and purely heroic detective and created a less triumphant, but more credible one, and he offered a more refined style in general (cf. McCann 48–49).

Lee Horsley suggests that, for reasons of greater verisimilitude, the employment of "more sophisticated ironies" as well as "ambiguity and complexity," and the "disruption of reliable narrative and of binary oppositions between good and evil, order and disorder," Hammett "has much the stronger claim to be seen as the progenitor" of American hard-boiled detective fiction than Daly (30).

Likewise, Cawelti argues that Hammett, more than any other person, invented the hard-boiled detective. He acknowledges that there were "action-filled, tough guy detective stories before Hammett came on the scene," but he allows that

> [i]t was he who licked the new story into shape, gave it much of its distinctive style and atmosphere, developed its urban setting, invented many of its most effective plot patterns, and, above all, articulated the hard-boiled hero, creating that special mixture of toughness and sentimentality, of cynical understatement and eloquence that would remain the stamp of the hard-boiled detective, even in his cruder avatars. (*Adventure* 163)

Thus, Hammett laid the path for subsequent writers such as Erle Stanley Gardner (1889–1970), James M. Cain (1892–1977), Cornell Hopley-Woolrich (1903–1968), Jonathan Latimer (1906–1983), Rex Stout (1886–1975), and W. R. Burnett (1899–1982), who largely adopted Hammett's concept.

Schmidt even compares Hammett to William Faulkner (1897–1962) and Ernest Hemingway (1899–1961) and claims that he is one of the most brilliant stylists amongst his American contemporaries (cf. 108–109). In his relatively short active writing career, Hammett published sixty short stories, five novels, as well as poems and book reviews. Among his most important works is his first novel, *Red Harvest*, which was published in 1929 and presents the character of the Continental Op and the *femme fatale* Dinah Brand. Equally important is his third novel, *The Maltese Falcon*, published in 1930 and presenting Samuel Spade as the detective and Brigid O'Shaughnessy as the central, deceitful female figure (cf. *The Maltese Falcon*).

4.4 Raymond Chandler

A writer who was as popular and esteemed as Hammett was, and who did not only resume, but also refine Hammett's patterns, was Raymond Chandler. He only came late to the writing of detective fiction in order to earn money. Although Chandler was six years older than Hammett, he published his first story when Hammett's fifth novel appeared and did not write his first novel until six years after Hammett had quit writing (cf. Schmidt 109). Thus, it can be presumed that Hammett's works directly influenced him.

This theory can be supported by the fact that the publishers of his first story, "Blackmailers Don't Shoot," which Chandler sent to *Black Mask* in 1933, immediately recognized him as a follower of the Hammett school. After its publication, there were enthusiastic reviews in such newspapers as *Los Angeles Times* (cf. MacShane 73). By 1939, Chandler had written nineteen more stories, but he owes his popularity, like Hammett, to his novels. Thus, his initial detective stories can be considered preparatory works in which Chandler gradually developed the patterns for his later novels.

This applies even more so since Chandler considered himself "a poor plotter and bad at construction," went back to his existing stories, and melted some of their plots and motifs with recent ideas in order to create his novels.[10] Chandler also designed his detective Philip Marlowe, who finally came forward in his famous first novel, *The Big Sleep*, in 1939, from existing characters (cf. *Speaking* 216). Overall, Chandler wrote seven novels, which all feature Philip Marlowe, and twenty-three short stories. His works were in high demand at the time and some were adapted into movies. Therefore, by the 1940s, Chandler started working as a screenwriter for Hollywood. In 1944, his important reflection on the genre of detective fiction, "The Simple Art of Murder," was published in the *Atlantic Monthly*.

Chandler was geared to Hammett's principles of writing, but he altered and refined several aspects of his predecessor's form. Although he equipped his detective with similar attributes, Chandler added more complexity to Hammett's character model. While Hammett's detectives are cool and quite selfish professionals, and rather flat characters, Chandler's Philip Marlowe is much more pleasant than Spade, for instance, because he is more sympathetic and selfless. He does not only work for profit, as Spade does, but also for the common good. Moreover, he does not have sexual intercourse with as many random women, but

---

[10] Philip Durham contributed a detailed analysis of which parts of different stories Chandler used for his later novels (cf. Durham 22).

he is more careful in his treatment of others. Marlowe is not a type, but a human individual.

This less emotionally detached, but more understandable and lifelike image of the detective that Chandler created is the one that would dominate in later detective fiction. Philip Durham explains: "Not only had Chandler described his detective hero, he had, and as artfully as it had ever been done, presented the American hero—the one who had been evolving in American fiction for more than a hundred years" (96).

Along with changes in character conception, the narrative pattern became different with Chandler. In brief, Hammett made use of a factual style and cool narration by employing selective omniscience. Sayers called this focus of narration "the Watson viewpoint," which mostly allows the readership to see and deduce the external actions of the detective (cf. Binyon 34). This prevents them from drawing quick and easy conclusions about his inner state of mind. Binyon explains that Hammett "describes in detail Spade's everyday actions—how he dresses, pours a drink, rolls and lights a cigarette—but never reveals his thoughts or emotions, apart from what can be gleaned from his words or the expression on his face" (40).

Marlowe, in contrast, is described through first-person narration. In this process, it is noticeable that, as Timothy Prchal points out, he serves two roles. On the one hand, he is the acting detective, and on the other, he serves as the narrator of his actions (cf. 33). Thus, one can draw conclusions about Marlowe from his actions and from dialogues with other people, and one has the chance to learn about his feelings directly from his interior monologues. Hence, the readership gets to know his consciousness and his private struggle, which was not at all the case with Hammett's Spade. The first-person narration is also the style that future authors of detective novels and female hard-boiled writers would adhere to. It is considered to "enri[ch] the texture of the writing and [to] giv[e] it a personality that cannot be provided by the omniscient narrator" (MacShane 69).

In terms of style, it is obvious that both authors had different skills. Hammett is particularly famous for his complex plots while Chandler's major achievement is his well-educated language. Chandler used a different language than ordinary American English. It was rather a mixture of the British English he had learned in the English public school and the American English he had to get used to in later years. Thus, Chandler claimed that every bit of slang he used was used deliberately (cf. *Speaking* 114).

In this context, Cynthia Hamilton rightly suggests that Chandler upvalued the detective novel and she states that his "awareness of the dynamics of style, his playful approach to language and his desire to push the formula to the limits of its capacity resulted in a style of great sophistication and flexibility, especially in his early books" (165). Not only are Chandler's descriptions linguistically sophisticated, but, according to Hamilton, they also "breathe life into the characters." She points out that "[i]t is Chandler's poetic descriptions, wisecracks and use of hyperbole which are the hallmarks of his style and which best convey his particular blend of humour, cynicism and sentimentality. Chandler is a master at wrapping a vivid scenario in a mood that makes the description take on a poetic quality" (168).

Suerbaum compares Chandler with Sayers and similarly argues that both writers made the detective novel overcome its boundaries and upgraded it to serious literature (cf. 140). Chandler also achieved this seriousness by providing a more positive world view and by using less action, bloodshed, and force than Hammett. Acts of violence in Chandler's works are rare and serve as evidence of Marlowe's courage (cf. Durham 83). This approach induces a "consistent lightness of tone" in Chandler's works, and further, due to Marlowe's "witty detachment with an underlying sentimentality," the atmosphere is much lighter than that of bleak pessimism in Hammett's works (cf. Horsley 35). Marlowe sees the prevailing corruption as a result of the circumstances of the time and not, like Spade, as part of the human condition (cf. Cawelti, *Adventure* 176).

Still, Marlowe gives an honest presentation of American society at the time, or rather, he offers a study of social life in Los Angeles between the two World Wars in distinct detail. Due to this realistic depiction of reality, the presentation of a complex character, as well as a narrative pattern and a refined style that later writers will resume, the following chapter will discuss Chandler's novel *The Big Sleep* as a representative American hard-boiled novel that will serve as point of reference later in the study. It is, next to *Farewell, My Lovely*, widely considered Chandler's best work, especially with respect to Marlowe.

4.4.1 *The Big Sleep*

4.4.1.1 The Prototypical Hard-Boiled Detective

Chandler wrote *The Big Sleep* in 1938. It is, according to him, mainly based on the plots and characters of two earlier stories, namely "Killer in the Rain" and "The Curtain" (cf. *Speaking* 243). Each story pictures an old man with an irresponsible daughter. Chandler followed this model in creating the main characters of the plot, namely General Sternwood and his daughters Carmen and Vivian.

Sternwood asks Marlowe to help him with blackmailer Arthur Gwynn Geiger, who is involved with Sternwood's younger daughter Carmen. Moreover, Vivian's husband, Rusty Regan, has vanished about a month ago, and Sternwood wants Marlowe to make sure that Regan is not entangled in the affair with Geiger. Marlowe finds out that Geiger trades in pornography and blackmails his customers and that Carmen once signed several warrants for Geiger. In addition, after Marlowe has turned Carmen down, she tries to shoot him dead. Marlowe awakens to the fact that Carmen did the same to Regan because he had rejected her as well. Vivian admits that she knew of the crime and covered the murder up with the help of her gambling acquaintance Eddie Mars for her father's sake. Mars, however, started to blackmail her shortly after. In the end, Marlowe promises Vivian not to call the police, if Carmen is institutionalized. Hence, Sternwood can continue to hope that Regan will return some day.

Chandler presents his concept of a hard-boiled, private detective, which he puts into practice with the creation of Marlowe, in his essay "The Simple Art of Murder" as follows:

> But down these mean streets a man must go who is not himself mean, who is neither tarnished nor afraid. The detective in this kind of story must be such a man. He is the hero, he is everything. He must be a complete man and a common man and yet an unusual man. He must be, to use a rather weathered phrase, a man of honor, by instinct, by inevitability, without thought of it, and certainly without saying it. . . .
>
> He is a relatively poor man, or he would not be a detective at all. He is a common man or he could not go among common people. He has a sense of character, or he would not know his job. . . .
>
> The story is his adventure in search of a hidden truth, and it would be no adventure if it did not happen to a man fit for adventure. He has a range of awareness that startles you, but it belongs to him by right, because it belongs to the world he lives in. (59)

Chandler made Philip Marlowe present these qualities.

Marlowe is thirty-three years old and he was born in Santa Rosa, California, but he presently lives in Los Angeles. He is an educated man who went to college and who worked as an investigator for an insurance company after that. Later, he was an investigator for the District Attorney, but he admits that he was fired for insubordination, which shows his wish to work independently (cf. *Speaking* 227–228). Now that he is a private eye, one can see that he is a common, but decent man, and "everything a private detective ought to be" (229).

Nevertheless, he is not concerned about a fine appearance and he has some bad habits. For instance, he is a heavy smoker. The reader gets to know that almost any sort of cigarette satisfies him (cf. *Speaking* 228). In addition, he often gets drunk when his life is dull. Marlowe likes any type of alcohol, and he likes

4.4 Raymond Chandler

it "[a]ny way at all" (6). He admits that he drinks "too much hot toddy" from time to time (30) and although he sometimes goes out and drinks in company, most often he takes a drink from his office bottle when he is alone and "let[s] [his] self-respect ride its own race" (90–91).

Being a loner who "has as much social conscience as a horse" (Chandler, *Speaking* 214), Marlowe lives in a single apartment with a bed which folds up into the wall. His office is "a room and a half on the seventh floor at the back," containing a faded settee, odd chairs, and "the boy's size library table with the venerable magazines on it to give the place a professional touch" (*Sleep* 39–40). This housing and office situation is due to the fact that Marlowe is relatively poor. He earns twenty-five dollars a day plus expenses, if he is lucky. Thus, he complains about the circumstance that "[y]ou can't make much money at this trade, if you're honest" (40–41).

Marlowe himself is indeed honest, but he is used to the deceptiveness of the modern world. He is realistic and points out: "I'm not Sherlock Holmes or Philo Vance. I don't expect to go over ground the police have covered and pick up a broken pen point and build a case from it" (151). When a problem seems too easy, he becomes suspicious and continues to investigate further, which mostly turns out to have been the right decision.

Marlowe knows how gangsters operate and he has a feeling for deceptive actions and for corrupt people instinctively. He points out several times that he does not know exactly why he acts the way he does, but his intuition mostly turns out to be correct. After following Geiger to his house, for instance, Marlowe states: "I didn't know what I was waiting for, but something told me to wait" (23). His instinct is indeed helpful at that point because Marlowe witnesses a murder a few minutes later. His intuition also tells Marlowe not to trust anybody. When he is offered a drink, for instance, he sniffs at it, watches his neighbor drink first, and rolls it around on his tongue until he is sure that "there [i]s no cyanide in it" (133).

Apart from his fine intuition, Marlowe possesses a profound knowledge of his tools. When Joe Brody, a former lover of Carmen's, points a gun at Marlowe, he immediately identifies that it is a Police.38 (cf. 56). Just as he knows weapons in theory, Marlowe is tough and has the necessary courage to use them. He even likes facing armed criminals. When Eddie Mars's hit man threatens him, for example, Marlowe reflects: "If it was a revolver he had, it might be empty. It might not. He had fired six times, but he might have reloaded inside the house. I hoped he had. I didn't want him with an empty gun" (143).

Marlowe is willing to compete with criminals all on his own, and he is forced to do so because he dislikes police officers. They are the ones whom he could cooperate with most easily, but he refuses to share his knowledge with them because he considers them inefficient. In his view, they are unable to protect members of society because they do not know the underworld and are therefore not capable of knowing how criminals operate. When he discovers that the corpse has gone from Geiger's house, for instance, he reflects that the police cannot have taken it because "[t]hey would have been there still, just getting warmed up with their pieces of string and chalk and their cameras and dusting powders and their nickel cigars" (30).

Marlowe also suspects the police of corruption, and hence he protects his clients. His attitude toward policemen is obvious when police officer Wilde asks Marlowe if he has told him in detail what he knows about the murder case. Marlowe replies: "I left out a couple of personal matters. I intend to keep on leaving them out, Mr. Wilde." When the police officer protests against Marlowe's discretion, the latter remains loyal toward his customers. He explains that his customer is entitled to protection and underlines that he is a private detective and that the word "private" has some meaning (cf. 80). As Wilde complains about how disappointing it is for a member of the police to be confronted with somebody who covers up facts, Marlowe replies dryly: "As for the cover-up, I've been in police business myself, as you know" (81). Thus, he indicates that the police cover up facts as well.

Apart from the reasons mentioned, Marlowe does not like the police, according to Chandler, because "Marlowe wouldn't be Marlowe, if he could really get along with policemen" (*Speaking* 248). To him, they are dishonest and take advantage of innocent people. Thus, they are portrayed as the exact opposite of the detective hero. For the restoration of order and for protecting society, a hero is needed who is familiar with the corrupt world and who has the courage to fight injustice, such as Marlowe.

Due to the fact that the system of order does not operate successfully, the upper class can abuse their power. It becomes clear that Marlowe despises them. Cynthia Hamilton observes that "[t]he possessors of wealth are judged unworthy, and the means to wealth are seen as corrupting and immoral." According to her, Marlowe clearly objects to the "bad morals, lack of dignity, and bad taste of the nouveau riche." He dislikes their "intellectual and emotional poverty as well as hypocrisy," (159) and he finally reveals their corruption and phoniness. Chandler points out: "P. Marlowe and I do not despise the upper class because they take baths and have money; we despise them because they are phoney" (*Speaking* 215).

Yet, Marlowe works for the upper class because they are unable to take care of their own affairs. As Cawelti rightly summarizes, "despite their power and success, these people need the hero" (*Adventure* 160). Therefore, Marlowe is the ideal detective for all social classes. He is fit for adventure, and he restores a certain amount of order by employing his honorable principles. Chandler concludes: "If there were enough like him, I think the world would be a very safe place to live in, and yet not too dull to be worth living in" (*Speaking* 59).

4.4.1.2 The Deceptive *Femme Fatale*

Apart from the detective, Sternwood's daughters play major roles in the novel. In the beginning, Marlowe describes Vivian and Carmen as follows: "Vivian is spoiled, exacting, smart and quite ruthless. Carmen is a child who likes to pull wings off flies. Neither of them has any more moral sense than a cat" (*Sleep* 10). Both women are characterized as being relentless and dangerous. While Vivian is smart, the use of a child as comparative parameter for Carmen belittles her intelligence and portrays her as being immature and irresponsible. The comparison of both girls with a cat underlines their lack of moral reason, which makes them possibly dangerous for Marlowe.

Marlowe's disdain, especially for Carmen, shows as he criticizes her reputed lack of intelligence and utters: "I could see even on that short acquaintance that thinking was always going to be a bother to her" (4). Later on, he underlines bluntly that her "slaty eyes [are] as empty as holes in a mask" (27) and that he "might as well have looked at a couple of bottle-tops" (154). All that Carmen does is giggle and say that Marlowe is cute (cf. 4). She even giggles at the sight of corpses and considers these cute (cf. 27). Repeatedly, Marlowe underlines the "stupid blankness of her eyes," and he describes her as a "pretty, spoiled and not very bright little girl who had gone very, very wrong" (47).

These examples show that Chandler makes use of traditionally presumed sex differences in language. Cheris Kramer explains: "English speakers believe—and linguists appear to be no exception—that men's speech is forceful, efficient, blunt, authoritative, serious, effective, sparing and masterful; they believe that women's speech is weak, trivial, ineffectual, tentative, hesitant, hyperpolite, euphemistic, and is often marked by gossip and gibberish" (157). Likewise, Marlowe makes clear that he despises Carmen by speaking in a blunt and offensive way while her speech is meaningless and marked by giggling.

Sternwood speaks and behaves in a similar way as Marlowe and it is obvious that he also does not take his daughters, and especially Carmen, seriously. When Marlowe asks Sternwood what Carmen thinks about her father's plan of hiring him, Sternwood replies deprecatingly: "I haven't asked her. I don't intend to. If I did, she would suck her thumb and look coy" (9). Here, Sternwood uses a similar picture as Marlowe—that of a childish figure that cannot be taken seriously.

Although the two male characters resemble one another in their attitude to women, Marlowe distances himself from Sternwood. Marlowe indirectly accuses Carmen's father of causing his daughter to behave like that because he did not do anything about it, and Marlowe concludes: "To hell with the rich" (*Sleep* 46). This, however, also indicates Marlowe's assumption that women need men's helping hands to point them into the right direction.

All in all, Marlowe's perception of women is one-sided, and he presents them as being good-looking, but not very intelligent or morally responsible. He reflects the traditional notion that women are the weaker sex and that they need male control over their lives. Chandler, with Carmen, portrays a woman who has too little guidance, therefore refuses "proper" feminine behavior, and uses her appearance and sexuality to deceive men in favor of her immoral intentions.

Marlowe is attracted by Carmen's looks. She is around twenty, small, and has a delicate figure. Her hair is a wave cut which is reminiscent of the former fashionable pageboy cut of the flappers. This sexually provocative appearance hints at her enormous dangerousness for traditional gender roles. When he observes her at close range in detail, Marlowe notes: "She was worth a stare. She was trouble. She was stretched out on a modernistic chaise-longue with her slippers off, so I stared at her legs in the sheerest silk stockings. They seemed to be arranged to stare at.... The calves were beautiful, the ankles long and slim and with enough melodic line for a tone poem" (13). Marlowe clearly objectifies Carmen, whom he later deprecatingly calls "just a dope" (26).

Moreover, he observes that "[s]he walked as if she were floating" and "she had little sharp predatory teeth, as white as fresh orange pith and as shiny as porcelain" (4). Again, due to her stalking movement and the description of her sharp teeth, Carmen seems dangerous and is indirectly compared to an animal that could attack any time. Marlowe seems to be particularly attracted by the danger she embodies when he describes that "her hot black eyes loo[k] mad" (14), although this again is a hint at her devilish nature. Moreover, the allusion to madness is an idea that can be found in earlier American literature. Women who refuse to act in a feminine way, but rather challenge traditional gender roles, are often found to be mentally ill.[11]

Carmen knows how to make use of her feminine charms and she acts in a tempting manner. Marlowe describes that "she lowered her lashes until they almost cuddled her cheeks and slowly raised them again, like a theatre curtain."

---

[11] Madness resulting from challenging patriarchal gender expectations can be seen in Charlotte Perkins Gilman's (1860–1935) short story "The Yellow Wallpaper" from 1892, for example.

4.4 Raymond Chandler

Then, "she put a thumb up and bit it.... She bit it and sucked it slowly, turning it around in her mouth like a baby with a comforter" (4). Afterwards, she tilts herself toward Marlowe on her toes and falls straight into his arms so that he has to catch her in order not to let her crack her head on the floor. Marlowe describes: "I caught her under her arms and she went rubber-legged on me instantly" (4–5).

Carmen's seductive behavior and her amorous approach are tempting for Marlowe, but in the end, he does not give Carmen the chance to seduce him. When he finds her naked in his apartment, he does not allow himself to be attracted by her. He states: "She looked at me under her long lashes. This was the look that was supposed to make me roll over on my back" (154). However, Marlowe keeps his self-control and follows his principles. He explains his refusal to Carmen: "It's a question of professional pride.... I'm working for your father. He's a sick man, very frail, very helpless. He sort of trusts me not to pull any stunts" (111). Rather than on his personal wellbeing, Marlowe focuses on his aim to help Sternwood and to restore the family arrangement in which the patriarch regains absolute control. The fact that Sternwood is weak hints at the disintegration of this concept. With the assistance of Marlowe, however, the traditional order is restored.

Apart from his loyalty to Sternwood, Marlowe feels that sleeping with Carmen would violate his home. He reflects that the room he lives in is all he has in the way of a home and that it contains all his memories. He cannot stand Carmen there any longer, throws her out, and tears his bed to pieces because "the imprint of her head [i]s still on the pillow and the mark of her small corrupt body [is] still on the sheets" (113). Although he eventually does not let Carmen invade his space, Marlowe reacts in an emotional manner and he is clearly irritated by such an ominous woman. After this event, he bluntly explains that he is fed up with women: "You can have a hangover from other things than alcohol. I had one from women. Women made me sick" (113). This disgust for women is probably an expression of his uncertainty and anger as a woman does not behave in the traditional way.

Vivian, Sternwood's older daughter, seems brighter than her little sister, but just as dangerous. Marlowe notices that she has a "taut, pale, beautiful and wild" face, "red and harsh" lips, and "wicked eyes" (105). She seems ominous to Marlowe, and the fact that she has been married three times and that the last marriage did not even last a month proves that being with her can be baleful (cf. 8).

Moreover, Vivian is described as acting in a dominant manner. When she is at the casino, for instance, she treats the croupiers in a bossy way. She commands forcefully: "Get busy and spin the wheel, highpockets. I want one more play and I'm playing table stakes. You take it away fast enough I've noticed, but when it comes to dishing it out you start to whine" (98). Then, she pushes her winnings "savagely" on to the layout. In doing so, her lips part and her teeth, catching the light, glitter like knives (cf. 99).

Due to her verbally as well as physically rather dominant and masculine behavior, the men around her dread Vivian. Mars, the owner of the casino, describes Vivian, whom he calls "the dark one," as "plain trouble." He explains: "She's a pain in the neck around here. If she loses, she plunges and I end up with a fistful of paper which nobody will discount at any price. She has no money of her own except an allowance and what's in the old man's will is a secret. If she wins, she takes my money home with her" (95).[12]

Toward Marlowe, Vivian behaves nicely at first, and she tries to attract his attention. When Vivian and Marlowe talk about nude photographs of Carmen, and Marlowe mentions that Carmen has a beautiful body, Vivian tells him that he ought to see hers. When Marlowe reacts in a positive manner, Vivian comments: "You're as cold-blooded a beast as I ever met, Marlowe. Or can I call you Phil?" As Marlowe agrees, Vivian offers him to call her by her first name as well. He, however, only responds: "Thanks, Mrs Regan" (44). By this, he clearly shows her that he is still the predominant interlocutor. Marlowe is not yet able to judge Vivian, and thus he is careful about her. Hamilton argues that "Marlowe builds a wall around himself verbally: through his rudeness he cuts himself off from obligations, expectations and sympathy" (163). In doing so, he represents the stereotypical male speaker.

Later in the novel, when the two are on their own, Vivian gets emotional and lets herself fall into Marlowe's arms, and she commands: "Hold me close, you beast." Marlowe kisses her "tightly and quickly" and presses his body against her (*Sleep* 107). However, as becomes clear shortly after, Marlowe only kisses Vivian in order to elicit some information about her relationship with Mars. As she has understood his intention, he affirms: "That's the way it is. Kissing is nice, but your father didn't hire me to sleep with you.... The first time we met I told you I was a detective. Get it through your lovely head. I work at it, lady. I don't play at it" (108). Vivian, just like her little sister, tries to use her sex appeal to manipulate Marlowe, but he does not let himself in for that and remains loyal to his client.

---

[12] The image of the casino reflects the changes of the time. In the 1920s, youth were granted greater freedom and especially the rich young became targets for the new leisure industries (cf. White 74). Hence, Vivian's hunger to live exquisitely reflects the wishes of young and wealthy people at the time.

4.4 Raymond Chandler

Another woman who has a beastly nature is the front girl of Geiger's store, Agnes. Her voice and movements hint at her dangerousness (cf. 67). Again, Marlowe is dazzled with her appearance and puts himself into danger because later in the novel, it turns out that Agnes belongs to the group of gangsters. In the end, she fights in a tough way. Marlowe recalls: "The blonde spat at me and threw herself on my leg and tried to bite that." Marlowe reacts to her violence in a brutal manner. He hits her on the head and kicks her off his feet (cf. 62).

In sum, all these women have no principles other than self-interest and they do not live up to male expectations of traditionally feminine behavior. Carmen openly uses her sexuality in order to deceive men, and Vivian and Agnes even partly act in a masculine and misogynist manner. They tempt Marlowe to violate his professional code of values, but he can eventually resist them and remains superior.

This plot construction can be explained with the change in gender roles in the first half of the twentieth century. Men started seeing independent women as competitive and feared that they could destabilize the social order. They felt threatened in both their professional and personal lives, and thus they tried to keep such women down. This is what Marlowe does with characters such as Carmen, Vivian, and Agnes. By not giving in to them and by helping Sternwood, Marlowe retains the traditional order of a patriarchal society, which is based on the belief that the male is the superior sex.

The only woman who acts according to traditionally feminine norms, and is consequently portrayed positively, is Mona Grant. She is the loyal and faithful wife of Mars. Mona hides in order to protect her husband, whom she probably does not believe or does not want to believe to be a gangster. In contrast to the other women in the novel, she is dependent, naïve and helpless. Marlowe nicely calls her "Silver-Wig" (141) and he thinks of her longingly in the end (cf. 164). She does not challenge the patriarchal order and thus, Marlowe is positively inclined to her.

Hence, although masculine behavior is demanded of the detective in the novel in order to preserve the traditional order, Marlowe's masculinity is beginning to crack. In contrast to Spade, who is continuously tough, Marlowe does finally turn out to belong to the predominant sex, but deceptive women such as Carmen temporarily irritate him and he reacts to their presence emotionally. Moreover, he longs for a female partner from time to time, as the example of Mona shows. Hamilton rightly points out that Marlowe acts like a hard-boiled detective, but "the voice of the narrator betrays to us his loneliness, his hopes and fears" (170) and hints at Marlowe's sentimental character. He is destined to remain single, accepts loneliness as part of his life, and seeks fulfillment in his job. Martin Priestman calls this phenomenon "deliberate self-exclusion" (172).

This exclusion is necessary for the hero in order to be successful in his job. Chandler explains that "a fellow of Marlowe's type shouldn't get married, because he is a lonely man, a poor man, a dangerous man, and yet a sympathetic man, and somehow none of this goes with marriage." Chandler further pictures that "he [Marlowe] will always have a fairly shabby office, a lonely house, a number of affairs, but no permanent connection." Marlowe is destined to walk "always in a lonely street, in lonely rooms, puzzled but never quite defeated" (*Speaking* 249).

Chandler's highly romanticized picture of the detective's destiny is rationally explicable considering the norms of the time. Durham plausibly argues that love and marriage are forbidden for the detective because "a man is less capable of freely offering his life in defense of others while he has a family at home depending on his continuance as a provider" (88).

All in all, Marlowe rates loyalty toward clients and business higher than personal desires. Thus, he turns Sternwood's daughters down. Hamilton argues that "Marlowe's loyalty is impersonal, often without warmth, but it is absolute" (161). When Marlowe last sees his client, he explains his professional convictions: "You don't know what I have to go through or over or under to do your job for you. I do it my way. I do my best to protect you and I may break a few rules, but I break them in your favor. The client comes first, unless he's crooked. Even then all I do is hand the job back to him and keep my mouth shut" (*Sleep* 151).

Despite the fact that Marlowe talks about breaking rules, he never seriously falls on the wrong side of the law. He is, as Durham calls it, "passionately ethical" (161). He never takes money for a job that is not completed. If he has already taken the money, he gives it back; as in the case of Sternwood. Marlowe returns the money to him in the end because, as he explains, it was not a completed job by his standards (cf. *Sleep* 152). Likewise, Marlowe does not take the fifteen thousand dollars Vivian offers him in order to hide Carmen's guilt (cf. 162) since he does not work for money in the first place, but he wants to fight injustice. Due to feelings of pity for Sternwood, he does more than he was hired for. He protects Sternwood's daughters, and he keeps the General from being disappointed by his relatives.

In that, Marlowe is more empathetic than Hammett's Spade. He is, according to Cawelti, "intensely sensitive, yet carries a shield of cynical apathy; he is disturbed to a point of near-hysteria by the moral decay he encounters, yet always effects a wise-guy coolness and wit; he is bitter, exasperated, and lonely, behind a veneer of taut self-control, sarcasm, and indifference" (*Adventure* 176). Marlowe offers a sensitive character under a hard-boiled façade.

4.5 Further Developments

It has been claimed that "[w]ith Hammett and Chandler the private eye novel had reached its apogee" and that "[d]uring the next decade there followed mainly a procession of epigones, usually distinguishable from one another only by the city in which they work" (Binyon 42). However, some distinctive writers represent the variety of approaches that were created after Hammett's novels and beside Chandler's latest ones. In general, these writers followed and further developed Chandler's sensitive model detective.

One exception is Mickey Spillane. In 1947, he created his famous New York City detective Mike Hammer, who makes much more use of violence than his predecessors and is thus often said to have maligned the subgenre (cf. Baker and Nietzel 70). However, his works were widely read. The glorification of violence does not stop when it comes to women, who usually serve as sexual consorts to the detective and are permanently available to fulfill his desires. They are often criminals and once Hammer has convicted them of the crime, he brutally kills them. In the same way as in earlier hard-boiled works, domestic women are spared while independent and especially working women are portrayed as evil (cf. Klein, *The Woman Detective* 150). This is probably a negative reaction of the author to working women during and after the Second World War. As mentioned above, at the time, women as independent workers were feared to overthrow the American family order. Spillane preserves this order, at least in literature.

Kenneth Millar, better known as Ross Macdonald (1915–1983), distanced himself from Spillane's violent style and chose a more subtle approach to portray independent women as negative. He began writing in the early 1950s and created another detective who works in California. Thus, Macdonald allowed the readership who had read Chandler to follow the development of California in postwar society. His Lew Archer is cultivated and has literary and artistic interests. Above all, one can see in his work that the style in the private eye novel changed from Hammett to Macdonald. Binyon explains that "[i]n Hammett's hands the style was classical; Chandler made it romantic; but with Macdonald it has become decadent" (43–44). Macdonald focused less on crime, but he was very much concerned with the breakdown of the family. His detective tries to preserve the core family and pieces together broken family ties. Moreover, he cares for mentally weak people. Women are not portrayed in a liberal manner, but their traditional role within the family is important. Those who do not adhere to this role are mostly delinquents. Regarding male characters, Macdonald often positively portrays sensitive and devoted husbands (cf. Cassuto 156–158).

Cassuto calls this tendency "hard-boiled sentimentality," a tone that focuses on the power of human connections and feelings (7). Binyon furthermore designates this approach as "mission towards social psychology" and explains the new ideal of the detective as follows: "If Hammett idealized the detective as the perfect private eye and Chandler as the perfect man, Macdonald idealizes him as the perfect parent, a surrogate father for the abandoned children he meets. The idea of detection as paid work has almost completely vanished" (44).

This changing character conception toward a caring detective can be ascribed to changes in American society at the time. In contrast to the 1920s, after the Second World War, many people sought stability in their personal lives. Women married at a younger age, the divorce rate that had increased in the years before the wars fell, and the birthrate rose (cf. White 105–106). The "revitalized cult of domesticity" that now included both men and women seemed the new secret to happiness and was to be sustained. In line with these changes, "hard-boiled writing from the thirties forward bec[ame] more and more sentimental in tone, more inclined toward emotional affect, and more explicit about its domestic concerns" (Cassuto 16). Cassuto specifies that "[t]he male heroes of the most fifties crime novels take responsibility to preserve the home during times of urbanization and suburbanization" (109). "[H]ypermasculinity" is no longer desirable, but the male hero is idealized as an upholder of sentimental domesticity in American crime fiction (cf. 110).

John Dann MacDonald (1916–1986) represents a different view on a meaningful social order. He started writing in 1964 and he then no longer believed in the value of the core family, but he depicted an alternative lifestyle. His detective Travis McGee also works privately, is an intelligent and moral middle-class man, is single, and leads a fulfilled life. In the first novels, he has quite a lot of affairs with women, but his partners become more experienced and the relationships become longer in the course of the series. He seems to learn to take women more seriously. However, Travis does not want to commit himself eventually, and he often endangers the women he becomes involved with (cf. Cassuto 158–159). This is due to his surrounding, which reveals current social ills, for instance corruption, drug trafficking, and blackmailing (cf. Baker and Nietzel 63).

Although the aforementioned authors still made use of some traditional conventions, the hard-boiled private eye's original nature was very much modified because the construction of a cowboy-like and tough hard-boiled loner was replaced by a caring character (apart from Spillane). Women were still portrayed

4.5 Further Developments

negatively if they tried to challenge the traditional distribution of gender roles, but in general, their presentation became less derogatory and superficial. The works of John Dann MacDonald and Ross Macdonald are rather profound novels of manners and psychology. The description of the milieu with its social issues outweighs the importance of the crime. John Dann MacDonald wrote a few years longer than Ross Macdonald. With their deaths, the private eye novels widely considered as classic ended.

Naturally, from that point onward there were still gifted writers who continued some lines of thinking, language, and setting of the classic hard-boiled detective authors. Dennis Lynds, who wrote under the pseudonym of Michael Collins (1924–2005) and presented his New York City private detective Dan Fortune, for instance, continued the aforementioned psychological approach. Critics claim that he modernized the genre and created a sociological approach to detective fiction. From the late 1960s onwards, Fortune investigated society's impact on people in detail and underlined the cruelty of domestic crime (cf. Baker and Nietzel 176–178).

There were also some female writers at the time, such as Will Oursler (1913–1985), who created two novels featuring Gale Gallagher in the late 1940 s. She invented a professional female detective who is as competent and successful as her male forerunners. She also shows some similarities in her habits; for example, she drinks and smokes. However, she has to face gender prejudices, especially by an old family friend, officer Hank Deery. He thinks that a woman is not supposed to work in such a dangerous business and that she should rather commit herself to the role of wife and mother. The fact that she frequently relies on him as well as on the wisdom of her deceased father limits her independence. Moreover, Gallagher has a romantic, but nonsexual, relationship with Bart Crane. He clearly embodies the masculine role while she is rather passive, being always available and grateful if he spends time with her (cf. Klein, *The Woman Detective* 126–130). Although Gallagher is not an independent detective yet, she can be considered a link between the amateur girl sleuths[13] and spinsters of the past and the female hard-boiled professional detectives to come.

Gloria (*1925) and Forrest Fickling (1925–1998), who wrote under the pseudonym G.G. Fickling, created Honey West in the late 1950s. She prepares the way for the female hard-boiled detectives of the 1980s even more because she is more independent that Gallagher, smart, tough, and sexually active. However, West often chooses criminals as her sexual partners and runs into danger that she

---

[13] Edward Stratemeyer (1862–1930) created Nancy Drew in 1930, a carefree amateur teenager who solved cases for her father.

cannot always escape on her own. Hence, she is repeatedly reminded that being a detective is not a suitable profession for a woman.

In sum, although they changed the sex of the detective and underlined female competence, these female authors did not revolutionize the genre because gender prejudices define their detectives' work and ultimately, the women cannot break free from patriarchal dominance (cf. 132–136). Portraying independent female detectives who free themselves from men altogether would probably have been too radical for the time. Female hard-boiled writers could only succeed with their self-determined female detectives in the 1980s because by that time, several changes in real life had taken place.

Female Hard-Boiled Detective Fiction 5

5.1 Changing Gender Conception in Real Life

Before the Second World War, women had achieved suffrage and had called attention to themselves, also as workers. The number of working women rose significantly during the Second World War when they were recruited into jobs that had been vacated by men; this also included married women and mothers. By 1941, women constituted one quarter of the workforce. In 1944, for the first time, married women outnumbered single women in the female work force (cf. Anderson 4). To support working mothers, day nurseries were installed for young children. Around nineteen million American women worked in war factories (a fact represented by the icon of Rosie the Riveter), but also in the services and in agricultural fields (cf. Oakley 58). Although women were paid less than men, their work made people even more familiar with the idea of female employment, and not only as a situation until women enter marriage, but also parallel to that.

After the war, in 1945, most female workers gave the returning soldiers their jobs back. Some women remained working alongside men, but married women were encouraged to return to their domestic spheres and to pay attention to their family duties, which was even supported by journals and the media (cf. Hartman 213). Single women were supposed to marry. Therefore, as mentioned above, the 1950s saw a large return to domesticity. Studies show, however, that this was not the wish of most women at the time. In 1945, around 80% of female war workers would rather have liked to stay in their jobs (cf. Hartman 24). In the years to follow, many women wanted to work (again) and took low-paid jobs in the service sector. Some women also sought higher education (cf. Bouchier 19–21).

© The Author(s), under exclusive license to Springer-Verlag GmbH, DE, part of Springer Nature 2024
S. Bernhard, *Gender Identity and Gender Relations Redefined*,
https://doi.org/10.1007/978-3-662-69867-9_5

In sum, the war marked a new era in many women's lives and a movement from the home into the public sphere. Even if many women resumed traditional places in the homes afterwards, during the war they had seen that they were capable of doing men's work. Once back within their family ties, many of them felt that they did not have the chance to follow their aspirations. Their frustration, on the one hand, but also the rising self-esteem on the other, initiated a revolt that became visible in the following decades and is referred to as second-wave feminism (cf. 3).

One early achievement was that in 1949, a Commission on the Status of Women by the United Nations issued a Declaration of Human Rights, which granted women and men equal rights during marriage and at its dissolution. In the same year, Simone de Beauvoir's (1908–1986) work of feminist theory, *The Second Sex*, appeared and underlined that women, through history, have been denied meaningful lives of their own because the construction of their identities has always been tied to the male sex (cf. Walters 97–98). As a consequence, the theory revealed the desire for romantic love as well as the cultural ideal of marriage as illusions and part of the patriarchal suppression of women (cf. Funk 101–102).

Because of such thoughts, in the 1960s, mostly middle-class, white women finally rebelled openly against traditional gender roles and expectations of female domesticity. Gail Collins points out that women had accepted those values for a long time because they had had a high standard of living and few of them had noticed their limited options. They had rather compared their own achievements with those of other women, instead of men (cf. 25). After they had entered the public sphere, however, they felt the need for a different aspect in life which could give them a sense of identity. That was the working world.

In 1963, Betty Friedan (1921–2006), writer, activist, and feminist as well as a leading figure in the women's movement, published her influential work *The Feminine Mystique* and underlined this claim. She did not support the former assumption that women can find fulfillment by caring for their husbands, children, and their home, but she suggested that such duties denied their needs. Thereby, Friedan revealed the image of the contented housewife and mother for middle-class suburban women in the US of the 1950s to be a myth. Living like this, according to Friedan, had a negative impact that led to such symptoms as feelings of nothingness, fatigue, failure, and, at worst, breakdown (cf. 43). Moreover, Friedan claimed that staying at home wasted women's potential. She suggested that the only recommendable commitment for a woman was her self-realization, which means the realization of her chosen lifestyle, which used to be a masculine

5.1 Changing Gender Conception in Real Life

privilege. In the end, she encouraged women to pursue higher education and make a career in order to achieve personal growth and self-esteem (cf. 91).

Due to this widely read work, either many women questioned the lifestyles that they had previously accepted, or, if they had already challenged them, they learned that they were not alone in doing so. Thus, they dared to express their irritations in public. However, these women did not take radical steps at first, probably amongst other reasons because they lived together with men and they could not fight against them (cf. Collins 104). Instead, they attached themselves to another movement.

Although American slaves had been liberated because of the Civil War and had been granted basic civil rights due to the Fourteenth and Fifteenth Amendments to the U.S. Constitution from 1868 to 1870 (cf. Jack E. Davis xvi), these rights had not been secured immediately. Struggles continued during the next century, leading to the Civil Rights Movement in the 1950s and 1960s in which the African Americans and their allies, especially from the younger generations, fought for social justice and equality for all races. Martin Luther King Jr. (1929–1968) most importantly led their mainly nonviolent protest. Like white women who had participated in the anti-slavery movement in the nineteenth century, they also took an active part in this movement and simultaneously underlined the need for their emancipation.

All this led to momentous changes in 1964 and 1965. Major civil rights acts were passed, amongst others the Civil Rights Act. Although it was mainly directed at racial discrimination, it included sections stating that discrimination in terms of sex is also prohibited (cf. Collins 38). It banned, among other things, segregation in public places, employment discrimination against colored people and women; the Twenty-Fourth Amendment, in order not to affect African American voters negatively, abolished poll taxes in federal elections, and President Lyndon B. Johnson (1908–1973) declared a war on poverty. Hence, the struggle of African Americans slowly turned into a movement that was not only about civil rights reforms anymore, but it extended into matters such as politics and economy, and it also focused on women (cf. xxi).

In 1966, Friedan created the National Organization for Women (NOW). Its key feature was the sense of solidarity that arose within this group. The women were no longer isolated from other women or even saw themselves in competition with each other, but they learned that they shared the feeling of being oppressed. They drafted a Bill of Rights for women and fought for the inclusion of women in all fields of American life—especially in education and career—in order to be able to live an independent and fulfilling life. It was an organization for women, not only of women, and its members were pleased to receive serious male support (cf. White 155). The organization is still active today, fighting for women's rights in the workplace.

Men back then, who had already been sensitized to the issue of equality by the struggles of African Americans, started to reconsider their attitudes toward women (cf. Bouchier 47). However, for some more radical feminists, this gradual consideration was not enough. They set themselves apart from visible, liberal feminist groups such as NOW because they did not believe that men would ever grant women more rights. After they had initially asked for dialogue with men and had not been taken seriously, these women became radical and anti-men (cf. 53).

Their feminist groups remained rather hidden because it was hard for them to gain acceptance. Nevertheless, they published feminist literature in both nonfiction, such as guides to the female body, and fiction, such as novels about modern women rejecting marriage. In this fiction, men come off badly. They are stereotyped as selfish fiends who neglect their families and search for sexual pleasure elsewhere (cf. 91). Such hatred of men led some of these women to lesbianism. In the 1970s, the so-called lesbian separatists became visible, who rejected any relations between women and men (cf. 160).

In sum, although being very different in their attitudes, the members of liberal as well as radical feminist groups had legally achieved equal pay as well as marriage and property laws by the 1960s (cf. 38). Within women's private lives, they were also attaining progress. Before the 1960s, not getting married or getting divorced was unthinkable for young women. Collins states that "marriage fever was in the air" (36) and that young women identified with the idea of being married. This idea only began to change in the second half of the twentieth century. In 1962, still 96% of married women spoke out in favor of marriage, and so did 77% of single women. Divorce was not seen as a right, but as a punishment that could be requested only by the innocent partner whose counterpart had done something wrong, such as adultery (cf. 36).

Hence, up to that point, the puritan ethic of their ancestors had still been in the people's minds—demanding a life of moral purity that would lead to future happiness. However, as Bouchier claims, "[a]s the puritan ethic faded, the search for happiness became an increasingly legitimate personal goal, and a bad marriage was a cruel obstacle to happiness" (cf. 31). People were no longer willing to sacrifice their personal fulfillment for an unhappy marriage. As a consequence, divorce became more common. From 1960 to 1980, the divorce rate more than doubled—from 9.2 divorces per 1,000 married women to 22.6 divorces per 1,000 married women (cf. Bradford Wilcox 81).

5.1 Changing Gender Conception in Real Life

Along with a rise in divorces, the 1960s saw more and more women marrying later, having fewer children, and making their own sexual choices. As mentioned before, Victorian attitudes toward sexuality had been challenged in the 1920s. Consequently, due to more liberal fashion styles for women, information on sexual matters, as well as female-controlled contraception in the form of diaphragms, female sexuality by the 1960s was no longer dominated by insecurity, fear of pregnancy, or social disrepute (cf. Bouchier 26). Sexual freedom especially gained popularity with the appearance of the contraceptive pill in 1961. Despite vehement objection to the pill, for instance by the Roman Catholic Church and anti-abortion activists, who saw the new sexual freedom as selfish, family planning quickly became an acceptable practice for married middle-class couples on the one hand, and a chance for single women to gain sexual experience on the other (cf. Allyn 7–8).

This new morality and the image of the New Woman[1] was also spread in popular culture, through films, books, and advertisements. Instead of presenting married women or mothers, the media increasingly showed independent, employed, single, urban, and glamorous women. This image slowly made its way into people's minds, and the 1970s saw the actual growth of a singles culture. People enjoyed their newly-won freedom, and women, according to Kevin White, were "free to behave badly as men had always been" and to separate sex from emotion (149). For single mothers, however, this lifestyle involved a loss of security and financial carelessness, and they usually had to take a job. In 1972, the number of women with school-age children who were in the labor force became greater than those who were not (cf. Bernard, Foreword x).

In sum, during the 1970s, the feminist movement could boast huge legal successes for women. In 1972, Congress approved the Education Act that prohibited discrimination in colleges and universities. It also approved the resubmission of the Equal Rights Amendment which sought to grant equal legal rights for women in general, for example, in matters of divorce, employment, and property. In 1973, the Supreme Court made abortion legal in limited circumstances (such as rape or incest) in 20 states. The Sex Discrimination Act was implemented in 1975, which protected women and men from discrimination on account of their sex or marital status. Finally, in 1978, the Pregnancy Discrimination Act made employment discrimination based on pregnancy illegal (cf. Bouchier 119).

---

[1] This ideal image, which was used by Henry James, amongst others, later on, was originally coined by writer Sarah Grand in her article "The New Aspect of the Woman Question" in 1894 (cf. 271).

In the 1970s, also black and working-class women were active in the feminist movement. They had not seen their sex as a reason for their oppression at first, but white middle-class women's commitment to the emancipation of women of all races and classes inspired them. In 1973, black women who stood up for their specific issues founded the National Black Feminist Organization. In 1974, working-class women who fought against sexism in the unions and women's inequality in general (cf. Reger 21) created the Coalition of Labor Union Women.

After 1975, the feminist movement lost momentum. Radical feminism had had its peak in 1971, but the groups had organizational and political problems with the partly radical theories that divided them (cf. Bouchier 98). In contrast, liberal feminism stayed visible, was open to anyone interested, and became part of the culture. Women concentrated on dialogue in every area of life. Therefore, women and men carried on advocating women's issues in governments, political parties, at universities, and in the media.

In general, a new consciousness and contentment among women had been achieved and could not be repressed anymore (cf. 177). They felt confident in their everyday lives and showed this newly-won self-awareness, for example, by wearing what they wanted. Again, the media underlined this image of the modern woman. Strong and confident American women such as Madonna performed in popular culture as role models. Moreover, women appeared in TV series as working equally alongside men (cf. Collins 297–298).

Polls show that, in the 1980s, the clear majority of younger American women were satisfied with their lives and believed they would meet their goals, which meant professional careers for most of them (cf. 294). In addition, women felt content because their wages were coming closer to those of men. Pay for full-time working women rose by 12% on average between 1979 and 1989 (cf. 302). The double burden of work and household, which employed women faced, however, was one point of criticism and is still one of the most prominent issues concerning gender equality today. Although men increasingly helped women in the households,[2] the new situation was challenging.

In the 1990s, third-wave feminism began, including diverse feminist study and activity. Part of the movement's agenda was to redefine what it was to be a feminist. Feminism had lost ground, among other reasons, because it embodied the image of skeptical, grim, and aggressive women. Hence, the new approach was to move away from theoretical and antagonistic tendencies, and to appeal to young, and not necessarily academic, women. Being a feminist no longer meant

---

[2] Numbers estimate that during the 1980s, husbands did 30% of the work at home, including childcare, up from 20% two decades earlier (cf. Collins 393).

5.1 Changing Gender Conception in Real Life

analyzing social structures or engaging in politics. Authors such as Caitlin Moran (*1975) postulated a more comprehensive approach. Just as in society, individual sensibilities and self-realization have become more important than political trends and societal analysis. Thus, according to her, feminism has to be real, rather than theoretical. It implies an open-minded and positive attitude to life (cf. Funk 54–55).

As a consequence, third-wave feminism rejected the notion of a collective identity. Its members advocated the acceptance of pluralism and aimed at including women of all ethnicities, religions, occupations, and sexualities. They campaigned issues that had not been solved during second-wave feminism, such as abortion rights or equal pay. Moreover, they sought to shatter the glass ceiling in business and politics, and to balance the double burden of work and family. In order to understand the different approaches within the movement better, Kathleen P. Iannello suggests differentiating between two major age groups.

According to her, mostly young women between fifteen and thirty years of age cared for the issue of social justice and asked for multicultural and sexually diverse perspectives, including gay, lesbian, bisexual, and transsexual ones. They perceived themselves less as a group of victims (as had been the case in the second-wave movement), but as powerful individuals who chose their lifestyles freely.[3] The young women focused less on political changes because they felt that important issues were being worked on. Rather than a feminist strategy, they employed their individual identities to fight any remaining sexism in society (cf. 70–74).

Considering women between thirty and fifty years, a crucial aspect of the discussion was a woman's relation to the family and her responsibility for housework, childcare, and other tasks related to this. Research shows that half of the wealthiest, best-educated women in the country stayed at home. Thus, members of the movement argued that women's responsibilities in the private sphere needed to be redefined because the home was as much of a barrier for women as the vote and the workplace had been earlier. Moreover, they hinted at an ongoing war between employed and stay-at-home mothers, which prevented them from working together and focusing on the real problem, which was patriarchy. Hence, women of this age group focused on collective approaches again. They wanted politics to help women cope with their duties, if they wanted both, employment

---

[3] Third-wave feminism, for example, was rather open concerning questions of how to treat women in pornography. While second-wave feminists had promoted that such activities were degrading and oppressing women, third-wave feminists encouraged women's individuality and sexuality (cf. 72).

and children, and not to burden them with the personal responsibility for their choice of raising children (cf. 74–77).

While women had gained self-awareness over the years, some (mostly white, middle-class, heterosexual) men had lost theirs. In the late 1970s, these men initiated the men's liberation movement because they felt that feminists had downgraded them. The movement soon divided into a conservative, anti-feminist wing and into a more moderate one.

The first group felt oppressed and feminized by the women's movement. Hence, they rejected feminist principles altogether and opposed societal changes requested by feminists. Moreover, they sought to correct gender discrimination in areas in which they believed to be disadvantaged or discriminated against, such as divorce, child custody, and paternity fraud. In addition, they underlined the male dominance they perceived as having been undermined by feminists and defended the traditional gender order in the family and in the workplace.

The more moderate group did not want to hinder feminism, but the men emphasized the importance of working together with women in order to confront patriarchy. Nevertheless, they wanted to make sure that their rights were equally kept in view. This group was more future-oriented and persisted, becoming more organized with the emergence of the internet. Today, men's rights websites such as "A Voice for Men" exist. In addition, political parties focusing on men's rights have been formed. In the past few years, also women have joined the debate (cf. Messner 255–256).

In 2017, following the MeToo movement, a term that was coined by activist Tarana Burke, fourth-wave feminism came into being and demanded further progress concerning the treatment of women. Apart from raising awareness for the problem of sexual abuse and sexual harassment, it was mainly a reaction to the fact that, in the 2000s, achievements for women had slowed, especially in business. The percentage of women in management jobs had stagnated and the narrowing of the gender wage gap had decelerated. The U.S. Government Accountability Office reported in 2010 that the share of women in management jobs in the thirteen industry sectors that accounted for almost all of the nation's workforce had increased by only 1% (from 39% to 40%) from 2000 to 2007. In that period, female managers went from earning 79 cents to a male manager's dollar to only 81 cents to the dollar (cf. Sherrill 2–3).

In the following decade, there was even a downward trend, and the share of female managers dropped between 2017 and 2018 (cf. Zarya). This is striking because in terms of women's education and participation in the labor force, the USA is well positioned. Women earned more than 57% of undergraduate degrees and 59% of all master's degrees in 2016 (cf. "Table 318.30") and of 144 countries, the United States ranked first in women's educational attainment in 2017, and accounted for 47% of the U.S. labor force in 2019 (cf. "Labor Force Statistics"). However, the USA has fallen sharply from its 2006 third-place ranking in women's economic participation and opportunity to place 19 in 2017. There are especially significant racial and ethnic inequalities in the rate of women's advancement (cf. Warner).

Concerning politics, the USA ranks 96th in women's political empowerment (cf. Schwab 334–335) and women only represent 24% of the members of Congress (cf. "2018 Election Night Tally"), which shows that there is still work to do. Hence, the goals of fourth-wave feminism, still today, are to represent women in the top levels of business and politics and to achieve equal pay. In addition, the third-wave-feminism objective to support working mothers is still in the focus, as well as to prevent domestic abuse, rape, and sexual assault. The technological age and the internet have produced new issues such as offensive, abusive, and threatening messages online or the misuse of private pictures of women. Hence, legislation that protects women against cybercrime is necessary since law enforcement struggles to react to such problems effectively.

Fourth-wave feminism also desires a better representation of women in the media, for example on television (cf. Chamberlain 111–115). Although an increasing number of successful films portray female talents, it is mostly men who create female images in the media. Furthermore, women's representation in the film and television industry is low. Only 18% of directors, executive producers, producers, writers, cinematographers, and editors who worked on the top films in 2017 were women (cf. Lauzen). The Center for American Progress disclosed that, when there are more women behind the camera or in other key off-screen roles, the representation of women on screen is better. They claim that films written or directed by women have a higher percentage of speaking female characters than films written solely by men (cf. Warner).

5.2 A Variety of Female Detectives in the Late Twentieth Century

Likewise, in literature, the presentation of women is generally more positive in works written by female authors. From the 1960s onwards, after the rise of second-wave feminism, the production and reception of American literature by women writers featuring independent female protagonists grew rapidly. Even those writers who distanced themselves from feminist activism, started to acknowledge and implement the achievements of the women's movement such as equal opportunity and economic independence in their presentation of female characters.

This is also true for detective fiction. In a genre in which there were successful female authors such as Agatha Christie and Dorothy L. Sayers, there is nothing unusual about women writers, but from the 1960s onwards, they presented exclusively female detectives as protagonists and moved away from traditional gender roles. According to Carolyn Heilbrun, these authors demonstrated an openness toward gender that "has found greater momentum in the detective story than in any other genre, and has recently gone further in the United States than elsewhere" (Heilbrun 5). She claims that "this openness about the prison of gender is one of the detective novel's great claims to fame and has been ever since Holmes's Irene Adler put on men's clothing for her own purposes." Heilbrun praises that "the English, who began by being courageously androgynous, are passing that torch on to Americans who today have shown wonderful new possibilities for the genre" (7).

These new possibilities included, above all, the introduction of self-determined female detectives. The readership at the time, with broadened horizons and a gendered consciousness, welcomed this approach. Kathleen Gregory Klein explains that these women detectives interpret the male world and define the female (cf. "Women Times Women" 6). They do not only solve murder cases, but they present the conditions and problems of the time from a female perspective. As Klein illustrates, the new female writers of detective fiction took the world by storm due to their brilliant timing in the second half of the twentieth century and changed the face of the genre:

> Their choice of women as main characters at this particular juncture in cultural history—a moment of feminist and equality centered writing both in the genres and outside has led women mystery writers to produce not simply conventional novels with differently gendered protagonists but gendered novels with noticeably different agendas. (11)

The female protagonists do men's jobs, and they do so successfully. Moreover, they are self-reliant and want no long-term commitments. Almost all of them are single or divorced, and they like it because they manage to cope without the help of men. However, despite everything, they speak about women's positions in society, and they address the struggles they have to overcome. Hence, the female detectives are reminiscent of their male forerunners in their work and lifestyles, but they also make the female living environment a subject of discussion.

5.2 A Variety of Female Detectives in the Late Twentieth Century

One major difference to male detectives is the women's nonprofessional status. Until well into the 1960s, the world of professional investigation was not available to women in real life (cf. Martin and Jurik 110–111). Thus, to portray them in a realistic manner, most female detectives in literature in the 1960s were amateurs. They join the ranks of amateur detectives—the first, and male, nonprofessional detective was created by the American author Jacques Futrelle (1875–1912) with his protagonist professor van Dusen in the early twentieth century. Moreover, as mentioned before, the British writer Dorothy L. Sayers introduced her female amateur detective Harriet Vane in *Gaudy Night* in 1935 and wrote four college novels. However, female amateur detectives only became independent in the 1960s. They can be categorized into different sub groups according to their principal activities. There were several finance officers, doctors, and authors, and there were academic detectives who form the largest group, probably because many authors came from that field. They will be looked at in more detail.

The most prominent American author of a female academic amateur detective is Carolyn Gold Heilbrun (1926–2003) who published her first novel, *In the Last Analysis*, under the pen name Amanda Cross in 1964. Heilbrun herself was an academic and she taught at several universities, focusing on feminist issues referred to in literature. Moreover, she belonged to elite groups formed around women's issues in which works on various aspects of feminism were published, and she was awarded several honorary degrees. Her works are characterized by her academic background and by her feminist beliefs and they are praised for being highly complex, clever and "most accomplished and engaging, and most plausible in presentation" (Craig and Cadogan 243).

Twelve of her novels feature Kate Fansler, a successful professor of Victorian literature. By choosing this profession, Cross presented equal opportunities at universities, although these were only legally recognized in 1972. The amateur detective Kate largely depends on her literary and psychological skills to solve the mysteries (cf. Cross 174–176), and her extensive use of literary allusion and name-dropping is apparent throughout the novel (cf. 72). Kate is graceful, but she rejects the expected destiny for a woman in the early 1960s, which was to stay at home and have children. Although she marries her partner Reed Amhearst later in the series, she does not depend on him emotionally or financially (cf. Craig and Cadogan 245).

Kate cherishes her profession, but she reveals its ills, which lie mainly in the patriarchal attitude of some male colleagues who do not take women and their work seriously (cf. Cross 4) and who objectify them (cf. 130). In all but one of Cross's novels, the victims are female, and all but one of the murderers are male, which shows how cruel men can be toward women (cf. Roberts 96).

The victimized women are mostly intelligent, like Janet Harrison. She was an outstanding college student capable of excellent work and thus she belonged to the group of women who threaten patriarchal orders the most (cf. Cross 88). Thus, Cross's novels portray patriarchal oppression of intelligent women.

Although she reveals male dominance as very serious or even devastating for some women, Cross presents an educated and independent female protagonist on whom hopes are pinned since she utters feminist criticism and fights patriarchy. In the course of the novels, the increasing acceptance of women as workers—even academic ones—and the growing equality awareness that was characteristic of the time can be traced (cf. Roberts 108–109). In sum, Cross's approach complemented and valorized the detective plot with academic and feminist considerations. Her novels cherish traditional good manners and grace, on the one hand, but demand a redefinition of gender prejudices, on the other. Susan J. Leonardi concludes: "She attempts heroically to save the language, order, and manners of the past—except, of course, that she wants equality for women" (116).

Cross's independent female detective, among others,[4] paved the way for fictional professional women in law enforcement from the 1980s onwards. Putting female investigators in roles such as police officers and private eyes reflected the expanded range of women's job opportunities and allowed for the trend toward more women in law enforcement (cf. Jackson 1). Although in the early 1970s only one per cent of American women worked as police officers, this number began to increase in the following years. One passage of the Civil Rights Act of 1964 prevented discrimination against women in hiring and employment, which was also binding for the police force and led to greater numbers of women in this profession (cf. Martin and Jurik 110–112). Likewise, professional, licensed women investigators became a reality, although they only formed a minority as well (cf. Mizejewski 18).

Female authors who portrayed their fictional women as independent and successful police officers and, more often, detectives exemplified these trends. The most famous professional female hard-boiled detectives were created by Sara Paretsky (*1947), Marcia Muller (*1944), and Sue Grafton (1940–2017) in the early 1980s. As already mentioned, there were professional female hard-boiled detectives before, such as Erle Stanley Gardner's (1889–1970) Bertha Cool in the 1930s and Forrest and Gloria Fickling's Honey West in the 1950s, but they can rather be seen as "a male fantasy in a male tradition" (Mizejewski 138). These

---

[4] American novelist, journalist, and professor Valerie Miner (*1947) was also a popular writer of female amateur detective fiction in the academic field and introduced assistant professor Nan Weaver, but only in the early 1980s.

authors did not create a tradition of female detectives, but their novels were male-centered and presented women as dependent on men (cf. Klein "Women Times Women" 12). Bertha, for instance, depends on her associate, Donald Lam, and is not very intelligent or self-confident (cf. Craig and Cadogan 134).

Only British author P. D. James created a rather independent young woman with her professional private eye Cordelia Gray in *An Unsuitable Job for a Woman*, published in 1972. Although Cordelia is only twenty-two years old and still on her journey to adulthood, she is about to find her full identity. The detective is as capable as male investigators, and she adds some qualities that are typically associated with women, such as empathy, that make her investigate successfully as well as protect vulnerable people (cf. Klein, *The Woman Detective* 156).

The approach of American female writers of hard-boiled detective fiction in the 1980s went one step further. They did not want to provide men with what they wanted to hear any longer. Almost simultaneously, the three authors mentioned published novels with professional and mature female private eyes as protagonists and they realistically presented women's experiences in a male-identified profession. The writers offered complex and lifelike female characters who are intelligent, competent, morally responsible, and independent. They feel complete without men, although most of them like to have good men around. The authors emphasized women's capacity to act and dismissed traditionally female roles as victim or seducer, which had still been present in Hammett's and Chandler's works.

With their works, there was a revitalization of detective fiction, and the number of female detective novels published in America has tripled every five years since 1985. Male authors such as Mickey Spillane and Lawrence Block continue to sell, but top-selling crime heroines who claim the bestseller lists have joined them. Hence, the 1980s are often called the start of the new Golden Age of the detective genre reinvigorated by the aforementioned female authors (Mizejewski 19) who will be looked at in the following.

5.3 Sara Paretsky

Sara Paretsky (*1947) had read Chandler before she started writing her first novel. In response to his male hard-boiled detective Marlowe, she wished for a more positively and realistically portrayed female detective because "[i]n all but one of Chandler's novels it's a woman who presents herself in a sexual way, who is responsible for everything that goes wrong." Apart from detective fiction, Paretsky found this negative depiction of women in general fiction, namely "women using their bodies to try and make good boys do bad things." She describes her vision in an interview: "I wanted a woman who could be a whole person, which meant that she could be a sexual person without being evil. That she could be an effective problem solver, as women are in reality but not very often in fiction or on the screen" (Richards).

Paretsky created such a female detective—Victoria Iphigenia Warshawski, a police officer's daughter who is of Polish and Italian descent. Victoria lives in Chicago and she is a lawyer-detective specialized in corporate crime. She is autonomous and successful in her job, and apart from her skills, she has a thorough knowledge of Chicago's power structure and its members.

In her private life, Victoria is equally independent. She was married and divorced at a young age, and since then she has been cautious concerning serious relationships with the opposite sex. Still, Victoria enters love affairs with some men. She is attractive, concerned about her outer appearance, and sexually active. Thus, Paretsky combines intelligence and sexuality in her female detective. Unlike male hard-boiled authors, who portrayed either attractive and fatal women, or unappealing ones, Paretsky advocates that women may combine both and that they may enjoy their sexuality as men do.

Victoria's lovers are often connected with the criminal cases. The relationships usually end after the cases are solved, and she does not appear emotionally dependent on these men. Mostly, they are rather undemanding, available to fulfill her desires, and they do not try to belittle Victoria's abilities or limit her freedom. Thereby, Paretsky portrays a strong female protagonist, on the one hand, and rather sensitive men, on the other. This constellation is the only one that works out for Victoria.

In *Indemnity Only*, Victoria has an affair with Ralph Devereux, who is rather dominant and does not believe in her skills as a detective (cf. 26). By the end of the novel, however, she saves his life. After that, he ends the relationship because he cannot cope with this loss of dominance since he feels that she does not need him (cf. 228). Thus, Paretsky depicts her detective as superior to the patriarch. He has to be rescued by Victoria, but he still cannot accept female capability and independence and instead of standing up to her, he escapes from this uncomfortable situation.

Victoria also has nonsexual connections to men, for example, to her elderly neighbor Mr. Contreras. He, however, is not used to female independence and he often worries about her safety. Victoria is annoyed by such behavior and she clearly cherishes her right to self-determination. Bobby Mallory, a friend and colleague of her deceased father, challenges this even more because he condemns her independent lifestyle. Victoria feels obliged to stay in touch with him in honor

5.3 Sara Paretsky

of her father, but his conservative attitudes upset her and repeatedly make her reflect on women's places in society (cf. Jackson 136).

The protagonist describes that she prefers to be in the company of women because among men she feels that she has to prove herself in order to be accepted. She often meets a close friend, Lotty Herschel, who is rather a mother-like figure for her. When Victoria is with her, she allows herself to be less tough and more authentic. Apart from Lotty, Victoria has several close relationships to equally independent and successful women and she works in social service in a women's shelter. There, Victoria cares for women who are less independent than she is. She strives to enable them to live a more autonomous life in the patriarchal surrounding (cf. 155–156). Thereby, Paretsky clearly advocates the second-wave feminist aim of mutual support between women.

In sum, Paretsky's novels portray a strong woman who represents the image of the New Woman—she is independent, employed, unmarried, childless, self-confident, and she enjoys her sexual freedom. Victoria advocates solidarity among women, and she mainly surrounds herself with moderate male characters. She clearly fights sexism and works against men who demand traditional gender roles. All these attributes and actions reflect the achievements and the notions of second-wave feminism and make Victoria a feminist detective. Her feminist background is even mentioned explicitly—she was active in the abortion rights movement of the 1960s and 1970s, and Paretsky herself was a feminist activist during her days at university (cf. Shuker-Haines and Umphrey 72–73).

Apart from presenting her feminist ideals, Paretsky largely reverses the original hard-boiled pattern and replaces the harsh male detective by a closely resembling and tough female one who appears rather androgynous as a result. When fighting patriarchal characters, Victoria makes use of verbal humiliation to fight her opponents. In addition, she is good at karate, often resorts to violence, and likes to use her gun—especially in order to hurt men whom she dislikes. Such scenes of violence toward men are explicitly portrayed and almost glorified in the novels since Victoria enjoys them (c. 58–59).

Thereby, Paretsky adopts the violent behavior of male hard-boiled detectives such as Spade and Hammer to construct her protagonist. Victoria also resembles them in that she speaks in a vulgar manner (cf. *Indemnity Only* 224). Paretsky portrays male characters as negatively as her male forerunners did with women, and all her villains are men connected to patriarchal institutions (cf. Klein, *The Woman Detective* 215–216). It has been criticized that every aspect of her novels relates to gender and that the reader is constantly made aware that she and her protagonist are feminists. Especially her later works have been criticized for being harsh on men (cf. Schmidt 281).

Paretsky had finished her first novel by 1980, but it took two years to be published (cf. Knight 169), which shows how controversially discussed her feminist detective was in publishers' views from the beginning. Authors such as Marcia Muller and Sue Grafton chose more moderate approaches in creating their female detectives and are more in Chandler's tradition. In order to examine them, the backgrounds of these two authors as well as selected novels will be discussed and compared with those of their male forerunners in detail in the following.

5.4 Marcia Muller

Marcia Muller was born in Detroit and grew up in Birmingham, Michigan. After graduating in English from the University of Michigan, she worked as a journalist at *Sunset* magazine, but she quit and followed her interest in creative writing. In the early 1970s, Muller moved to California and began writing mystery novels, her favorite reading material. As Alexander M. Howe points out, Muller had an early love for reading, especially for the fiction of Raymond Chandler, Ross Macdonald, and Dashiell Hammett (cf. 2).

As mentioned above, however, the publishing market in the late 1970s was not used to professional female detectives and her first three manuscripts were rejected. In 1977, Muller's first novel, *Edwin of the Iron Shoes*, was finally published by David McKay, but they canceled their mystery list and her struggle went on. Her second novel, *Ask the Cards a Question*, was not published before 1982 by St. Martin's Press. Sara Paretsky's and Sue Grafton's first novels appeared in this same year.

To this day, Muller has published thirty-five novels presenting her detective Sharon McCone, three other series of novels, five stand-alone mystery novels, and two series of short stories. Muller is married to detective fiction author Bill Pronzini, with whom she collaborated on several novels. Together with him, she also edited some anthologies and a nonfiction book on the mystery genre. In 2005, Muller became the Mystery Writers of America's Grand Master, and Pronzini was named Grand Master in 2008 (cf. Lindsay 181–182).

The couple's home, San Francisco's Bay Area, is the setting of Muller's novels. Hence, she writes about a place that also Hammett and Chandler used as setting for their writings. Due to her early reading of male hard-boiled classics, Muller was familiar with the standards of the genre when she started writing her first novel. In order to present a female viewpoint in this fiction, she created a hard-boiled female detective and carefully negotiated the standards of the original genre with the needs and particularities of a woman detective. Muller insists that she had no interest in creating a female version of the stereotypical hard-boiled detective. Rather, she wanted her protagonist to be lifelike (cf. Howe 2).

Likewise, Muller's topics are authentic. The investigations often lead to the exposure of social injustice and draw attention to issues of gender, ethnicity, and class. In addition, as Muller claims in an interview, each of her novels focuses on a current issue in American society (cf. "The Time was Ripe" 263). These include social debates such as on euthanasia (cf. *Games to Keep the Dark Away*), environmental issues (cf. *Where Echoes Live*), national security (cf. *Coming Back*), and terrorism (cf. *A Wild and Lonely Place*). The following analysis will focus on three novels that are especially related to the issue of gender.

5.4.1 *Edwin of the Iron Shoes*

5.4.1.1 The Innovative Female Private Investigator

Edwin of the Iron Shoes is the first novel about Sharon McCone. She is staff investigator of Hank Zahn, her employer as well as good friend, at All Souls Cooperative, a legal organization. One night, she is called to an antique shop where the body of shop owner Joan Albritton has been discovered. Sharon knows the victim due to some past incidents of arson and vandalism in the neighborhood. Homicide detective Lieutenant Greg Marcus, whom Sharon later starts a relationship with, investigates the murder. Shop owner Charlie Cornish additionally entrusts Sharon with looking into the case to find out if it is related to the previous incidents in the neighborhood. Sharon unveils love relationships between Joan and Charlie as well as between Joan and bail bondsman Ben Harmon, who was assisting the victim in some legal trouble. Although Charlie is the main suspect, it finally turns out that estate agent Cara Ingalls killed the shop owner because by these means, she could force the antique dealers out and sell the land.

Sharon had been in department store security before she started working for Hank, but after a couple of years, she did not want to continue to spend her life "snooping through racks of dresses with a walkie-talkie in [her] purse" (*Edwin of the Iron Shoes* 25), and so she started studying sociology. Thus, Muller creates an educated female protagonist who represents women's newfound educational opportunities. After university, Sharon did not find a job straight away because "[n]obody wants a college graduate with a lot of vague textbook knowledge" (25). Hence, she worked in security first and eventually started to do some detective work in one of the big outfitters in the city. However, Sharon did not have the chance to deal with many criminals there, which had been her actual aim.

The detective agency eventually fired Sharon because she had refused to follow a special assignment that would have harmed an innocent man (cf. 25). This act is reminiscent of Marlowe, who also followed a strict moral code that included never harming uninvolved people. After that, Sharon started working for All Souls. With this institution, Muller intentionally gave her protagonist a social surrounding and did not make her a loner, as male hard-boiled detectives used to be (cf. Muller, "The Time was Ripe" 361).

Sharon, like her male forerunners, does not have close family ties. We learn about her original family that she is half Indian and that her father was a Navy Chief. Sharon's mother Saskia had been very young, poor, and about to start college on a scholarship when she became pregnant with her, and thus Saskia arranged to have Sharon adopted. Sharon seems to have a trustful relationship with her adoptive mother, because in the end of the novel she tells her about her relationship with Greg. Her adoptive mother is very interested, but she warns Sharon: "Well, just don't you go getting pregnant" (*Edwin of the Iron Shoes* 194). We learn that this is one of her adoptive mother's chief worries because Sharon's two younger sisters have several children each. Sharon concludes that she loves her family, but that conversations like these make her glad that she lives over five hundred miles away from them (cf. 194).

Sharon is clearly contrasted to such mother figures as her sisters because she, like Marlowe, is single and childless, and she rather concentrates on her job. Sharon lives on her own, and she does not need much space or many belongings. She has a small studio apartment (cf. 22) and the only extra item she possesses and cherishes is her red sports car (cf. 17). Consequently, Sharon clearly stands out from women who concentrate on domesticity and embrace their roles as devoted and neat wives and mothers. Instead, Sharon feels at ease with her minimalist lifestyle and with herself in general, as the following example shows.

Sharon is self-confident and not very concerned about her outer appearance. Even if, at times, she wonders if she should change her looks, she concludes that she should stay just the way she is:

> I pulled my long black hair back in a tortoise-shell barrette and wondered, as I did several times a week, if I should get it cut. In spite of my almost thirty years and the gray streak that had been there since my teens, the hair still made me look very much the ingénue. Then, annoyed at the conservative notions I was developing, I yanked the barrette out, brushed vigorously, and went off to the SFPD [San Francisco Police Department] with my hair blowing free in the breeze.
>
> Might as well be yourself, Sharon, I thought. (22)

Matters of beauty never hinder Sharon in any way. When she hears of a murder in the middle of the night, she starts straight away without caring for her appearance (cf. 2). Despite this, she knows how to dress up for special occasions and, unlike Marlowe, she is willing to adapt to societal rules. Before she goes to a meeting with the police, she reflects: "I needed to change, since the soft red jumpsuit, the nearest thing at hand when I'd dressed earlier that morning, didn't seem decorous enough for police headquarters" (cf. 22). Muller makes looks a subject of discussion since a certain appearance is expected in this professional surrounding. Sharon knows about such expectations and lives up to them when necessary, but she prefers to be herself.

Likewise, instead of acting in a traditionally feminine and cautious manner, Sharon, like male hard-boiled detectives, has bad habits and never refuses a drink of Bourbon (cf. 105) or gin, for instance at a business cocktail party. She explains: "I set my empty glass on a passing tray and picked up two fresh ones. I would need fortification to get through this" (45). This behavior hints at the freedom that the feminist movement has achieved for women, and Sharon embodies the New Woman who is free to behave in any way she wants. Drinking, since the 1920s, has become tolerated for women.

Her bad habits also apply to food. Rejecting to be a domestic woman, Sharon does not care about healthy food or cooking. She likes fast food such as a cheeseburger and a Coke (cf. 93) or other quick snacks: "On the way out of the kitchen, I grabbed a handful of cookies from the big jar that was always full of chocolate chips. They would be my dinner" (62). Sharon generally does not care about what other people think of her habits. When she is at Greg's place and he offers her a bagel, for instance, she states: "When Greg returned with bagels smothered in cream cheese, I practically leaped at mine, not caring if I looked starved." Later on, she munches on the bagel and licks her fingertips as politely as she can while he is watching her with amusement in his eyes (cf. 167).

Such behavior shows that Sharon is an independent woman who does not try to live up to former feminine ideals such as gentleness and subtlety, but she is authentic and self-confident enough not to pretend. However, she is not as indifferent to what other people think as male hard-boiled detectives used to be. She seems more life-like in that she adapts to social standards. This can also be seen in her language, which is not always gentle. Sometimes, it is blunt, which is reminiscent of the traditional male manner of speech. When Sharon gets up from under a table in the antique shop and hits her head, she curses: "Damn it!" in a loud voice, but she simultaneously reflects on her behavior: "I must have been making an interesting impression on whoever was out there" (cf. 76). Sharon knows that she is part of a society in which certain patterns of behavior are expected of a woman. Although she often challenges them, she shows that they are still present in people's minds.

In the night after the murder, Sharon does not go to sleep at all, but she drives to All Souls and reads over her files on the vandalisms (cf. 17). She states that she likes All Souls and the premises, especially the kitchen, but she doubts that she would last in such a communal situation for more than two days (cf. 22). This shows that, like Marlowe, she rather likes to be on her own. Especially in the patriarchal institution in which Sharon works, she faces gender prejudices and tries to challenge them by being hard-working.

Sharon is as dedicated to her job as early male hard-boiled detectives used to be. Another night, she sleeps in the antique shop and she does not mind any inconvenience: "My watch showed three fifteen in the morning, and I was exhausted. I could go home, but it didn't seem worth the effort, so I found an afghan on a chair near the cash register, wrapped myself in it, and curled up all five-foot-six-inches of me on the mauve settee, next to Clothilde [a dressmaker's dummy]" (69).

Apart from being hard-working, Sharon is confident about her work and she knows about her strengths. When Greg mockingly asks her if she tries to become a super-sleuth, she claims that she is competent and that her strong point is "knowing how to ask the right questions without trying to cram [her] words into other people's mouths" (26). This statement includes two crucial aspects of Sharon's character. Firstly, Sharon implicitly criticizes the police's manipulative techniques and she contrasts her own moral standards with theirs. Secondly, Sharon self-confidently emphasizes the fact that she has a professional way of communicating, which is indeed one of her major skills. These traits will be further analyzed in the following.

In general, Sharon is on better terms with the police than male hard-boiled detectives used to be. This is probably due to the fact that, compared to the 1920s and 1930s, these institutions have become more professional and trusted. Nevertheless, Sharon criticizes the police's partly misleading procedures, especially because they stand in contrast to her own honesty, which can be traced repeatedly in the novel.

For instance, when Oliver van Osten, the salesman from whom Joan used to buy many of her antiques, offers to give Sharon money for one of the unidentified paintings in the shop, she does not take his offer because she is not allowed to conduct business (cf. 81). This is reminiscent of Marlowe's refusal to take money from his clients when the case has not been solved according to his standards. Even if, for the purpose of solving the case, Sharon sometimes pretends to belong to a certain group in order to gather some information, for example at a cocktail bar (cf. 44–49), honesty is certainly one of Sharon's virtues and she never seriously falls on the wrong side of the law.

As mentioned above, another skill is Sharon's professional way of conducting conversations. Greg observes Sharon in some interviews, and he is indeed amazed that she picks up many details about Charlie's and Joan's relationship just by asking neutral questions (cf. 27). In general, when she interviews someone in connection with the case or even when it seems that she only makes small talk, the reader can observe that Sharon thoughtfully leaves space for people to give her information (cf. 94). It is also due to her conversational skills that Sharon mostly detects flawed people since they often are caught up in contradictions, as the following example shows.

First, Charlie tells Sharon that he and Joan have just been casual friends and then, to explain why she wanted to sell her shop to him, he claims that they have been extremely good friends (cf. 107–108). Sharon concludes that he is not very smart, asks him about the contradiction, and gets the right answer, namely that he has had an affair with the murdered woman (cf. 108). This ability to professionally conduct conversations was less pronounced with male hard-boiled detectives. It takes account of the notion of women being attentive and empathetic and it makes Sharon more lifelike and includes a new facet into the figure of the detective.

Another new facet is emotionality since Sharon works on a case she is emotionally committed to. She reflects: "Even though I hadn't known Joan Albritton very long, she was the sort of person who quickly made her way into your affections and brightened your world with her mere presence. Her death hurt me, much more than I was willing to show in front of Charlie" (11–12). This can be seen in the very beginning of the novel, when Sharon is at the crime scene. Unlike the Lieutenant, who turns away and "motion[s] to a uniformed officer" (3), Sharon is affected by the identification of the victim, which will be shown in the following.

With cold fingers, Sharon asks Hank who the victim was and utters her sympathy softly. Consequently, she begins to shudder and cannot speak for a little while (cf. 3). During her work, Sharon tries to ignore the blood stains on the carpet because they bother her, as well as the "wicked-looking" blades of the weapon—a knife. Sharon swallows hard and sighs several times, and she mechanically touches some of the victim's beloved items (cf. 5). All this shows that Sharon is strained by the situation. This makes her appear vulnerable, but also life-like. Nonetheless, she continues with her work and questions the friend of the victim in a gentle manner (cf. 10).

Sharon is generally comforting toward others in difficult situations. When Charlie is very emotional during the investigation process, for instance, Sharon manages to calm him down and bring him back to work: "But we can waste all the time we want in recriminations, and it won't get us any closer to the killer. Do you want me to find him or don't you, Charlie?" (13). Later, at a bar, Charlie tells Sharon about the fight he and Joan had before her death, and he almost breaks down. Sharon holds his hand, comforts him, and listens to him carefully (cf. 156). In sum, she conceals her own emotions and acts in a rational and consoling manner.

Sharon's behavior is a clear contrast to the depiction of women in male hard-boiled novels. Women, in these novels, were portrayed as being little rational, driven too much by their emotions, and needing guidance. Muller has clearly altered this former prejudice. Sharon keeps calm and helps other people when she feels needed. Moreover, she is good at fighting her own fears with rational thinking. For instance, as Ben threatens her, she discloses her inner struggle: "I put down my terror and thought of the moves I'd practiced in self-defense classes.... I shot my right leg back around his, then rolled my hips and pitched forward with all my strength. He toppled, flipping and hitting the ground on his back, grunting heavily. Shocked that it had actually worked, I stared down at him" (116). Even in serious situations, Sharon stays calm and she sometimes surpasses herself in terms of physical ability.

In contrast to earlier male authors, Muller does not often portray violent scenes, but she chooses them well to show that Sharon is capable of overpowering men, if necessary. However, Sharon does not like to be involved in physical confrontation and she generally avoids getting into danger. If she is involved in a precarious situation, she does not act as tough as male hard-boiled detectives did. One night, when Charlie offers her to go out the back way of the house, she states:

> Damned if I would go into the alley with Charlie's Old Father Death lurking in the dark!
>
> It was bad enough to pass through the roomful of junk on the way to the front door. Several times, I glanced from side to side but saw nothing more threatening than a huge, ugly armoire with gorgons carved on its doors. Just the same, I was glad to get out of there. I waited long enough to make sure Charlie shot the bolt, then raced for my car. Fumbling with the keys.
>
> I needed light, and reasonable, sober people to dispel the gloomy foreshadowing of my own uncertain death. (59)

5.4 Marcia Muller

More than her male forerunners, Sharon realizes her limits and relies on the comforting company of people.

To make up for this weakness, Sharon is wary and very precise in her observations since her experience in security service has taught her that this is a crucial part of investigation. The fact that she immediately spots the significant items at the murder scene, such as the window and the glass cabinet the knife was taken from (cf. 4), shows that she has a passion for detail and works effectively, almost like early English detectives. Furthermore, she observes every detail of her surroundings and the people in it, and, using her intuition, she draws important conclusions from that information. For instance, one day, in front of the antique shop, she sees a black vehicle and immediately spots that it is an unmarked police car. Therefore, she can avoid being observed (cf. 81).

Likewise, Sharon makes use of her intuition concerning people. When she first visits Charlie, she notices: "A moment later a tall, gray-haired man of about fifty-five, clad in old army fatigues, opened [the door]. Charlie Cornish's tiny eyes were rimmed with red, and his long mane was tangled, as if he'd been clawing at it with his fingers" (9). Here, she compares Charlie to a dangerous lion. This impression makes her consider him a suspect, which leads to important information about the case. In a nutshell, Sharon is less courageous than early male hard-boiled detectives, but she makes up for that by observation that is more precise. In the end, she is just as successful as they used to be.

Like her forerunners, Sharon is not satisfied with superficial answers, but she keeps on investigating until she is sure to have found out every detail. When she suspects some credit union of the vandalism because the leaders wanted to use the property for their own purposes, she observes: "[W]hen I found some of their pamphlets in a mountain of trash littering Charlie Cornish's sidewalk, I felt I was on the right track. This, however, was not the concrete proof I needed, and it might just have been evidence of someone else's cleverness" (20–21). Doubts like these make her, unlike the police, investigate further and end up with the right solution.

Moreover, Sharon often treats herself rigorously. She is self-critical when reflecting on her own work and she sometimes blames herself for not being more successful. It occurs to her in a conversation with a suspect that, had she been more effective with her investigations on the vandalism in Salem Street, Joan might still be there (cf. 36). This thought is devastating to her. Likewise, Sharon is modest and admits when she has been wrong or ineffective. As Charlie blames her for not having found out who was responsible for the vandalism before, she agrees that she lacks proof (cf. 12). Earlier male hard-boiled detectives did not show such discernment.

They also did not show any interest in educating themselves further in unfamiliar topics. Sharon, in contrast, in order to increase her chances of successfully solving the case, states that she wants to learn all about antiques, although this is actually not an object of her interest, except as a possible motive for murder (cf. 28). She realizes how little she knows and decides to get some books on the subject from the library as soon as she starts investigating the case (cf. 32–33).

Despite her good general knowledge and manifold interests, Sharon is ignorant of art (cf. 137). In this case, however, she has a friend to help her: Paula Mercer, who can identify the painters of the paintings in the antique shop. When Paula finds out that her friend has a stolen Bellini painting in her trunk, it is obvious that Sharon has never heard of that matter, but Paula helps her out and makes her detect that Joan was a smuggler (cf. 146). This passage is reminiscent of the strong bonds that started to exist between women during second-wave feminism. Since the link between Sharon and her friend helps her solve the case, it is presented in a positive light in the novel. Relations like these were not existent in male hard-boiled fiction. In the end, however, when Paula considers taking the painting into her museum, Sharon focuses on her case and hands the painting over to the police. Again, she is determined and does not let herself get distracted.

In spite of her motivation to work hard, it is obvious that Sharon would like to have more free time and the possibility of spending more time with female friends. This can be seen as she refuses to have tea with Paula because she has to work on the case. Sharon regrets: "As we passed the Japanese Tea Garden, I looked in longingly. Fuchsia and lighter-pink flowers bloomed among the carefully sculpted trees and stone lanterns, and gold and white carp swam in the pool. I wished I could take a few minutes to sit in the tea house, drinking from a white porcelain cup" (143). In such situations, the reader can detect that her job is not always easy for Sharon and that it is very time-consuming, if it is done compassionately. Here, she seems weak and longs for being comforted by a friend and by nice surroundings, but she does not give in. Sharon clearly has a greater longing for company than male hard-boiled detectives do, but she is professional, and she prioritizes more on her job than on her comfort.

In the same way as Sharon describes the Tea Garden in close detail, she observes items around her carefully. When she enters a cocktail party, for example, she notices that "a flower stand at the corner... added gaiety to the scene, but its early spring daffodils were offset by a nearby sculpture..." (43). Male hard-boiled detectives did not make such commentaries. Here, it is obvious that the female perception of the world plays a crucial part in the novel.

In summary, Sharon is an independent, self-confident, and natural woman who is as devoted to her job as early male hard-boiled detectives used to be. She uses her analytical and conversational skills and her intuition to investigate. More than her male forerunners, she is caring and comforting to others. Although Sharon is mostly physically and emotionally strong, she can also be vulnerable at times. This results in a complex picture of a modern woman who shares her concerns and interests—not only relating to her surroundings, but also to the people, which the following chapter will show.

5.4.1.2 The Stubborn Male Main Character

Sharon is particularly interested in Lieutenant Greg Marcus. At their first encounter, Greg learns that Sharon is the detective who has been investigating the vandalism in the area, and she curiously observes his reaction to this piece of information and notes: "Greg hesitated, the corner of his mouth twitching, and I braced myself for one of the variants of the usual remarks, along the lines of 'what's-a-nice-girl-like-you-doing-mixed-up-with-an-ugly-business-like-this?'" (2). Greg actually just announces that he wants a statement from Sharon the next day, but the fact that Sharon is used to such commentaries shows that a woman in the detective business was still considered unusual and even ridiculed by the 1980s because of the notion that women were too gentle to work in such a potentially harmful surrounding.

Greg follows this view and feels that he needs to protect Sharon and give her a comforting feeling. In doing so, Greg is quite pushy. When Sharon goes down to the shop because she wants to take a look around the crime scene, she stumbles and gratefully feels Greg's hand at her elbow steadying her, but she moves away from him as she realizes that his hand is still on her elbow when she looks through the shop (cf. 4). Sharon simply ignores such harassment, which shows that she still accepts her role as the weaker sex in a male-dominated business.

Probably due to such bodily approaches, Sharon even takes an interest in Greg as a man, although she does not think that he might be keen on her. Before she sees him in his office to give her statement, Sharon wonders what to wear and she decides to go for comfortable clothing, adding to herself that Greg is not going to like her no matter what she does (cf. 22). Additionally, she goes through her vandalism files the whole night to prepare for the meeting, and she admits: "I realized I was worried about making a good impression on the man, and I felt a flash of annoyance with myself. Look, I thought, you're not normally an anxious-to-please type, so stop fussing over this statement" (21). Sharon, instead of trying to change the hierarchy, is humble and tries to impress a dominant police officer in a patriarchal system.

In their meeting, Greg clarifies straight away that he only considers letting Sharon join the case for the sake of his friend, Hank. In fact, Sharon has sought for Hank's permission to work on the Albritton case, which shows that a woman in this business was dependent on men's good will. Greg allows Sharon to join the case, but he demonstrates that he is in charge: "We are... to be informed of whatever you find out. Immediately. And completely. Do you understand?". Sharon emphasizes that he has shown his supremacy and responds: "You've made it clear" (24).

Although Sharon has made it into the detective business, the novel exemplifies that men did not treat women equally in this business. Greg's commanding manner of speech is rather reminiscent of the male police officers in hard-boiled novels half a century earlier. With him, Muller presents a man who reinforces his dominance at a time when traditional gender roles are being undermined, and he probably does so in order to defend those roles and to oppose societal changes. Greg does not like a female detective interfering with his case and thus, he keeps her down.

Sharon explains that she only sees the chance to back down: "Greg Marcus was not a man I cared to tangle with. Everything about him was tough and disciplined: the controlled quality of his speech; his tight, economical movements; the lean, trim body—a damned good body for a man who must be in his early forties" (24). Sharon is similarly cowed and attracted by Greg and she does not fight his dominance. Sharon acts in a reasonable manner for the situation because she is caught up in patriarchal structures and has to get along with the men around her since she relies on them for income.

Sharon's cooperative approach pays off little by little. Against her initial feeling that Greg dislikes her, he turns out to be interested in her origin and in her professional career. He questions Sharon about her past, but he cannot let go of scornful commentaries about her professional suitability as a detective. For instance, he asks her whether she knows all there is to know about criminals from her sociological studies and mockingly raises an eyebrow (cf. 25). As they get closer, however, Sharon more and more likes Greg's sarcastic nature because she observes that it is often humorous: "His usual sarcastic expression was in place by the time he got to the door: the familiar mocking quirk of the mouth, one dark-blond eyebrow raised" (83).

His humorous nature allows them to negotiate several topics on jocular terms. When Sharon criticizes Greg's carelessness, for example, because he hangs his wet coat on an antique chair, Greg reacts in a sarcastic manner: "He looked at me in exaggerated surprise, then picked up the coat, ostentatiously wiping a few drops of water from the chair," saying: "Jesus, we wouldn't want to damage one of these valuable antiques, would we?" (84). With an ironic undertone, Sharon states: "Not that particular one. It's genuine, and there are very few other things of any real value in this shop" (84). In their conversation, Sharon and Greg play with traditional gender roles and the notion that the woman minds about the supposedly female sphere of the home.

This humorous style, however, does not make up for the fact that their conversations are not on an equal footing. Greg responds to Sharon's assessment of the chair: "Yes. Papoose, I can see you're learning a lot. It's a pity it hasn't improved your temper—or your appearance, for that matter. You look like you could use a bath" (84). Here, Greg shows a dismissive attitude in a number of ways—he makes fun of Sharon's professional skills by comparing her to a learning infant, criticizes Sharon's mood and looks, and he is racist.

Ignoring the comment about her appearance, Sharon remarks that the nickname "papoose" annoys her. He explains his reference: "That's what they call little Indians, isn't it? Or would you rather I called you 'squaw'?". Sharon, at that moment, is shaking with anger, but she keeps her voice level and replies: "You have no business calling me either. I don't have to listen to your comments on my ancestry or on the way I look" (84). The fact that Sharon utters her anger in an unagitated, but controlled manner, seems to impress Greg. Her subtle resistance prepares the ground for a more equal relationship in the following—although this is still a long way to go.

When Sharon later describes a shop break-in and the intruder of the past night to Greg, in a neutral and focused manner, he questions her professional abilities and her rationality once again: "Sounds more like a woman's intuition than logic" (86). Sharon is angered about such a stereotypical statement and thus, she shifts on the stool and starts fiddling with her hair. She states: "My fingers tangled in the ribbon, and I jerked it out savagely, letting my hair fall to my shoulders. Why did Greg feel he must oppose everything I said?" (86). Again, Sharon does not utter her anger in an aggressive way, but she expresses her point of view in a subtle manner. She keeps her voice calm and repeats that this still is what she thinks has happened.

Winter S. Elliott concludes that Sharon, throughout the novel,

finds herself in situations which represent the very problems second wave feminists contested. Confined within a benign patriarchy, Sharon doesn't actively resist its limitations until its strictures cease to be comfortable. Sharon constantly challenges Greg, who as a police officer aptly figures the power fought through political activism in the 1960s and 1970s. She finds her physicality, her strength, and her professional abilities challenged throughout the book—always on the basis of her femininity. Thus, while Sharon might not qualify as a feminist herself, the challenges she faces are undeniably informed by that same activist feminist movement. (17–18)

Elliott rightly claims that, as long as authority feels comfortable, for example, with Hank, Sharon does not resist it. But as soon as it becomes disagreeable and especially when she finds her professional capacity to be diminished on account of her sex, Sharon objects, albeit in a subtle manner.

Sharon also intervenes when she senses that the investigation process might be hindered. Concerning the choice of people to be interviewed on the case, Sharon criticizes Greg's lack of accuracy, and she turns out to be right. Instead of being open to constructive criticism, however, Greg demonstrates his power and makes clear once more that Sharon is dependent on his good will: "Watch it, Ms. Sharon. You're here only because I say so, you know" (*Edwin of the Iron Shoes* 88). In addition, he continues:

> Now, I have something to tell you, Ms. Sharon, and I want you to listen carefully. You have forty-eight hours, exactly, to finish this inventory and get out of the shop. By noon, day after tomorrow, you are to be gone.
>
> If I see or hear of you talking to anyone involved with the case, if you harass anyone, like the Hemphill people or Mrs. Ingalls, I'll see that you never work again in any investigatory capacity. You will go back to guarding dresses in department stores, where, in my opinion, you belong! (88)

Greg threatens her, and in the end, he clearly utters the male worldview of the time, namely that women do not belong into the detective business.

After this monologue, Sharon takes a step backwards, and she is speechless. Nevertheless, Greg goes on: "In addition, I'm putting a twenty-four-hour guard on this building, in case your so-called murderer returns. I don't want it on my head if you get yourself stabbed to death while inventorying this trash" (89). Greg clearly devalues Sharon's work. Although he finally takes her concern seriously and allows for a security guard on duty, Sharon is angry: "He had ridiculed my suggestion that the intruder and the killer were the same person, but he thought it important enough to put a man on the shop" (89). Sharon finally takes revenge for being bossed around by showing Greg that she is able to outwit him intellectually. She tells him that his calculation of the deadline for her work was wrong and she observes him: "Several emotions warred for possession of his face: anger, disgust, and a trace of admiration. Disgust won out" (89). Sharon does not back down completely any longer and at least to some extent, Sharon's subtle and witty resistance impresses Greg.

Sharon leaves the office feeling relaxed because she is sure that Greg has overestimated the time finding Joan's killer would take her (cf. 89). This shows that Greg's clear announcements do not intimidate her, but they seem to encourage

5.4 Marcia Muller

Sharon to work even harder in order to prove her strength to him. She, representative of many women at the time, is not demoralized by men's strength, but she considers it a challenge to live up to their requirements and to show them what women are capable of. And indeed, Sharon's plan works out, and she is successful in finding the killer. After that, her relationship with Greg becomes more equal and trusting. Sharon and Greg exchange their findings on the case, he allows her back on it, and they even joke (cf. 140). Greg also shows Sharon that he cares for her: "Call me any time, either at the Department or at home" (141). At this point, Greg has acknowledged Sharon's professional capacity.

Due to their more trusting relation, Sharon's interest in Greg comes up again, and there are first signs of jealousy on Sharon's side. When they meet her friend Paula, Sharon watches "Greg's eyes appraise her" and she feels "a tiny, unreasonable stab of jealousy" because "[h]e looked at Paula as a woman, a way he'd never look at [her]" (141). Sharon realizes her feelings and concludes: "I had no business getting interested in the man, I told myself sternly" (141). Later, when Paula asks her who her company was, Sharon utters that he is a cop who despises her, and she goes on: "I'm sure he'll do something to make me despise him again before the day's over. Now let's go look at those paintings" (142).

Sharon's prioritization of the case, which can be witnessed repeatedly in the novel, finally makes her solve it. Although Greg has tried to prevent her from doing so, Sharon breaks into Oliver's office and finds the missing information for the solution of the case (cf. 159–160). Hence, due to her solo run based on her intuition and her courage, she is successful. In general, Sharon is willing to cooperate with the authority, but as soon as her sense of social justice or her determination to investigate are infringed, she does not listen to anyone. Because she solves the case as a result, this kind of independence is advocated in the novel.

A few days later, Sharon visits Greg at home, and for the first time, he considers her as his potential partner: "Say, you and I could become lovers, and then you could add something to the house, too." When Sharon is taken by surprise, he goes on: "Don't look so horrified. I've been told I'm not all that bad." He then asks her how she would improve the room they are in, and she replies in an intentionally irritating, unwomanly manner: "With a gun collection." He jokes: "It's the little feminine touches that make a home," and she concludes: "We grinned at each other warily. Our brief acquaintance had taken an unexpected turn" (166–167). Greg and Sharon play with traditional characteristics of being female and male and dissolve them. This again shows that gender is performative.

Greg also increasingly accepts Sharon's independent and curious character. When they get a call informing them that Oliver is dead, Sharon immediately takes her jacket in order to join Greg, and he says in a bemused tone: "I never knew a young woman with such a fondness for looking at dead bodies, but if that's what you want to do, come on along" (172). For the first time, he accepts her wish without protesting, probably because she has proven by solving the case that she can perfectly deal with any kind of situation. When they arrive at the scene and Greg notices that Sharon stops and breathes hard as she sees all the blood, he briefly squeezes her shoulder in a comforting manner and says gently: "Don't like dead bodies as much as you thought you did?" (175). Again, Sharon is authentic and vulnerable, but she soon acts in her usual professional manner and discusses her findings with Greg. Despite her sensitive nature, he acknowledges her skills, and they work together closely.

After they have left the scene, in the car, Greg asks Sharon to join him for a drink, but she refuses because she is tired. He puts his arm around her and says that he would like to see her again after the solution of the case, nonprofessionally. He promises her to teach her all about Rembrandt and Cézanne and acknowledges that there are things she can teach him as well, "[t]hings about a strong man and a strong woman [and] [a]bout how two such people can be together without diminishing each other or tearing each other apart" (180). The fact that Sharon has proven to be strong and independent has clearly fascinated Greg and thus, he accepts her as an equal partner. This statement is a very important message to the reader, female as well as male, because it mirrors the completion of women's fight to reach equality and the major goal—to live together and get along with men, on equal terms.

As a result, Sharon replies that she would be willing to meet him again. Then, Greg kisses her and she describes his rather subtle body language: "His kiss was an offering, not a demand. I accepted. I leaned my head against his arm, exhaustion and desire mingling." In contrast to his initial behavior, Greg now allows for Sharon's feelings and her wishes and he is clearly less challenging, but they remain on their joking terms, as Sharon describes it: "Like me, however, Greg was unable to remain on his good behavior for long." He utters: "My God, papoose. I can't tell whether you're succumbing to my charms or falling asleep!'". She replies: "For a detective, you're not very observant. And will you quit calling me that ridiculous name? It's a racial slur!'". He adds: "When you think about it, it's also sexist and agist" (180). Here, Muller shows that at least some men are well aware of their patronizing comments toward women.

As Sharon gets out of the car, Greg says with a sarcastic grin on his face: "The course of our relationship is not destined to run smoothly." Later, Sharon reflects: "If anyone had told me two nights ago that I'd ever let that bastard kiss me, I'd have said they were insane!'". The term Sharon uses to talk about Greg

5.4 Marcia Muller

is characterized by their usual teasing interaction. However, Sharon is indeed still skeptical when she thinks of the "new relationship [she] seemed to have contracted with the lieutenant." She states: "Contracted was a good word for it, too: as in contracting a disease, I didn't think it would be healthy. Greg Marcus was a headstrong, domineering man, and I was an equally self-willed woman. He might talk of two such people co-existing in harmony, but I suspected he and I were more the tearing-apart type" (184). Sharon, more than Greg, questions that women and men who both know what they want in life may live together in harmony.

Indeed, when Greg comes to pick Sharon up to meet with the customs inspector the next morning, he drops a kiss on the top of her head and walks into the apartment "with an air of confident possession," which she obviously does not like (cf. 185). He comments: "Nice place, for a papoose." When Greg sees Sharon's narrowed face, he replies jokingly: "Uh, oh. Don't go getting mad at me. It's too early in the day" (185). Greg still plays with diminishing comments, proving that he is well aware of their effect.

Repeatedly, Sharon and Greg discuss gender stereotypes, and they partly do so in a serious manner. When Greg asks Sharon if she had considered becoming a cop before she decided to be a detective, she replies: "I did, but at the time there wasn't much opportunity for women. Lady cops were confined to typing, taking shorthand, and the juvenile division" (187). Although, after 1964, women legally had the right to enter the police forces, Muller hints at the fact that there was no equal distribution of tasks among women and men. Rather, the woman was seen as the office agent who does not have the ability to act independently and who can, if anything, care for young people.

When Greg supposes that Sharon does not have any "womanly skills like typing and shorthand," she replies that she's "a mean shot with a .38, and [she] bake[s] terrific bread." Greg replies: "If you'll bake me some, I'll take you to the police range next week" (187). Sharon purposely plays with a stereotype—namely that of the woman as housemaker and cook. However, she does not dismiss this as untrue, but she claims that, apart from this, she can also be strong and handle a gun. Hence, she is not willing to dismiss earlier female occupations, but she wants the freedom to choose by herself what she wants to do, and she emphasizes an individual identity. Greg jokes that he will only introduce her into "his" male sphere once she has fulfilled her "female" duties. In the end, Sharon and Greg both play with gender stereotypes. They are highly aware of such cliches, but they are willing to question them since they feel that they are outdated.

By the end of the novel, when Sharon and Greg are at an industrial port in order to find one of the important paintings from the antique shop, they appear as equal partners. Although Greg protects Sharon physically, he accepts her independent decisions, as can be seen in the following example. Greg leads them through the stacks of cargo, and he puts his hand around her shoulder to protect her from splintering wood. As she utters that she would like to help the stevedore find the important painting in the crate, Greg motions her forward without hesitation and encourages her to do so. When the stevedore later naturally gives Greg the knife to unwrap the painting, Greg approvingly says: "It's Ms. Sharon's case," and he gives her the knife (cf. 189). Hence, Greg acknowledges Sharon's success and makes others see it as well.

In the final confrontation of the novel, in contrast, Sharon feels that Greg lets her down. Cara is about to attack Sharon with a knife, but Sharon bravely knocks Cara backwards and takes away the weapon (cf. 205). During the following fight, however, Sharon's hand is hurt and she cannot reach her gun. Again, the female detective is not portrayed as physically indestructible. As Greg enters, Sharon expects him to help her because she exclaims that Cara is the murderer, but he does not intervene. It is Sharon herself who has to go after Cara and stop her. When she has successfully pulled Cara down and keeps her on the floor, Sharon requests Greg to act, but only his colleague helps Sharon up and captures Cara (cf. 206). Later, Sharon reflects: "I felt Greg had let me down, first at the shop and next by turning coldly professional on me at police headquarters. I had needed support, injured and shocked as I was, but he had offered none" (210).

Eventually, Greg's inability to act becomes comprehensible. It is unveiled that Greg was Cara's lover and the reason for the divorce from her former husband, which is probably why he did not want to harm her. As Hank informs Sharon about this circumstance, she feels a flash of jealousy and immediately a flash of annoyance at her jealousy, probably because she is still not convinced that a relationship with Greg would be rewarding for her. Hank specifies that Greg did not marry Cara back then, although she was willing, because "Greg found he couldn't handle the idea of a wife who made more money than he did. It was hard for him to accept that Cara didn't need him in any of the traditional ways women need men" (211).

Additionally, her plans for him were bizarre. Hank explains: "Mrs. Ingalls couldn't be married to a cop—it would never do in her social circle. Greg was to quit the force and devote himself to the finer things in life, like servicing Cara and broadening his interest in the arts when she was busy elsewhere. She even offered to pay for painting lessons" (211). This shows that Greg still hangs on to the traditional view of the man being the provider of the family. He is not willing to live with a woman on unequal terms, this time disadvantaging the man, and he turns Cara down. Nevertheless, he apparently favors women who utter their wishes. Sharon is such a woman—but she is not as demanding and superior as Cara. Thus, Greg is willing to enter a love relationship with her.

Sharon, in contrast, raises doubts about her emotional bond with Greg. Hank calms her: "Greg's initial reaction to you was colored by his experience with Cara. He sensed the same strength and independence in you, so he set out to put you in your place. Fortunately, you wouldn't stay put" (112). Sharon's subtle resistance has smoothed the way for an equal relationship between her and Greg. She, in contrast to Cara, does not try to put him down. The fact that Greg rejected Cara but enters a relationship with Sharon shows that he responds much more positively to less radical women who utter their views, but who only demand one step at a time instead of a complete reversal of gender roles. This makes Muller portray active feminism as unproductive.

To summarize Sharon's and Greg's relationship, it can be noted that Greg is skeptical about a female detective at first and he tries to challenge Sharon by being dominant and by ridiculing her work, mostly due to his former experience with a dominant woman. However, he seems interested in her rather self-confident manner from the beginning. Sharon tries to impress Greg at first, but she utters her concerns more and more openly and feels that he takes her demands more seriously. She does not resist his diminishing comments in a radical manner, but instead, she cooperates and works hard in order to convince Greg that women are capable of being successful detectives. She shows him that she is intellectually as well as physically capable of solving the case on her own, and in the end, they work together on equal terms. With Sharon, Muller offers a subtle way for women to gain respect in a former male-dominated profession.

In the end, Sharon forgives Greg for letting her down concerning the arrest of Cara because she concludes that "Greg had hidden in his professional disguise at police headquarters out of embarrassment at my part in Cara's arrest" (214). However, the relationship with Greg does not endure long because Sharon develops further and needs more independence than he is willing to allow her.

5.4.1.3 A Variety of Minor Characters

Another man whom Sharon appreciates is Hank Zahn. He founded All Souls in order to provide quality legal service at reasonable prices to its member clients (cf. 7). He is thirty-five years old and has been practicing family law for nine years. The character trait Sharon values most about Hank is his concern for other people, most likely because she shares this ideal. As Sharon states, he never got cynical nor lost his empathy for his fellow humans (cf. 10). The two of them work together on a friendly basis. Thereby, Muller shows that traditionally feminine characteristics are not limited to women any longer, and she presents this in a positive light.

Sharon also becomes connected with Ben Harmon. When she first meets him, she admires his neat looks and observes that he holds out a large, neatly manicured hand and that he is wearing a flashy suit, and looks as fresh as if it were morning (cf. 104). Her rapport to Ben, however, soon gets worse because he tries to dominate her. When she interviews him about his relation to all sorts of people involved in the case, she is the superior conversation partner at first, and she discovers that he contradicts himself. He, in contrast, presents himself as the dominant sex and states: "I don't like being badgered by little girls playing detective" (109).

Despite this downgrading and sexist comment, Sharon remains seated and goes on with the interview. He, though, does not want to be questioned by her much longer and threatens her: "Listen, you nosy little bitch, I'm not taking any more crap off of you." The fact that his contradictions are about to be discovered makes him angry and insult her in vulgar language. Sharon, in contrast, remains professional and keeps her voice from revealing her fear, even when she is led away by his bodyguard Frankie (cf. 111). Only when she has backed through the swinging door and across the sidewalk toward her car, she has to fight down nausea:

> Frankie's threat hadn't particularly bothered me, but the touch of his body literally made me sick. It was important I remain here, though, waiting for Harmon's next move. I was surprised at how much our conversation had thrown the bail bondsman off, and it was possible he might panic and do something revealing. If he did, I wanted to be on hand for it. (111)

Ben indeed comes out ten minutes later, and Sharon can follow him in the car.

Hence, Sharon's courage and her resilience make her solve the case. Although at first sight it seems that the two men have won the argument because they have thrown Sharon out of the office without letting her finish her interview, she is the stronger character because she has gotten the information she wanted. Sharon is physically weaker and cannot fight men, but her cleverness makes up for that and lets her outwit men who consider themselves superior just because of their sex and their physical strength. Hence, Muller shows a subtle, but effective way of female opposition to patriarchy.

Oliver van Osten is another pushy person. Sharon describes him as goodlooking and bright on their first encounter, but she dislikes his behavior because

5.4 Marcia Muller

"[h]is gaiety struck a discordant note in the light of Joan's death" (29–30). Moreover, he is brash toward women. When he follows Sharon to see Charlie and puts an arm around her shoulder, she is startled and warns herself to watch out because "this one's a not-too-subtle charmer" (30). Sharon continues to substantiate her assessment:

> When I had met van Osten the previous October, I realized within minutes why he had the reputation of being a good salesman. He greeted me warmly, wrapped me in an easy flow of conversation, and quickly let me know he thought me a very special person. Only later, when I was away from his dominating presence, did I realize how carefully calculated his whole act was. That, to me, made him someone to be wary of. (30–31)

Although Sharon feels flattered at first, with a little distance, she is capable of recognizing Oliver's calculating approaches.

Later, when Oliver offers to go through Joan's antiques records with Sharon to see what values to assign to which pieces, she is again distrustful and hesitates: "Van Osten didn't strike me as a man who would be helpful unless there was something in it for him.... He wasn't there because he had always had a desire to be Ellery Queen" (80). Sharon judges his character: "I watched van Osten, disregarding his carefully constructed facial expressions and looking straight into his eyes. Instinctively I stepped away from him, closer to Charlie. I was recoiling from what I had seen, for despite his sympathetic words to Charlie, his eyes were totally devoid of emotion" (32). Oliver lacks humanity and is rather selfish. Therefore, Sharon does not accept any help from him. Her intuition and her knowledge of human nature keep her from dangerous acquaintances.

Likewise, Sharon is careful about Cara Ingalls, although she interests Sharon because she is a power behind many of the large real-estate deals. "[W]omen didn't generally get in on the big operations," Sharon muses (41). This shows that, in the late 1970s, there was still discrimination against women in certain professional spheres and in higher positions of the free economy (which is not to say that this problem does not exist anymore). Despite Cara's pleasant outer appearance, Sharon realizes at an early stage that the real estate agent is not as kind as one might think:

> Ignoring the substance of her words, I studied her.
>
> Ingalls was tall and slender, but her body gave the impression of well-toned muscles and strength. The classic loveliness of her face provided a sharp contrast to the determined, predatory set of her features as she spoke of the Yerba Buena Center [a

community center in San Francisco]. She was feline in a way that reminded me that not all cats are domestic; some are dangerous. (46)

The cat metaphor is reminiscent of Chandler's description of the two *femmes fatales*, Carmen and Vivian, who are pretty, but just as well compared to amoral cats (cf. *The Big Sleep* 10).

This figurative language hints at the fact that Cara has cruel plans. And indeed, although Sharon appreciates Cara's looks and lifestyle, the detective soon finds out that Cara lacks kindness. Sharon describes Cara's outer appearance: "I crossed the street, admiring Ingalls's cashmere coat-dress that met brown leather boots at mid-calf.... [T]oday she wore a little wine-colored felt job tilted rakishly over one eye. She made me, in my simple pants and corduroy jacket, feel like a mere slip of a girl" (*Edwin of the Iron Shoes* 128). Sharon admires Cara's impressive and stylish appearance.

In addition, she likes her independence: "I was beginning to enjoy talking with Cara Ingalls. She was my kind of woman, one who made her way on her own steam and refused to be held back. That was what I had always done, although without anything near her financial success" (129). To Sharon, Cara is a modern woman who has chosen her individual lifestyle, like herself, and she has even earned much money with it.

This appreciation fades, however, when the women talk about the property in Salem Street; Cara claims that she wants to buy it, and she explains: "Look at the trash that moves into those places. Each family with dozens of unruly kids writing on the walls—if they can write at all—and dirtying the place up. Those people shouldn't be allowed to live here" (130). Sharon is irritated by that statement and describes her emotions: "Her tone was matter-of-fact, and it shocked me." She calls Cara's attitude "rather calloused" (130), but Cara replies in a patronizing and derogatory manner: "Miss Sharon, let's have none of your girlish liberal sentiments. The world is a big, harsh place" (130). Sharon, ignoring Cara's dominant manner of speaking, returns in a self-assured way: "I try to hang on to my ideals" (130).

This again proves Sharon's strict moral code, which advocates humanity. She concludes about Cara:

> It was a shame about Cara Ingalls, I thought, as I started down the sidewalk to the place I'd left my car. She was an intelligent, strong woman, and strikingly attractive, but in spite of that I couldn't help pitying her. In her rush to make it, she had left a part of her humanity behind, and her desperate reaching out to me signaled that she felt its loss. (132–133)

Sharon clearly sets herself apart from Cara and demonstrates that making a career, regardless of the social surroundings, is not advisable for women or people in general, and does not make them happy. As demonstrated with Greg, Cara has a general disdain for men. In the end, Sharon is annoyed with such people as Cara, and she is rather alone than joining them.

Sharon is not hostile toward men, but in the following novels, she gets romantically involved at times. Her longest relationship is the one with Hy Ripinsky that starts in Muller's 13th novel (cf. *Wolf in the Shadows*). Sharon continues to work as an investigator for All Souls. She is successful in her work, but the firm has grown and is no longer small and informal. It has new legal partners and Sharon's headstrong investigations are no longer accepted. She is offered a raise in salary, but this would limit her to office work and she decides against it. Instead, Sharon opens her own business (cf. *Till the Butchers Cut Him Down*), which shows that she knows exactly what kind of work she wants to do and she is self-confident and brave enough to become a freelancer. By the 22nd novel, *The Dangerous Hour*, published in 2004, the firm is successful and has a growing staff as well as plenty of work to do.

5.4.2 The Dangerous Hour

5.4.2.1 The Mature Female Detective

In the beginning of the novel, Sharon claims that she is satisfied because her San Francisco firm has tripled in the last two years and it has bright future prospects. Sharon's nephew, Mick Savage, leads their new computer forensic department, and they are looking for assistants to extend their areas of activity (cf. *The Dangerous Hour* 3). Sharon reflects on her career: "Not a bad situation for a woman who once worked out of a converted closet at a poverty law firm" (4).

Despite her success, Sharon is down-to-earth, and she sometimes misses her idealistic and light-hearted old self and "those days when [her] generation [held] the firm conviction that [they] could change the world" (4). Now, Sharon is more mature and realistic and she knows that she can only make a little difference with her investigations. As a reminder of the past times and of her professional fortune, she has an old armchair in her office, covered by a throw to make it fit into the new surroundings. Hence, she cherishes past times and knows that her former experiences have made her into the person she is today—a successful freelancer. In the course of the novel, however, Sharon's agency and her career are threatened.

Julia Rafael, one of Sharon's new employees, is accused of credit card fraud against a recent client, Alex Aguilar, but it turns out that she is innocent and that Alex has simulated the fraud. His dubious past leads Sharon to two murders: Scott Wagner, Alex's business partner, died, supposedly in a hiking accident. Sharon finds out that he was a drug dealer. Johnny Duarte, another drug dealer, allegedly fell off a cliff while walking, which makes Sharon draw the line to Scott's death. Her partner Hy Ripinsky is also involved in solving the case, and he warns that the harassment might stem from one of Sharon's former clients, which places her on the right track.

Years ago, Sharon tracked down Reynaldo Dominguez, a drug distributor in the San Diego area, and she convicted him of murder. Sharon finds out that, when he was released, he killed Johnny to take control of the drug business. For the same reason, he killed Scott. It turns out that he finally wants to take revenge on Sharon for putting him into prison. In the end, Sharon faces Reynaldo and overpowers him. Although he pretends to be mentally insane, Sharon, in an interview, provokes him to admit his crimes. Eventually, he is found sane, the case is solved, and Sharon and her agency are out of danger.

Sharon's professional change has also led to alterations in her private space, and she lives in a more sophisticated way than before. She owns a spacious house with an alarm system and a cleaning service that copes with her untidiness—when Sharon gets home, she uses to drop her clothes carelessly on the floor (cf. 131). Moreover, the facts that she is three weeks overdue picking up her dry-cleaning and that she mostly eats meals from the microwave when she does not eat out show that Sharon is still not willing to fulfill the traditionally female domestic role. Instead, she has advanced her career and kept her independence—apart from two cats, Alice and Ralph, she still lives alone (cf. 31).

Yet, compared to the first novel, Sharon has become more social, which contrasts her to male hard-boiled detectives. Adah Joslyn, for example, who is also an investigator, is a friend Sharon likes to go swimming with and whom she admires for her professionalism (cf. 163). Daphne Ashford is another friend—a graphic artist who helps Sharon to work on portraits of suspects so that she can solve the case at hand more easily. Connections to other women, who are similarly strong and independent, are clearly portrayed as being helpful. While Sharon rather longed for such connections in the first novel, she has realized them by now.

Apart from friends, Sharon's family plays a bigger role in her life. Sharon's brother has committed suicide with an overdose of drugs and alcohol the year before (cf. 59). Sharon is quite realistic about his death. When an old friend of her brother's, Gary Viner, expresses his sympathy to her and blames himself for not having contacted his high-school friend for so long, Sharon replies:

> Oh Gary, nobody heard from him, and nobody could've helped, even if they had made the effort. . . .
>
> For a time there I beat myself up for not trying to save him, but now I realize that people who push everybody away can't be dragged back. They need to want to save themselves. Joey didn't. (211–212)

Sharon acts in a mature and stable manner and implies that she is now aware of the fact that she cannot help everybody. Hence, she is a strong woman who can assess personal and emotional events rationally. Nonetheless, she often thinks of her deceased brother (cf. 109), and she feels that grief about the loss of her son has made her adoptive mother cling to her more tightly (cf. 103), which shows that Sharon is more influenced by her family now than she was in the first novel of the series.

Nevertheless, Sharon does not depend on anyone, and she focuses primarily on herself and on her career. As a result, she has developed from a staff member in a patriarchal system into a manager who runs her own company. With this depiction of Sharon, Muller reflects the reality of the time. At the turn of the century, it was natural for many women to lead independent and successful lives. In preceding years, sex segregation in most professions had declined, the gender wage gap had narrowed, and the percentage of women climbing the management ranks had risen steadily. In 1980, there were no women in the top executive ranks of the top 100 companies in the United States, while by 2001, 11% of corporate leaders were women (cf. "Fulfilling the Promise"). Thus, it was not unrealistic anymore to portray a female manager who performs well in her position.

In contrast to the first novel, Sharon now mostly wears suits that "presen[t] the proper image for the owner of a successful and growing agency" (*The Dangerous Hour* 54). Although she admits that she still prefers jeans and sweaters (cf. 55), Sharon represents her position adequately, and she is more prepared for every occasion in terms of her outer appearance than she was years ago. Before she goes to a bar to spy on Dan Jeffers, a drug dealer, she rummages through several outfits before she chooses some leather pants and a leather jacket in the end (cf. 126–127).

Sharon reflects on her looks:

When I was dressed and surveyed myself in the full-length mirror on the back of the door, I had to admit I looked like a woman any self-respecting drug trafficker would be eager to meet. The long, red enamel earrings that matched the silk tee were a particularly nice touch. Before I left the office, I took my .357 Magnum from the safe and slipped it into my bag. I didn't like to carry the gun under normal circumstances, but tonight I'd feel better with it close at hand. (127)

Being dressed in a feminine and appealing way, Sharon feels vulnerable and has the urge to protect herself from her potentially dangerous companion.

Her concerns are unfounded, though, because when Sharon is at the bar, drinks wine, and talks to Dan, she outwits him by pretending to be interested to work for him (cf. 129) and by twisting him around her little finger. When he utters that he is enamored with women who have high cheekbones and black hair in ponytails, like Sharon, but that he does not like red lipstick and earrings, she plays along, rubs her lipstick off, and gets rid of her earrings. In the end, Sharon gets much more information from him than he is aware he has given away. She concludes triumphantly: "When under the influence of a considerable quantity of single-malt Scotch, even the most streetwise drug dealer is no match for this private investigator—wine or no wine" (130). Sharon is self-confident and exactly knows when to play with her feminine charms in order to attract men and make them give out information.

Apart from just playing the feminine role, the female detective introduces some new characteristics into a formerly male position in an authentic manner. Unlike Cara Ingalls, from Muller's first novel of the series, who has lost her humanity in the course of her career, Sharon is benevolent, caring, and supporting to all her staff members—especially to Julia, a young woman with a criminal past who is now accused of credit card fraud. Sharon describes her feelings about Julia: "Sometimes, she's a truth teller. She's also a bit of a con woman—but then, so am I. Nobody who doesn't possess a sneaky, shifty side gets very far in our business. You walk a little to one side of the line, a little to the other, and hope you don't stray too far" (86). Sharon admits that the detective business requires some cunning characteristics, and she refuses to distance herself from the young woman: "I don't want to give up on her. She's come far since I hired her" (87).

Instead of making decisions over Julia's head, Sharon decides to talk to her and asks her everything she needs to know. In the end, Sharon assures Julia: "The agency is behind you one hundred percent" (118). When Sharon feels that the young woman is still discouraged, she comforts her in a professional and rational manner: "I've analyzed what surface facts we have, and I think the charges against you—and the agency—are the result of a carefully orchestrated plan on the part of

5.4 Marcia Muller

Aguilar. We need to know the reason behind it" (119). In the following, Sharon questions Julia further: "Now, I'm going to ask you some questions, based on things I've found out over the past couple of days, and I want you to think carefully before you answer them" (119). Sharon has developed her skills of conversation further, and she is more mature than in the first novel because she takes on a leading role.

This also shows later in the novel, after Reynaldo has tried to shoot her nephew Mick. While all the others prove unable, Sharon is the only one who can really comfort him. She is rational as well as understanding, pats his hand, and tells him that his behavior in the precarious situation has been really good (cf. 264). At all times, Sharon acts in a professional manner and she is up to the tasks she has to face.

In everyday situations, Sharon is also caring toward her employees and she attends to their issues. Although she has plenty of work to do, she feels responsible for the wellbeing of her staff at any time and thus, she adequately fulfills her role as a manager. Nevertheless, Sharon can also be moody if something is done against her order or behind her back, but soon after that, she usually apologizes for her behavior (cf. 206). Thus, Sharon knows that she is the boss and she can meet these requirements, but she does so in a rather prudent manner.

Apart from being caring, Sharon is straightforward toward her employees. She trusts every single one of them, and she does not deny them access to any department in the agency (cf. 7) or to any piece of information (cf. 48). This helps her create a trusting atmosphere. Her employees also appreciate that they can often be on a humorous basis with Sharon, which can be seen in several conversations (cf. 103–104). Consequently, they like working for her and they work very hard, if necessary. Sharon appreciates this and she is rewarding toward them. When they work extra hours toward the end of the case to find Reynaldo, for example, she decides: "When this situation was wrapped up, I would treat my staff to one hell of a celebration" (218). And indeed, she does have a celebration with all of them after the case has been solved (cf. 290).

This shows that Sharon is determined to solve the case, whatever it takes. When she learns that it involves her own agency as well as one of her employees, she balances: "I was equal to the task, wasn't I? Look at the cases I'd solved single-handedly. Look at what the agency had collectively taken on. And it didn't matter that this case was deeply personal; I'd solved that type of case before" (82). Although Sharon is realistic and does not portray herself as a heroine, she is self-assured and takes on the case. In the course of her investigations, Sharon becomes convinced that Reynaldo has committed the murders, and she is intent on tracking him down on her own although Mick warns her not to do so. Sharon courageously replies that she is not alone and pats her bag containing her .357 Magnum (cf. 225).

This proves that Sharon does not match the traditional notion that women are too weak for such a potentially harmful job. Quite the contrary—the following passage is reminiscent of descriptions in early male hard-boiled novels. This time, however, a woman walks down the mean streets:

> A dark, half-block-long Mission-district alley that, so far as I knew, didn't have a name. Near the projects, where men loitered on the sidewalks doing drugs and drinking from bottles in paper bags. Sirens wailing in the background—police cars and ambulances speeding toward S.F. General. Busy night in the mission, and by now the emergency room I'd left earlier would be filling up with its victims. But here in the narrow space between two old warehouses silence prevailed.
>
> I walked along, hand on the .357 Magnum in the outside compartment of my bag. Listened to the crunch of my shoes on gravel and broken glass. The cold wind whipped down the alley and blew the hood of my sweater off my head, bringing with it the smell of garbage, urine, and feces. On the street behind me tires screeched, there was a thin crash, and then the vehicle sped away. (229)

Muller depicts perfect gender equality here, showing a strong woman who is absolutely independent and effective in a job that was exclusively available for men in the past. Sharon, just like Marlowe, navigates through the underworld in a self-assured manner. Compared to the first novel, she has a more professional self-conception now and doing that job feels much more natural for her. Also, her surrounding accepts a woman in this position, as her connections to the criminal underworld show.

Sharon meets her informer, Claude Cardenas, street name Cowboy, in a bar. In her contact with Claude, Sharon shows that she is aware of the manners of the criminal underworld and that she can adapt herself to them. She knows how to approach him discreetly: "He glanced at me, registered surprise, then looked away. I turned and went back outside. After a few minutes he came through the door and started down the alley; I followed him into the shelter of a Dumpster behind the warehouse" (230).

When they talk, Claude utters that he is glad that Sharon needs a cowboy again, and it is obvious that he is still stuck in the notion that the weak woman needs the strong male hero to succeed. He does not recognize that Sharon only uses him to get some information, but disrespects him for his crooked actions. Sharon does not protest, probably because she is aware that it is not worth discussing the matter with someone who is caught up in such traditional gender roles (cf. 230). A feminist would certainly not have ignored this sexism; Muller's protagonist, however, being a powerful woman, concentrates on taking advantage of him.

After Sharon has all the information she needs, she hands Claude forty dollars, which is their usual upfront arrangement (cf. 231). After that, he asks her if all this had to do with the rumor that some woman was going to die. He adds that he is surprised to see her at the bar because the potential victim sounded like her (cf. 232). Sharon is outraged and thinks to herself: "The little bastard! All these years I've put money in his pocket, treated him like a human being. He hears there's a contract out, suspects it's on me, and doesn't give warning." But she concludes: "Well, what do you expect from a scumbag paid informer? Loyalty?" (232). Sharon needs people like Claude to get certain information about criminals, which is why she does not start a dispute, but it is obvious that she despises his sexism, carelessness, and amorality.

In contrast to early male hard-boiled detectives, Sharon does not feel to be a part of this criminal underworld, although she has a good knowledge of their activities, which can be seen in the conversation with Darrin Boydston, the owner of a gun shop. Sharon is aware that he makes illegal deals, and, by verbally blackmailing him, she forces him to tell her about the purchase Reynaldo has made (cf. 245). Darrin, according to Sharon, is an old-school Texan, and she remembers that years before, when she gave him a ride because his car had broken down, he told her that she drove "right good, for a girl" (244). In a similarly degrading manner, he calls Sharon "little lady" (cf. 245). Sharon protests, but it does not seem worth fighting his stereotypical images. Sharon uses a subtle approach instead and tries to create a better understanding of what women are capable of. She tells him that a friend of theirs has just published a novel, and Darrin concludes: "Women these days—ain't it amazin'" (246). Female intellectual capability surprises him.

It is for this reason, as well as for their crooked actions, that Sharon disdains men such as Claude and Darrin. Nevertheless, although her own actions are more ethical, Sharon herself does not hesitate to be dishonest from time to time when it helps her in the case. For example, she pretends to be a freelance writer who is creating an article about a certain organization, and she uses the name of her half-sister, Robin Blackhawk, to get admission and information (cf. 52). However, Sharon does so "with mental apologies to [her] half-sister" (129). Sometimes, Sharon acts intuitively, and she only realizes that her actions are unlawful when it is almost too late. When she squeezes through a fence to get into a building, for example, she thinks to herself: "Criminal trespass, Sharon. You get caught, you'll be in even more trouble." But instead of turning around, she concludes resolutely: "Then I won't get caught" (234).

Despite this commitment to the case, Sharon is human and encounters problems at times. When she visits Alex's building to interview his employees about him, for example, Sharon is afraid when she walks to her car in the dark and hears sounds (cf. 73). And indeed, when she arrives at the car, she sees that the convertible top has been slashed and that her briefcase has been stolen, and she laments: "I inspected the damage to the top, saw it was not repairable. They probably didn't make tops for this model anymore; I would need a costly custom job—and at a time when I could least afford it. Jesus, how could everything in my life turn to shit in such a short time?" (74). The case at hand and the resulting fact that her career is at stake obviously strains Sharon.

In addition to her professional life, Sharon's personal life does not run smoothly either. After her boyfriend Hy has asked Sharon to marry her and she has requested for some time to think it over, she describes her feelings: "Everything seemed to be crashing and burning around me. Hy had suddenly changed from the easygoing man I'd fallen in love with to a man with a mission. My cat had diabetes. I was riding across the bridge—which was now totally socked in—in a car whose top was held together with duct tape. My life felt as if it could use duct tape" (82). Such admission of weakness makes Sharon lifelike and distinguishes her from her male forerunners.

Aside from such powerless moments, Sharon is still determined to convict Reynaldo, and she wants do so by herself instead of risking anyone else getting hurt. Even in challenging situations, Sharon is caring and she leaves warnings with people that might be in danger (cf. 258). Only when she is certain that nobody in her surrounding will be harmed, does Sharon fully concentrate on solving the case:

And here I was, at close to eleven. Waiting.

I got up, began pacing. I was exhausted but wired. Wanted to be doing something, needed motion, action.

I paced some more. Returned to the armchair. Stared at the fog. Again went over the details of what had happened from the day Reynaldo Dominguez had arrived in town to the events of a few hours ago. He was out there somewhere, and I –

Sudden jolting thought. I grabbed my bag and jacket and ran for the MG. (268–269)

Sharon is absorbed in the case and her unusually staccato phrases reflect her inner turbulence.

Later, after Sharon has found Reynaldo, he is following her. Sharon tries to dial the emergency number, but she realizes that she is out of reach and concludes:

5.4 Marcia Muller

"Okay, I wouldn't panic. The night was clear enough, and the security spots on the old adobe guided me. Soon I'd get to my car and drive to a place where the cell worked. Or find that dinosaur of the communications industry—a pay phone" (283–284). Sharon keeps calm and rational and considers what she can do. She is even humorous in such a dangerous situation. Thus, she is more mature and self-assured than in earlier novels of the series.

When she cannot make it to the car and Reynaldo gets closer, though, Sharon decides to hide behind a rock and stays there for a while. However, as she realizes that this could go on all night, she is brave, takes the offensive, and shows Reynaldo where she is, risking her life to finally solve the case. She eventually fights and overpowers him, although she is hurt and in pain (cf. 286). Later on, Sharon is annoyed at herself for having taken such a foolish risk to face him on her own. Unlike early male hard-boiled detectives, she admits mistakes. "All the while I was beating myself up for falling for Dominguez's ruse. Chalk it up to impatience, a desperate desire to bring the matter to a conclusion before anybody else got hurt. But I'd been damned stupid, and it could still get me killed" (284).

A few days after solving the case, Sharon has an interview with Reynaldo because the court wants to find out whether he is sane or not. Reynaldo repeatedly calls Sharon "puta," which is "whore" in Spanish, and Sharon concludes: "You don't like women, do you, Dominguez?... You like that kind of word, don't you? Puta.... They're [those words are] obscene, degrade the woman whom they're directed at." And she continues: "Let's talk about other words—or actions—you like.... Humiliation. Torture. Rape. Murder. Acts of a coward who's really afraid of women" (297).

Sharon provokes Reynaldo by implying that he humiliates women by verbally or physically attacking them because he knows that he is intellectually inferior to them. Thereby, she names physically palpable manifestations of patriarchal structures. The fact that a man who puts such crimes into practice is the criminal in the novel portrays male dominance as evil and inexpedient. Sharon knows how she has to speak to Reynaldo to make him get indignant. In the end, she threatens him that eventually all his crimes will be uncovered and he will be put into jail for the rest of his life or be given a lethal injection if he does not speak. As a result of Sharon's skillful interviewing, he panics and admits his crimes (cf. 297–298), which proves that he is indeed intellectually inferior to Sharon.

After the interview, the psychologist asks Sharon if she wants to talk about the event, but she refuses, thinking: "If I start talking to a shrink about all the trauma I've endured over all the years, I'll be on the couch for the rest of my life!" (299). Despite all the setbacks of recent years, Sharon is a strong woman who is able to cope with her problems on her own.

Her positive depiction as well as the favorable presentation of her educated and independent female friends in the novel stand in contrast to the negative portrayal of most men in the novel. They are often sexists, drug dealers, murderers, and immoral members of the criminal underworld. One male character, who is presented as being human and considerate, however, is Sharon's boyfriend Hy Ripinsky, who will be discussed in the following chapter.

5.4.2.2 Rewarding Partnership and Marriage

In the beginning of the novel, Sharon reveals that Hy has asked her to marry him. Although she loves him, the thought of marriage fills her with dread and thus, she has requested some time to think about the proposal. In order to give her this time, Hy is on vacation at his ranch in the countryside, waiting for her decision. It is obvious that Sharon knows Hy well because she can tell what he would do at the different times of the day (cf. 44–45). Moreover, she is convinced that he is thinking about her and she emphasizes that they have a strong bond: "Hy and I had always shared an odd psychic connection, and now I could feel his mood as if he were beside me." Sharon explains further: "Today he was contemplative and patient. Biding his time without feeling particularly anxious. Giving me the chance to decide what direction I wanted our future to take. No pressure, and thus no call" (45).

Sharon reflects on her reluctance to marry him:

> So why did I feel pressured? And why couldn't I bring myself to call him? Normally, given what had happened during the past two days, I'd've been on the phone to him, seeking his input and reassurance. But now …
>
> I glared at the phone.
>
> Why did people want to change things that were functioning perfectly well to begin with? Why did they want more, when less was enough—?". (45)

Sharon allows that Hy gives her comfort in difficult situations. The relationship with him is rewarding because they support each other at eyelevel. However, being an independent woman who can easily make a living with her job and who has a social surrounding that satisfies her, Sharon dislikes the notion of committing herself to another person. She prefers to keep her independence and lead a fulfilling relationship in addition.

Hy finally calls Sharon and asks her out for a picnic, but she has too much work to do. She reflects: "Take me on a picnic in an isolated place; hold me hostage till I'll talk about our future. Somehow, the idea didn't alarm me as much

5.4 Marcia Muller

as it would have a week ago, and genuine regret crept into my voice as I turned him down" (164). Sharon clearly feels pressed and even associates marriage with captivity, but she realizes that she gets used to the thought of it more and more. Not wanting to make a decision yet, Sharon tells Hy that there is a work-related problem she could need his input on, and he offers to meet her to talk about the issue in the evening. Sharon is pleased:

> The idea appealed to me. We'd have a nice evening, a productive exchange of ideas about the situation with the agency, and a good time in bed. Now that I could anticipate Hy's arrival, I realized how much my body had been aching for his. And Sunday we'd have brunch at a favorite restaurant, attend the book signing, spend more time in bed.
> Maybe I'd even get away without a discussion of marriage. (165)

This statement clearly contradicts traditional notions of the desires of women, such as marriage, domesticity, and noble reserve. Sharon, in contrast, cherishes intellectual exchange at eye level, and sexual, culinary, and cultural satisfaction. She focuses on experiencing different facets of life with her partner and rejects marriage (still at that point). Hy rather is the one who longs for a fixed relationship and who presses the woman, although he treats her with respect and grants her time to make her decision. Thus, the notion that the pursuit of a certain lifestyle is tied to the sex of a person is denied.

When Hy visits Sharon that night, she feels comforted: "Suddenly I wanted to insulate the two of us in a warm cocoon where no problems—his or mine—could touch us" (177). They have sexual intercourse first and then they talk about the case. Sharon is pleased, but as Hy calls himself a potential stepdaddy for her cat, he feels that she tenses. Hy then assures Sharon that he does not want to talk about the proposal again since he has uttered his wish, and now, he is waiting for her decision. Sharon asks him what they are going to do if the wishes are not the same, and Hy replies: "Sharon, we love each other. We'll negotiate something." Hy assures Sharon that he loves and respects her, unaffected by her decision for or against marriage. This relieves her because he does not take the "all-or-nothing stance" she has feared (cf. 178).

The way in which Sharon talks to Hy and openly expresses her feelings and concerns shows that their relationship is trusting and at eye level. Moreover, Sharon is more mature and self-confident than in the first novel. Her former partner Greg was much more dominant toward Sharon and although she tried to revolt against some of his behavior subtly and often jokingly back then, their relationship did by far not reach the equality and harmony as the connection with

Hy. Nevertheless, Sharon still has a close connection to Greg, as the following conversation shows.

Greg tells Sharon that he is going to get married again, and she asks him how he has decided to do so. Greg replies that it just feels natural for him and Sharon wonders why it is not natural for her. She explains her concerns to him:

> In case you haven't noticed, marriage isn't what the Sharon family does best. My parents divorced; my brother John divorced; my brother Joey never even got close to marrying. Charlene and Ricky broke up; my youngest sister, Patsy, has three kids by three different fathers, none of whom she considered tying the knot with. Bad track record, all around. (183)

When Sharon realizes, however, that her birth parents had a happy marriage, and Greg underlines that heredity is as important as environment and prompts her to think the matter over again, she is pleased.

Later, Hy offers Sharon to stay in town longer to support her further in the case, but underlines that there is still no pressure on the personal front. Sharon concludes: "God, he was a good man! When I compared him to most of my much-loved but problematic relatives, I couldn't understand why I hesitated to allow him into my family." Then she considers honestly: "Because you can't lose your family. Them, you're stuck with for life. But if a marriage doesn't work out, you could very well lose Hy" (186). Sharon cherishes her current relationship with Hy, and she is afraid of spoiling it with a fixed commitment, probably because she fears that this involves restricting each other. Too much restriction was also the reason why she broke up with Greg years ago, which makes her fear comprehensible.

The fact that Sharon's relation to Hy is rewarding shows repeatedly when she describes her affections toward him: "My stomach was growling empathically when I looked up and saw Hy standing in the doorway. His hazel eyes were shining in a manner usually reserved for fine aircraft" (195). It is not only his outer appearance that she admires, but also his comforting nature. One evening, when she is on her way back home, she admits: "During recent years, I'd experienced greater and greater pangs of loneliness when Hy departed on one of his business trips or went alone to his ranch or our Mendocino County seaside retreat" (202). Nevertheless, Sharon still hesitates about marriage: "It's such as risk, and I'm not sure I can afford that big a one" (202).

As Sharon is about to solve the case, she listens to a message on the answering machine saying that Hy is going to be back the following day, and she thinks to herself: "Hurry home, Ripinsky, I need you" (272). Especially in difficult situations, she is grateful for his support. This again distinguishes Sharon from early hard-boiled detectives who were less strained by their cases and appeared to be more heroic. Sharon is vulnerable and life-like and she cherishes comforting company. Thus, after the case has been solved, Sharon and Hy fly off for a weekend.

At first, Sharon is afraid that Hy might talk about marriage again, and she still does not know what to reply. However, in the course of the flight, she reflects: "Since I'd been with Hy, he'd enriched my life in so many ways: with the flying we loved; the remote and beautiful places he'd shown me; but mostly with his love, support, and understanding." Finally, he asks her to marry him again, and she agrees, thinking: "You've risked your safety time and again. You've risked your life, too. Why not risk happiness?" (304). Although Sharon is still skeptical about the concept of matrimony, she shows that it does no longer mean subordination for a woman. Instead, it should consist of common hobbies, broadening the horizons together, loving, and respecting each other. Under these circumstances, Sharon is willing to enter into marriage.

Although Hy has a dark past of corrupt entanglements that challenges their relationship at a certain point (cf. *The Ever-Running Man*), Sharon and Hy are happily married, and in the 32nd novel, they finally settle into their new home after losing their former house due to a fire (cf. *Someone Always Knows*). In the 33rd novel, *The Color of Fear*, published in 2017, Sharon has to solve a racially motivated attack on her family.

5.4.3 *The Color of Fear*

5.4.3.1 The Female Detective and Her Private and Professional Partner

San Francisco private detective Sharon is personally involved in the case at hand because her dad is beaten up in the beginning of the novel. Sharon first thinks that it was a racist hate crime and further incidents in the area that seem to have been motivated by racial hatred underline this assumption. It turns out that the same group of racist teenagers has committed them all, with their leader being Rolle Ferguson. As more assaults occur, however, Sharon realizes that the attacks have also been motivated by hatred against her. Sharon's house is broken into, and messages of racial hatred are written on the walls, she receives a racist call at Christmas, and her company is hacked and blackmailed. Moreover, her employee Julia's car is bombed, and Mick's house is defaced with racist graffiti.

Sharon investigates Ferguson's premises and finds a dead man in the bathtub. He is Hispanic and has been beaten to death by the group. Shortly after that, Sharon overhears that the attacks against her and her father were indeed committed out of racist reasons, but also because she sent a friend of one of the boys into prison years ago. They are even planning to murder one of her employees if they do not get three million dollars. Sharon manages to sneak out of the house, but Jerzy Capp, one of the boys, follows her. Sharon overpowers him in self-defense, calls the County Sheriff's Office, and they find the boys still on the premises and arrest them. In the end, one of their laptops is found and becomes evidence of their racist activities. Sharon and her agency are out of danger.

Sharon's personal and professional circumstances have changed. Meanwhile, she and Hy live in a comfortable home with leather furnishings, a native-stone fireplace, and a big flat-screen TV, just to mention some of the conveniences. In addition, they merged her agency with his international executive protection firm into one entity and their elegant offices are located in an ancient building with a roof garden in the thriving financial district (cf. *The Color of Fear* 23). Their firm is a 24–7 open operation, and they have busy employees (cf. 105). However, at the end of the novel, Sharon decides that they need support. She is tired of spending most of her time in the office because, as she says, she is an investigator, not an administrator (cf. 259). Not being willing to retreat into office work, Sharon makes Will, a friend, work for them.

Sharon and Hy often cooperate. In the beginning of the novel, for example, the two of them investigate the area in which her father was attacked (cf. 77). This stands in contrast to Sharon walking through the streets alone, as was still the case in "The Dangerous Hour." Nevertheless, Sharon is still independent and most of the time, she works on the case by herself. The couple often only meets in the office late in the day to exchange their findings. Even so, Hy's companionship is a support to Sharon because he acknowledges her intellect, and he assists her in a subtle, but effective way. For instance, he encourages her to rely on her senses concerning potential suspects (cf. 87). Hence, unlike in earlier novels, female intuition is portrayed as a positive characteristic by a male character.

Moreover, Hy sometimes stops Sharon from working when she is absorbed in the case and thus, he helps her balance her working and her private life so that they can spend more time together. Sharon and Hy lead a harmonious relationship, and they share similar moral concepts in life, for example, in that they donate money to charities (cf. 10). It is also obvious that they want to belong together. For instance, they have got matching terry cloth robes (cf. 7). The following situations give proof of how their relationship has developed into a loving, mature, and supporting life partnership.

5.4 Marcia Muller

Sharon describes Hy as being easygoing and good-natured, with a sly sense of humor and an edge that complements her own (cf. 94). These characteristics can be traced when Sharon shops before Christmas. As Hy finds the trunk full of bags, he jokingly asks her when she went binge shopping and hugs her (cf. 140). He is also considerate and caring. One morning, he lets Sharon sleep long because he feels that she is exhausted. However, as Sharon criticizes Hy for this because she needs to work, he apologizes for being overprotective. Hence, Sharon insists on being treated equally and Hy respects this wish.

In return, Sharon allows him privacy. When Hy works hard on a solution to a case, for example, she does not disturb him and she tells others not to do so (cf. 72). Sharon also grants him his privacy and freedom in general, but sometimes, Hy is unreliable and Sharon is annoyed when he does not answer his phone (cf. 101). Still, they only rarely have arguments, but they talk to each other about problems in a mature way (cf. 116). Sharon does not seriously worry about Hy if he cannot be reached because she trusts in his capabilities to do his job successfully, and vice versa (cf. 189). Nevertheless, it is difficult for Sharon when Hy leaves for longer business trips because she knows that it may take a while until he calls her (cf. 170). Despite their equal relationship, Sharon sometimes seems vulnerable, and she has to accept that she cannot change his habits.

Hy can also play the dominant, masculine role. On Christmas Day, he instructs Sharon to wear "that killer blue velvet shirt" he gave her, mocks her, and advises her that she should just not slop gravy on it (cf. 156). Sharon does not react negatively to this rather provocative statement concerning her appearance and her clumsiness, probably because she knows his humorous manner. This situation reflects the conviction of third-wave feminism that men are free to underline their sexual desires as long as they treat women respectfully in general.

Hy does so and he takes on a protective role from time to time. In the middle of the night on Christmas Eve, there is a knocking on the door, Hy takes his gun and heads downstairs, and he tells Sharon to stay where she is. She, however, refuses and goes down the stairs with him (cf. 163). This shows full gender equality. In situations that require professional ability, Sharon wants to prove herself. In private surroundings, in contrast, she does not mind being comforted. After the resolution of the case, for example, Sharon describes her state of mind: "I was curled up on the sofa in front of a crackling fire when I heard him come in. He dropped his travel bag on the floor, crossed the room, picked me up, and held me tight. I clung to him for a long time before he set me down" (251). Sharon willingly accepts to take on the gentle role and to be sheltered by Hy.

Hy knows that Sharon likes to feel valued and respected, and he sends her a weekly rose on Tuesdays. He started out with a yellow rose when they did not know each other well, and now that their relationship has deepened, it is a dark red rose. Sharon explains that, every time she receives a rose, she is thrilled (cf. 167). On Christmas Day, Hy buys a mistletoe and kisses Sharon, and he also offers Champagne, a paté, and other snacks she likes in order to have a private Christmas dinner before they join their friends and family (cf. 155). Sharon treasures such moments, which shows that she is both a gentle woman who likes to be appreciated by men at eye level and an investigator who fulfills harsh work and who is master of most situations.

In terms of relationships, in summary, Sharon has developed significantly in the course of the novels. In the beginning, she is submissive and tries to please Greg, a rather dominant police officer, who questions her strength and skills as a detective. By and by, Sharon begins to be true to herself, and she utters her demands. Thus, Greg respects her more and more, gets less dismissive, and realizes what she is capable of. However, she eventually ends the relationship because she wants to keep her freedom.

Hy, in contrast, offers Sharon a rewarding relationship at eye-level. She demands her needs more clearly than before, and they discuss personal as well as professional issues and work together closely. Although Sharon is skeptical about making a commitment, she marries him and the marriage does not involve subordination of anyone. They both act in a mature and loving way, Sharon enjoys taking on the gentle part, and she likes to be comforted by Hy at times. Although she remains independent and can care of herself, she is soft within and likes to be sheltered. Her emotional needs are being met by a relationship with a man.

With regard to her profession, Sharon has become more independent, strong-willed, and responsible. She works for a legal organization in the first novel, turns into the manager of her own successful firm later, and she eventually merges it into one entity with her husband's company. Sharon is skilled and dedicated to her job at all times, but she becomes more and more self-assured and accepted as a female detective. As a freelancer, she has responsibility, and she manages to create a trusting work climate in her company. Thus, her employees like working for her and they do a good job. In problematic situations, Sharon is mature and supporting toward them.

5.4.3.2 Remaining Gender Conflicts

Sharon does not experience gender inequality in her relationship with Hy, but she still encounters patronizing men from time to time, as the following two situations show. When she talks to a bartender in the area in which her father has been attacked, the man explains that there was a group of boys in his bar, and that they talked in a vulgar way. He states that these days, this is normal

5.4 Marcia Muller

and even common with women. He concludes: "If you ask me, broads have filthier mouths than the guys sometimes" (79). The bartender naturally uses this derogatory name for women. Sharon does not intervene, probably because she can see that she would not get anywhere with him because of his lack of critical reflection concerning matters of gender.

In professional and more sophisticated contexts, however, Sharon is annoyed by gender inequality. When police officer Priscilla Anders interrogates Sharon and Hy about former clients that might want to harm them, she questions Hy first. Sharon observes: "My back was up; Anders was following a standard routine of ignoring the female witness while catering to the male" (17). Later during the conversation, Sharon points out that she thinks that the attack might have been motivated by racial hatred, and she observes: "Anders nodded as if I were a schoolkid who had given the right answer to a tricky question" (18).

Muller portrays, in formerly male-dominated institutions such as the police, women who are still taken less seriously than men. It is interesting that even a woman who works in that area seems to have taken on this condescension toward her own sex instead of trying to change it. Anders seems to accept and imitate certain male terms of behavior and their routines without questioning them. Sharon has worked hard over the years to emancipate from such patriarchal structures and especially the fact that a woman obstructs gender equality because she does not seem to reflect on her actions seems to concern her (cf. 18). Sharon esteems people who are aware of remaining sexism and resist it, but in a subtle way.

It becomes clear that Sharon does not support radical groups when she looks for organizations that commit hate crimes. Apart from groups she has heard of, Sharon finds groups sounding as if they were "the do-good variety," but she reveals that "the profilers' summaries of their activities showed their true dark sides" (99). Sharon refers to "the "Society of Men" that is clearly misogynist, devoted to smearing the reputations of women in positions of power in business or politics. She also finds "The Sisterhood," an organization that is targeting men, and "Women for Equality," who do not seek equality for the male gender (cf. 99).

Hence, Sharon hints at the existence of hate groups of either sex and she sets herself apart from their radical ideas. Instead of demonizing the other sex, she rather tries to help increase female equality, which the following example shows. Kendra Williams, one of her employees, cancels her contract and Sharon suspects that she did so because she cannot handle her big family and her job. Sharon does not want to lose her, and she knows that Kendra's financial needs cannot be met without the job. Thus, Sharon modifies Kendra's working hours so that she can combine work and family (cf. 96). Thereby, Sharon supports one major goal of third-wave feminism, which is to help women balance their responsibilities for housework and childcare with their work. In the following, Sue Grafton's female hard-boiled detective will be analyzed in three novels of the series in order to trace related developments.

5.5 Sue Grafton

Sue Taylor Grafton was born and raised in Louisville, Kentucky. There, she also attended the university and graduated in 1961 with a degree in English Literature, Humanities, and the Fine Arts. After her studies, she married and moved to California. Grafton held different jobs and started writing novels, but she was not successful at first. Only two of her seven novels were published.

In the early 1970s, having to raise three children on her own after having been married and divorced twice, Grafton accepted an offer to write the screenplay for one of her novels, *The Lolly-Madonna War* (1969), in order to earn money. Although she kept on writing screenplays for the next fifteen years, it did not satisfy her because she wanted to be her own boss instead of having to write by committee. Thus, she returned to writing fiction in the late 1970s. Bruce Taylor claims that this was her "antidote to the work in Hollywood" and "[e]verything else has simply been part of the journey to get to this place" (cf. 5).

Grafton, whose father was a mystery writer, explains that she decided to write detective novels because she loved the material as well as its form, "which is difficult, subtle, complex, and challenging" (cf. *Letter to the Author* 2). She describes how she has been especially attracted by the novels by John D. MacDonald and Harry Kemelman and by the coherent titles of their works. Inspired by this idea, Grafton created a series of novels based on the alphabet with the letters representing a thematic content of each novel (cf. "A Conversation with Sue Grafton 1996").

All of Grafton's twenty-five novels of the alphabet series are set in and around the fictional town of Santa Teresa, California, and present the female private investigator Kinsey Millhone. Grafton's first novel, *"A" Is for Alibi*, published in 1982, drew immediate attention. Readers recognized that Grafton consolidated and expanded the new form that Marcia Muller had introduced. Like her, Grafton specifies that she intended to offer a progressive approach to male hard-boiled detectives. She explains: "I'd been reading a great deal of mystery fiction and I finally got bored with male detectives who drank, smoked, and imagined that all women were wildly attracted to them. I could see hard-boiled detective fiction turning into pure male fantasy and the monotony wore me down" (*Letter to the Author* 2).

Grafton aims at showing that women are capable of doing the same jobs as men and that men can be deceptive and "fatal" as well. Like Muller, Grafton focused on the authentic depiction of her fictional detective and constructed a less heroic investigator than their male forerunners. She claims: "I want her [Kinsey] to be life-sized. In the stories I construct, the fate of the Free World doesn't rest in her hands. She's a small-town private eye, trying to make ends meet" (3).

Apart from her fictional detective, Grafton herself has become well-known. As Linda Mizejewski claims, "the usage of the author herself has become more common for trade-book marketing since the 1980s" (21). The scholar argues that "[p]opular authors are expected to be available to fans not just in occasional print and television interviews, but on regularly updated Web pages, many of which offer an email address for feedback or interaction" (22). More than Muller, who also has her own website, Sue Grafton met these demands. Her face has become a familiar icon of her detective novels. Before she passed away in 2017, she was frequently available for interviews and online interaction on her website, and she replied to personal letters, which are quoted in this study selectively.

Because of this strong presence of the authors, readers often try to find out the biographical truths of the authors' fictions. In Grafton's case, there are striking parallels to Kinsey's surrounding and her biography. The fictional Santa Teresa where Kinsey operates is based on Grafton's Santa Barbara where she maintained a home in a suburb. Kinsey's disciplinary problems at school and the dislike for too much bureaucracy that made her quit her job as police officer stem from Grafton's own character. Moreover, the fact that Kinsey lost her parents early is taken from Grafton's life, as well as her having been divorced twice. In addition, like Kinsey, Grafton jogged frequently and she loved fast food. She even owned a VW like Kinsey that bore the license plate with her protagonist's name (cf. Mizejewski 22).

As Mizejewski claims, "she both is and is not Kinsey" (34). Grafton underlined this assessment by stating that Kinsey was less domestic and more courageous than her, but she felt that Kinsey was her alter-ego: "I think of her as the woman I might have been had I not married young and had children. In fact, I live two lives, hers and mine. Of course, hers is the more adventuresome" (*Letter to the Author* 2).

Grafton added that she often asked herself in real life whether Kinsey would take certain decisions and that Kinsey's growth was parallel to her own in that they both kept changing and exploring themselves. Grafton talked about Kinsey as if she was a real person and this made her so lifelike to the reader. Grafton even predicted that the identification between her and Kinsey was so strong that by the time she wrote "Z," the last novel, there would be no Sue Grafton. There would only be Kinsey Millhone (cf. Kaufman and McGinnis Kay, 253). Unfortunately, because Grafton passed away before she could write this very last intended novel of the series, there is some truth in this statement.

Apart from the construction of her protagonist, Grafton built on Muller's model and made hard-boiled detective fiction more realistic in general, offering a diversified view. Grafton claimed that she was interested in the psychology of crime: "As far as I can tell, crime isn't restricted to one ethnic group, one sex, one income bracket, or even one educational level. I'm curious about the mindset of criminals who are often so cleverly disguised that once they're caught, we learn we've been living right next door to them" (cf. *Letter to the Author* 1–2). Hence, apart from gender, Grafton explored social circumstances, which the analysis of three of Grafton's novels will show.

5.5.1 *"A" Is for Alibi*

5.5.1.1 The Self-Sufficient Woman Detective

Private investigator Kinsey Millhone works in Santa Teresa, California. After high school, Kinsey received formal training at the police academy, and she used to be a police officer with the Santa Teresa Police Department, but she quit after two years because of the patriarchal attitude toward women officers and the bureaucracy there (cf. *"A" Is for Alibi* 64). This suggests that there were still patriarchal structures in law enforcement in the early 1980s. Although she does not fight such structures actively, Kinsey is aware that they exist, and she is independent enough to step out of a surrounding in which she does not feel esteemed and self-determined.

After that, Kinsey held a variety of jobs before joining a small private investigate firm for two years. She then obtained her license and opened her own office in an insurance building close to her apartment with no need to pay any rent, but in exchange for investigating two or three cases for the owners each month (cf. 6). Hence, compared to Sharon, Kinsey becomes an independent freelancer earlier.

In the novel, Nikki Fife, who has just come out of prison, visits Kinsey. Her husband, Laurence Fife, a prominent divorce lawyer, was murdered eight years ago and Nikki was falsely blamed for the murder. Now that she is free, she hires Kinsey in order to find the real murderer. During the investigation, Kinsey detects that Laurence had left his first wife, Gwen, for Nikki, but Gwen and her

5.5 Sue Grafton

ex-husband were still having an affair. Gwen does not only admit to the affair, but also to having murdered Laurence. Shortly after her confession, however, she is found dead.

In addition, Kinsey investigates Charlie Scorsoni, Laurence's former business partner. Kinsey finds out that Laurence's death is connected to that of his apparent business friend and accountant Libby Glass. Both died from oleander in capsule form that was switched with their allergy medication. Through further investigation, Kinsey discovers that Charlie was having an affair with Libby. He killed her when she discovered that he was embezzling money. Charlie dispatched Libby the same way that Gwen had killed Laurence to make everyone assume that there was only one murderer. Bit by bit, Charlie feels that Kinsey has detected his true character, and he finally tries to kill her, but Kinsey shoots him dead, despite their love affair.

Kinsey is thirty-two years old and has been twice divorced. Her marriages were brief, and, according to Grafton, they ended because the men were wrong for her (cf. *Letter to the Author* 3). The fact that Kinsey was married clearly distinguishes her from early male hard-boiled detectives. They did not even mention their marital status because it was taken for granted that they were single. Kinsey mentions her relationship status explicitly, which hints at the fact that readers may still understand women to be dependent. Kinsey, however, is now self-determined and free. She enjoys single life in her one room bachelorette and specifies that she has neither children, nor pets, nor houseplants (cf. *"A" Is for Alibi* 5).

Kinsey does not seem to consider being single a loss of security, as many women in the 1970s still did. She does not need to have men around; in contrast, she has experienced that a bad marriage is an obstacle to happiness, which is her utmost goal. Hence, Kinsey embodies the independent woman that stands in contrast to Gwen's recapitulation of the limitedness of her married life: "[I]n those days I was the dutiful wife.... I cooked elegant meals. I made lists. I cleaned the house. I raised the kids.... I wore my hair up in this French roll, not a pin out of place, and I had these outfits to put on and take off, kind of like a Barbie doll." Gwen explains that she is angry at herself for "buying into the whole gig" and she describes that she was totally unequipped to deal with the real world because her husband made the major decisions (cf. 43–44). These considerations reveal marriage as part of the patriarchal suppression of women.

Kinsey, in contrast, is absolutely self-determined in both her private and professional life and she chooses freely how to behave. For instance, she does not cook (cf. 99). Kinsey, like McCone, embodies the image of the New Woman—she is employed, single, childless, and not domestic. The fact that Grafton constructs her protagonist in this way without social disrepute shows that those trends, which had arisen in the 1960s, were present in the minds of the people by the 1980s.

Kinsey's love of freedom might result from her upbringing—she lost her parents in a car accident when she was five years old and was raised by her aunt Susanna, who taught her to be autonomous (cf. 146). In the first novel, there is no more information about her family, but Kinsey, like Sharon, is more social than her predecessors, and she likes to spend time with friends who offer emotional support. For instance, Rosie, the owner of the tavern in her neighborhood, is a trusted friend and a mother-like figure for Kinsey. Moreover, her landlord Henry is important for Kinsey, and there are coworkers and clients she cares about (cf. 21–23).

However, Kinsey does not allow friendships to become all-consuming in her life, and she hates to be reliant on someone. She enjoys the fact that she can take care of her own affairs, even if they are simple. She claims: "I stopped for gasoline, using the self-service pump and thinking, as I always do, what a simple but absurd pleasure it is to be able to do that sort of thing myself" (39). In addition to affairs of her everyday life, Kinsey is her own boss in terms of her job. For example, when she has worked hard, she allows herself to take days off for good behavior (cf. 113). Mizejewski accurately describes Kinsey as "the professional woman who needs space, time, silence, and control of her agenda" (23).

Kinsey embodies a new consciousness and works alongside men without feeling inferior or dependent. Kinsey, unlike male hard-boiled detectives, is willing to cooperate with the law enforcement. However, she is still faced with rather patriarchal structures there as becomes evident when she tries to win Lieutenant Dolan over: She explains: "I don't know what kind of gripes you have with the other private investigators in town, but I stay out of your way and I've got nothing but respect for the job you do. I don't understand why we can't cooperate with one another" (*"A" Is for Alibi* 84).

Dolan, in contrast, does not want to treat Kinsey as serious business partner at first because he is skeptical about a female investigator. He downgrades her intellectual capacity and suggests: "You'd get more out of me if you'd learn to flirt" (84). Dolan is more used to women who fish for his attention than to independent investigators and thus, female power irritates him. Kinsey, however, shows in this conversation that she is not going to behave in a submissive way. She states: "No I wouldn't. You think women are a pain in the ass. If I flirted, you'd pat me on the head and make me go away" (16).

After a while, Dolan admits: "I don't think you're a bad investigator. Young yet, and sometimes off the wall, but basically honest at any rate" (19). Since leaving the Santa Teresa Police Department, Kinsey has developed further and due to her self-confidence and respectability, Dolan soon takes her seriously. This basis of mutual respect paves the way for their frequent cooperation in the course of the novels, which stands in clear contrast to the investigative approaches of early male hard-boiled detectives.

Like her forerunners, though, Kinsey has financial problems. Her wage, namely thirty dollars an hour plus mileage (later on, she asks for around 50 dollars), leaves her relatively poor (cf. 26). Hence, Kinsey is often astonished about the carelessness in which other people give out thousand-dollar checks (cf. 27). Nevertheless, she likes her ordinary middle-class life. She appreciates living in a small space, just as she likes her car cramped. Since Kinsey often has to travel for her job, she always keeps a packed overnight case in her VW in order to be flexible. She explains: "It just makes me feel secure to have a nightgown, toothbrush, and fresh underwear at hand" (11).

As she is given a clue in the beginning of the novel, Kinsey is indeed spontaneous and she immediately drives off to Las Vegas (which is around six hours drive). She does not mind driving, also at night. Kinsey, in this respect, resembles the lonely frontier hero. She appreciates her independence and she prefers solitude to big cities. Once Kinsey arrives in Las Vegas, it is obvious that she dislikes it. She disapproves of gambling and she cannot stand the smell of cigarette smoke and spilled scotch. According to her, the atmosphere in the gambling halls is "that of a crowded Woolworth's at Christmas" (cf. 119).

When Kinsey is not on the road, most of her days are the same and consist of "checking and cross-checking, filling in blanks, detail work that [i]s absolutely essential to the job but scarcely dramatic stuff" (37). Kinsey is hard-working and highly professional. She is intellectually sharp and works in an analytical manner, but she also listens to spontaneous hints and uses her intuition concerning people around her and the world she lives in.

Even if Kinsey cannot prove her assumptions, they are mostly correct. After the case Kinsey has actually been hired for is solved, for example, she still feels uneasy about the situation. She states: "There was something not right and I couldn't put my finger on what was bothering me. There was no feeling of closure" (246). The continuation of her investigations makes her reveal the second murderer, Charlie. In the final scene with him, Kinsey proves that she is physically and psychologically strong, and she shoots him dead.

Yet, Kinsey can be disillusioned at times because people around her are morally corrupt. She never falls on the wrong side of the law, except for breaking and entering when it is necessary. Like Marlowe, Kinsey has a moral code, but like him, she is also realistic and knows that dishonest people often get away with their behavior. She observes: "The ludicrous fact of the matter is that in this day and age, a white-collar criminal can become a celebrity, a hero, can go on talk shows and write bestselling books. So what was there to sweat? Society will forgive just about anything except homicide" (262). Kinsey is aware that she cannot restore full order.

Being less heroic than her male forerunners, Kinsey can be weak and strained at times. For example, she acts quite emotionally when she is confronted with death. When she finds Sharon Napier, Laurence's former secretary, dead, Kinsey feels pity for her, and she wants to hold her hand and bring her back to life. Actually, Kinsey knows that this is "misplaced sentiment" (133), but still, her hands shake so badly that she can hardly manage to drive her car (cf. 135). Furthermore, it often makes Kinsey nervous when she does not have a quick solution to a problem (cf. 67). As a consequence, just as all other hard-boiled investigators do, she often has a drink in such situations—but instead of hard liquor, Kinsey prefers wine (cf. 20).

When Kinsey is stressed by her job, she also finds relaxation in running. Apart from the fact that Kinsey thinks that she might need fitness in an emergency one day (cf. 113), she likes it: "It hurts and I'm slow but I have good shoes and I like the smell of my own sweat" (64). Unlike some women who just exercise in order to lose weight, Kinsey is in harmony with her body, and she shows little sympathy for thin women in magazines with "one foot arranged in front of the other, as though weight loss also involved the upsurge of charm and modeling skills." Kinsey wonders if everybody in California is obsessed with self-image (cf. 161). She is not subject to this cultural slimness ideal. On the contrary, Kinsey eats without guilt. She loves fried food "drowned in ketchup" with French fries, preferably from McDonald's (cf. 114).

Kinsey is also not too much concerned about her outer appearance, but in her daily life, she dresses comfortably and cuts her hair with manicure scissors. She specifies that she dislikes women who "spen[d] about forty-five dollars having a free makeup demonstration in some department store" and whose "fingernails [a]re long and painted the approximate shade of cherry syrup in the sort of boxed candies you wish you hadn't bitten into so eagerly" (63). Kinsey is not influenced by societal expectations for women concerning their outward appearance, but she makes deliberate choices according to her preferences, and she favors function before appearance. This strong self-awareness represents the notion that there is no longer a collective female identity, but individual wellbeing is the utmost goal.

Some women in the novel, however, stand in clear contrast to this. When Kinsey meets glamorous Charlotte Mercer, an ex-lover of Fife, for the first time, she observes: "She had to be fifty-five years old and there was no way she could

5.5 Sue Grafton

have looked that good without a team of experts. There was an artificial firmness to her jaw and her cheeks had that sleek tucked-up look that only a face-lift can provide at that late date" (78). Indeed, Charlotte later advises Kinsey to have her eyes done in a couple of years, but Kinsey replies that she likes lines and that she earned them (cf. 83). By emphasizing this, she criticizes society's expectations of feminine beauty. She underlines that trying to live up to them leads to artificiality.

Although Kinsey rejects supposedly feminine ideals of beauty, she has some knowledge about activities that used to be attributed to domestic women. When she enters Charlie's office, she recognizes the wool skirt of his secretary immediately and detects that she must have knit it herself. Kinsey observes the skirt and calls it "a masterpiece of cable stitches, wheat ears, twisted ribs, popcorn stitches, and picot appliqué." Thinking of knitting, Kinsey remembers her youth and, hence, she feels connected to this woman straight away. Kinsey explains that "[s]he and I became instant friends when I recognized the aforementioned—my aunt having raised me on a regimen of such accomplishments—and we were soon on a first-name basis" (32).

This valorization of women's domestic skills shows that Grafton includes a female perspective in her works. Kinsey aligns with Charlie's secretary and demonstrates that women can share interests and be friends. They are no longer portrayed as competitors for men, as was mostly the case in male hard-boiled novels.

In summary, Grafton, more than Muller, picks up characteristics of the early male hard-boiled novel, but in her construction of the female detective, she goes beyond her male forerunners and experiments with the genre. Grafton constructs Kinsey as a complex character who is personally and professionally independent, skilled, and determined to solve her cases. Her professional way of investigating even allows her to gain the respect of patriarchal police officers and to cooperate with them. Kinsey is generally strong, but she also has her foibles and weaknesses, which makes her a round, lifelike character. Knowing that she is not perfect, Kinsey is still at ease with herself and she prefers to be on her own instead of defining herself in a relationship to a man.

5.5.1.2 The Deceptive *Homme Fatal*

Although Kinsey does not like to commit herself, she does not reject occasional love affairs with men. Even though he is still on her list of suspects, she is interested in Charlie Scorsoni. When Kinsey first meets Charlie, she describes him as conservative middle-aged man (cf. 31). Kinsey specifies Charlie's appearance: "His collar was open, his tie askew, sleeves rolled up as far as his muscular forearms would permit. He was tilted back in his swivel chair with his feet propped up against the edge of the desk, and his smile was slow to form and smoldered with suppressed sexuality" (33).

Kinsey's explicit observations are reminiscent of the male detectives' carnal descriptions of women in the hard-boiled novels of Hammett and Chandler. The fact that Grafton undertakes a role reversal and that it is now a woman who describes a man in this manner reflects realities of the time. By the 1980s, women increasingly separated physical from emotional love and objectified male bodies. This is exactly what Kinsey does.

However, Kinsey does not debase Charlie, as many radical feminists did with men, but she depicts him as strong and masculine and notices Charlie's hard traits and "that barely suppressed male animal [that] seemed to peer out through his eyes" (36). The hint at Charlie's beastly nature evokes parallels to the negative descriptions of the deceiving women in early hard-boiled novels and indicates his future role as a murderer. Male hard-boiled detectives had to face the same challenges. The *femmes fatales* were sexually attracting, but baleful.

Charlie seems to be interested in Kinsey as well because he eyes her in close detail so that she feels embarrassed (cf. 33). As they talk about the case, however, Kinsey observes that "[t]he sense of sexuality that had seemed so apparent at first was seeping away and [she] wonder[ed] if he could turn it off and on like a heater" (33–34). Kinsey and Charlie are both factual and Charlie listens to Kinsey's observations with interest. Nevertheless, she has the feeling that he knows exactly how much he wants to tell her about the case and what he wants to hide from her (cf. 34). Kinsey is rather polite and undemanding in the conversation because she specifies that, "[a]gain, that barely suppressed male animal seemed to peer out through his eyes" (36). Kinsey senses that Charlie might pose a risk to her and her investigations, and thus she is cautious.

Nevertheless, Kinsey is attracted to Charlie. She admires his "thick, sandy hair" as well as his "solid jaw, cleft chin, [and] his blue eyes magnified by big rimless glasses." Kinsey is astonished at her own positive reaction toward Charlie. She reflects: "I'm a real hard-ass when it comes to men. I don't often think of a forty-eight-year-old man as 'cute' but that's how he struck me" (65–66). Indeed, Kinsey cannot resist Charlie's sex appeal. When he leaves her office, they shake hands and Kinsey notices: "I didn't know why—maybe just an excuse to touch" (69). She admits: "Even a contact that casual made the hairs stand up along my arm. My early-warning system was clanging like crazy.... I got a long time between men and maybe it was time again. Not good, I thought, not good" (69–70). Kinsey speaks as openly and explicitly about her sexual desires as men used to do.

5.5 Sue Grafton

Despite Kinsey's sexual interest in Charlie, when he visits her one day and asks her out for dinner, she is not prepared and she is embarrassed about looking "like shit" (cf. 187). As Charlie naturally gets a bottle of beer out of her refrigerator, she is additionally upset by his arrogance. Therefore, she tries to discourage him from staying and argues: "Look, I've got laundry to do. I haven't been to the grocery store for a week. My mail is piled up, the whole place is covered with dust. I haven't even shaved my legs since I last saw you" (187). Kinsey is not in the mood to have a date with Charlie and she looks for excuses and seems to be concerned about her looks and about housework, which she is usually not.

To make matters worse, Charlie adds that she needs a haircut as well (cf. 187). Instead of appeasing Kinsey, he acts in a dominant manner and he downgrades her because of her looks. Kinsey is belligerent and points out that her hair always looks like this. He then smiles, tells her to get dressed because he is not going to take her anywhere looking like that, and determines that they are going to go out. Although Kinsey protests, he insists, offering to go grocery shopping for her while she is getting dressed. As Kinsey refuses, he promises to take her to the supermarket after dinner (cf. 188).

Charlie is the dominant conversational partner and the one who decides what to do. Although Kinsey resists, he does not give in, but the fact that he offers to go shopping for her shows that he is willing to support her. Kinsey, however, does not like anyone to interfere with her habits and refuses. Both of them want to prove their decisiveness. Later, at the restaurant, Charlie shows that he is aware of Kinsey's independent nature and that he respects it, at least to a certain extent. He asks her in an ironic tone: "Shall I order for us or would that offend your feminine sensibilities?" (188). The term "feminine" is used in an inadequate way by Charlie since in traditional notions of femininity, male dominance would be appreciated. He does not seem to notice that Kinsey's wish for independence is progressive and emphasizes that gender is performative.

However, his confident manner seems to attract Kinsey. During dinner, she watches Charlie in detail and emphasizes his masculine traits. Moreover, she admiringly describes Charlie as being "relaxed, in possession of himself, a man of sophistication and grace" and she contrasts herself as being "doltish and tongue-tied" and she feels that he does not expect anything of her because he talks about trivial topics (cf. 190). This shows that Kinsey feels inferior to Charlie. She describes him as being self-assured, intelligent, and having good manners while she perceives herself as insecure and timid. Thereby, at least to a certain extent, she emphasizes traditional feminine and masculine characteristics.

Kinsey also appreciates Charlie's calm nature: "He seemed to operate at half speed, taking his own time about everything. It made me aware of the usual tension with which I live, that keyed-up state of raw nerve that makes me grind my teeth in my sleep.... With Charlie, I could feel my time clock readjust, my pace slowing to match his" (190). Hence, similarly to Sharon, Kinsey feels positively decelerated and protected by a man's presence. Kinsey likes Charlie being in control, and she is even willing to abandon her tough character when he is around, which makes her authentic.

After dinner, Kinsey asks Charlie if he has ever been married and he explains: "I never had time for that. I work. That's the only thing that interests me. I don't like the idea of giving someone else the right to make demands" (192). Kinsey realizes that she feels the same way, which makes him even more attractive to her (cf. 192). Since they are both not interested in a serious relationship, their connection is primarily sexual. Kinsey cannot resist Charlie's "oddly sexual [look], full of a strange, compelling male heat as though money and power and sexuality were all somehow tangled up for him and fed on one another" (192). His "smoldering sexual signals" make the air crackle between them (cf. 193). Kinsey portrays traditional notions of masculinity as desirable and thereby, she underlines patriarchal gender roles.

Still, Kinsey is cautious and tries not to say anything flirtatious because she is not sure about Charlie's intentions toward her. She reflects: "What if I fell on the man like a dog on a bone only to discover that his meaning was merely friendly, absentminded, or impersonal?" (193). Again, although Kinsey still presents herself as inferior to Charlie, her description of her own behavior is sexual and she does not hide her desires, which Charlie reacts to. Back in the car, Kinsey utters that she feels languid and Charlie takes her hand and presses it between his legs.

As they get home, they have sexual intercourse, and Kinsey describes that it was "as though a channel had been opened between [them], sexual energy flowing back and forth without impediment" (194) and that she enjoyed the natural and undemanding manner in which he made love to her. Afterwards, they go to sleep, and Kinsey describes how his big arms pin her to bed: "But far from feeling trapped, I felt comforted and safe, as though nothing could ever harm me as I stayed in the shadow of this man, this sheltering cave of heat and flesh, where I was tucked away until morning without waking once" (194). Since Charlie is not commanding, but treats Kinsey with respect, she takes on the conservative role and allows to be sheltered by him.

In the course of the novel, Charlie's attraction on Kinsey does not decrease, and she repeatedly emphasizes his sex appeal. Charlie's outfit reminds Kinsey of a "Peanut Butter Cup with a bite taken out and [she] wanted the rest" (212). Despite

5.5 Sue Grafton

this, Kinsey maintains her freedom. When Charlie picks her up for dinner again, for instance, she follows him in her car because she does not like "to be stuck without [her] own wheels" (220). One evening, when they meet, Charlie has the impression that Kinsey interrogates and only uses him in order to find out more about the case. Kinsey is annoyed by his sensitivities and leaves, concluding: "I'm too old to take any guff from anyone" (226). In this situation, she is the dominant character.

Charlie, in the following, asks her if she has never heard of compromise, and Kinsey replies: "That's when you give the other guy half of what's rightfully yours. I've done that lots of times. It sucks" (227). Kinsey does not let go of her beliefs, and Charlie complains that she keeps him "at arm's length," and that sex is the only time that she lets him get close. He analyzes that she does not seem to be used to having anyone in her life and although he accepts this and he lives in the same way, he cannot cope with her rejection well (cf. 228).

This situation presents a reversal of traditional gender roles since the man is sensitive and aggrieved whereas the woman is not interested in an emotional connection, but rather in sexual intercourse. Kinsey acts uncompromisingly and pragmatically. Although Charlie attracts her, she never really trusts him, which turns out to have been the right intuition. As Kinsey advances in her investigations, she notices that Charlie remains a major suspect, and she worries: "This was not good, not cool. As a rule I scrupulously avoid personal contact with anyone connected with a case. My sexual wrangling with Charlie was foolish, unprofessional, and in theory, possibly dangerous" (230).

Thus, she decides to break out of the relationship in order to maintain her professional work. She reasons: "[T]he fact remained that I was still in the middle of an investigation and he still had not been crossed off my list. I didn't think our physical relationship had clouded my judgment about him, but how could I tell?" (230). Hence, Kinsey phones Charlie and tells him that she is not willing to see him until the case is solved. He reacts in an offended manner, but he accepts her decision, and Kinsey affirms: "There were no declarations between us, no commitments. I'd been to bed with him twice. What did I owe him? I don't know what love is about and I'm not sure I believe in it anyway (cf. 236–237).

In contrast to this statement, Kinsey later admits that she also broke up with Charlie in order to prevent herself from being disappointed: "It had been too long since I'd cared about anyone, too long since I'd taken that risk and I'd already invested too much. I just had to slam the gate shut emotionally and move on, but it didn't sit well with me" (262). Kinsey is guided by her emotions, more than male hard-boiled detectives used to be.

Even shortly before Charlie tries to kill Kinsey, she does not want to believe that he has a thoroughly evil nature. After a chase on the beach, Kinsey hides in a trash bin. When she hears Charlie approach and call for her, she wonders: "Was I just imagining everything? He sounded like he always did" (277). When he opens the lid, however, she sees that he holds a big butcher knife and she "bl[ows] him away" (278). Like her male forerunners, Kinsey only survives thanks to her detachment and toughness. In the same way as Sam Spade had to turn his former lover Brigid O'Shaughnessy over to the police in the final scene (cf. *The Maltese Falcon* 211), Kinsey has to shoot her lover in self-defense.

Despite of her strength, Kinsey seems life-like at the end of the novel because the reader can see traces of fear in her character. When she has a vague idea of the danger she is in, she feels uncomfortable: "I couldn't prove it, of course, but I wondered if I was getting close enough to the truth to be in danger myself. I wanted to go home. I wanted to retreat to the safety of my small room" (*"A" Is for Alibi* 175). When Charlie chases Kinsey, she delineates the situation as follows: "As long as I was running, the fear seemed contained, adrenaline driving out every sensation except the urge to flee" (274). When she is in the sea, however, she is scared of Charlie: "Now that I was forced into immobility, the fear took up where it had left me, ice spreading across my lungs, pulse beating in my throat" (276). Kinsey even feels tears rising (cf. 278). In the end, she is so afraid that she hides in a trash bin although she is half-naked and has to bring herself to touching the garbage with her skin.

Kinsey is also upset by her act of self-defense, which makes her a realistic character who sets herself apart from violent male detectives. The fact that she has killed somebody "weighs heavily on [her] mind" (5) and she states: "The shooting disturbs me still. It has moved me into some camp with soldiers and maniacs. I never set out to kill anyone." However, in the end, Kinsey is optimistic and strong: "I'll recover, of course. I'll be ready for business again in a week or two, but I'll never be the same. You try to keep life simple but it never works, and in the end all you have left is yourself" (279). Kinsey's character evolves due to her experiences, and she accepts herself without constraints, knowing that such experiences leave their marks on her.

Thus, in the end, entering an affair with Charlie turns out to have been a serious mistake. From the beginning, there are clues that he is inappropriate as a lover for Kinsey in that he sometimes bosses her around, seems arrogant, and is dominant. He is a typical handsome *homme fatal*,[5] very reminiscent of the *femmes fatales* in earlier hard-boiled novels. Like them, Charlie is deceptive because he

---

[5] French counterpart of *femme fatale*, which means "ominous man" (cf. Mizejewski 19).

embezzles money, he sleeps around with women, and he poses a threat to them. It follows that Grafton reverses the gender of the villain and shows that men can be just as deceptive and dangerous as women.

5.5.1.3 Diverse Male Side Characters

In addition to dangerous men, Grafton presents men who cannot be taken seriously—just as Hammett and Chandler did with some women—because they are feeble and inferior to Kinsey. Libby's ex-boyfriend, Lyle, for example, is handsome and reminds Kinsey of James Dean in early years (cf. *"A" Is for Alibi* 104). She is attracted by his looks when she watches him laying brick and reflects that his chest muscles are well formed like those of someone who lifts weights (cf. 100). When Kinsey approaches him with a gun later on because she suspects that he might have murdered Libby, however, Lyle is not even capable of talking to Kinsey, but he starts to weep and sob, which shows that mental toughness is not necessarily a male characteristic. Kinsey recalls: "He might have been nine years old, looking squeezed up and frail and small.... He hugged himself, rocking back and forth in misery, tears streaming down his bony cheeks again" (254). Kinsey compares this male character to a child, just as male hard-boiled detectives did with some women.

In addition to either deceptive or vulnerable men, there are those who are not attractive and thus, uninteresting for the protagonist. Officer Con Dolan, for instance, is in his late fifties "with the aura of the unkempt: bags under his eyes, gray stubble or its illusion, a pouchy face, and hair that's been coated with some kind of men's product and combed across a shiny place on top." Kinsey observes that "[h]e looks like he would smell of Thunderbird and hang out under bridges throwing up on his own shoes" (14). Moreover, Kinsey's power unsettles Dolan, and he would probably not be ready to put up with her.

The only man whom Kinsey has a harmonious relationship with is Henry Pitts, her landlord. He is eighty-one years old and a former commercial baker. He now makes a living by devising crossword-puzzles, and he trades baked goods to a nearby restaurant (cf. 21). Kinsey admires his vigor: "[H]e seems totally concentrated, like a basic stock boiled down to a rich elixir" (195). To Kinsey, it does not matter that there is almost a fifty-year-difference in their ages (cf. 196). Henry is both a fatherly friend and a guardian for her, just as older secretaries used to be to early male hard-boiled detectives. He is the only man she fully trusts.

In the following novels, Kinsey still gets involved with men from time to time. She meets Sergeant Jonah Robb, who works in the Missing Persons Division and is later promoted to the Homicide Division of the Santa Teresa Police Department.

They start an affair in *"D"* (cf. *"D" Is for* Deadbeat), but in *"G,"* Kinsey decides to end it because she feels that he is still tied to his wife (cf. *"G" Is for Gumshoe*). In *"D,"* Kinsey's second husband, Daniel Wade, who had surprisingly left her, returns. He, a musician, appears and wants to leave a guitar with Kinsey for a few days. She allows him to do so, but she does not seem willing to revive their emotional relationship. In the end, she discovers that there are bugs inside his guitar, and he reveals that he has an affair with a man (cf. *"D" Is for* Deadbeat). After this encounter, she is more determined than ever to be careful with romantic relationships.

This becomes evident with Robert Dietz, a private investigator from Nevada. In *"G,"* Kinsey hires him as her bodyguard when she is the target of a hit man. He moves into her apartment and they become sexually involved. They actually are a good match because they are both tough, independent, and humorous, but Kinsey is hesitant about defining themselves as a couple (cf. *"G" Is for Gumshoe*). Hence, although there are loving moments, also again in *"M,"* in the end they work better on professional than on private terms, and he leaves for a job in private security work (cf. *"M" Is for Malice*). Therefore, overall, none of these men stays in Kinsey's life for a long time, and she does not like to define the relationships in any way.

Kinsey continues to live in her apartment, but in *"E,"* it is bombed by a killer and it is rebuilt by Henry (cf. *"E" Is for Evidence*). In addition, her office is renovated in the same novel, but in *"H,"* she leaves the place because she does not get along with the new efficiency expert (cf. *"H" Is for Homicide*). In *"I,"* she finds an office close to her home (cf. *"I" Is for Innocent*). In the course of the novels, Kinsey has become more successful. She is now an independent contractor for attorney Lonnie Kingman, of "Kingman and Ives". In the following, Grafton's 15th novel, *"O" Is for Outlaw*, published in 1999, will be discussed because it gives insights into Kinsey's first marriage and outlines her development.

5.5.2 *"O" Is for Outlaw*

5.5.2.1 The Nonconformist Detective

In the beginning of the novel, Kinsey is exhausted because she has just finished a time-consuming job and she hopes for some time off. However, she is called by Mr. Rich, a storage space scavenger, who tells her that the owner has abandoned one of his storage units and that his belongings will go into an auction, including one cardboard box that has her name on it. As Kinsey only owns few personal keepsakes, she collects the box, and she finds that it contains old memories of

5.5 Sue Grafton

her first ex-husband, Mickey Magruder, alias John Russell. Through old friends and his lawyer, Kinsey detects that Mickey has been the victim of a shooting and that he is now on life support. The police even suspect Kinsey of the shooting because Mickey was shot with the gun he had given her for the wedding back then.

Kinsey learns that Mickey was on the track of the killer of a recently returned Vietnam veteran, Benny Quintero, because he himself had been suspected of this crime. Kinsey finds out that Mickey was innocent and that he was together with his affair, Dixie Hightower, that night. She investigates at the places Mickey went to shortly before he was shot, and she talks to Dixie herself and to Mark Bethel, another veteran and Mickey's lawyer on the manslaughter charge. Kinsey finds out that Mickey was last looking into Benny's connections to journalist Duncan Oaks. Duncan, a former classmate of Mark's wife Laddie, was wounded in Vietnam, and disappeared in transit for medical treatment.

Kinsey concludes that Mark found out that Duncan and Laddie were having an affair, and thus he killed Duncan by pushing him out of the medical helicopter, witnessed by Benny. Benny started blackmailing Mark, who killed him consequently and made Mickey look suspicious by using the gun he had sold him. After that, Mark shot Mickey with the same gun and implicated Kinsey. She tries to make Mark confess, but this rather makes her his target. In the end, Benny's brother, the biker Carlin Duffy, who has been accusing and chasing Mickey, understands that Mark is responsible for the death of his brother, kills him, and saves Kinsey.

Kinsey still lives alone in her small and rather plain apartment. She enjoys her autonomy, but she remembers that she has not always been so self-congratulatory about her single and childless state, and that she occasionally kept an eye on the kids of her friends when their parents were gone (cf. *"O" Is for Outlaw* 51). Hence, she is not unaffected by her surrounding and by societal expectations, but in the end, Kinsey chooses her own lifestyle and concentrates on herself and on her wellbeing.

Kinsey has started lifting weights again after two years, which she always does after her runs, three times a week before work (cf. 2). She states that running helps her to relax, and she claims that, in general, "[i]ntense exercise is the only legal high [she] know[s]," except for love (cf. 187). Thus, Kinsey exercises because she enjoys it, unlike many other women at the gym. She observes "the extremely lean fitness fiends, who trash themselves daily, and the softer women who arrive after any food-dominated holiday." She concludes that the latter never last, but that it is good for them anyway, and she pictures herself somewhere in between (cf. 188).

Just as Kinsey does not exercise in order to fulfill any ideals of beauty, she is not concerned about dieting. She describes that, in the course of the day, her "flirtation with good health is overrun by [her] tendency to selfabuse, especially when it comes to junk food." She pictures that "fat grams are [her] downfall, anything with salt, additives, cholesterol, nitrates[,] [b]readed and deep-fried or sautéed in butter, smothered in cheese, slathered with mayonnaise, dripping with meat juices" (188). Throughout the novel, Kinsey indeed often eats fast food, and she is always excited about it (cf. 323).

She even compares fast food to sex: "It's pitiful to have a life in which junk food is awarded the same high status as sex. Then again, I tend to get a lot more of the one than I do of the other" (131). This statement shows how utterly at ease Kinsey is with herself. She admits that her lifestyle might not meet society's expectations, but she does not miss sexual intimacy with a man. She rather likes being on her own, enjoying fast food on her couch while watching junk TV (cf. 323). Kinsey describes it as a virtue of being single that one does not need to explain to anyone "the peculiarities of one's appetite in moments of stress" (30). Kinsey enjoys not having to give account to anyone about her habits. She behaves as she pleases, using paper towels as both napkin and plate, joking about doing the dishes by throwing them away afterwards (cf. 165).

Likewise, Kinsey does not let her outer appearance run her life. She is often self-ironic about her looks, for example, when she explains that her hair "was mashed flat on one side and sticking up in clumps on the other like dried palm fronds" (281) and that she uses nail scissors for the occasional emergency haircut (cf. 297). In terms of clothing, Kinsey only owns one dress in which she can attend all kinds of events (cf. 81–82). She is more concerned about her clothing style for functional reasons, and she often changes her appearance for purposes of investigation (cf. 19). As long as Kinsey is at home or at work, she does not question herself in terms of her outer appearance. In public, however, Kinsey occasionally does so.

At the Honky Tonk, a bar, for example, Kinsey looks at herself in the mirror and observes: "The fluorescent lighting gave my otherwise unblemished skin a sickly appearance, emphasizing the bags under my eyes. My hair looked like thatch. I wore no lipstick, but that was probably just as well, as the addition would have played up the yellow cast in my aging complexion." Then she decides to delete her ego from the situation and scrutinizes the place from Mickey's point of view (cf. 174). Hence, her work is more important to Kinsey than her looks.

The following experience reinforces Kinsey in her behavior, and it even shows that being too concerned about one's own outer appearance can turn out pathological. Later on, in the bathroom, Kinsey hears a woman throw up while another one encourages her, and she concludes: "If I'd even heard of it in my day, I'd have assumed Bulimia was the capital of some newly formed Baltic state." When she sees the women, Kinsey observes that they are both "thin as snakes" and when one of them brushes her teeth, she reasons: "In five years the stomach acid would eat through her tooth enamel, if she didn't drop dead first" (174).

Hence, Kinsey presents and criticizes the negative impact of social expectations concerning women's external appearances. These expectations result from a traditional, patriarchal society, but some women seem to have internalized them and thus, they allow them to continue. Kinsey herself is not influenced by such beauty ideals, but she, in sum, is a self-assured woman who feels at ease with herself and her single life. She pursues her passions, and she seems to feel most content while being at home or at work on her own. This character trait is reminiscent of male hard-boiled detectives, who were loners as well. Nevertheless, Kinsey is more life-like because she is not immune to her social environment. She is also more sociable than her male forerunners.

Kinsey is still friends with Rosie and Henry and she feels comfortable in their presence. However, she does not allow them to get too close, and she dislikes when they act as guardians for her. Rosie, for example, often makes mocking comments about Kinsey's weight, hair, and marital status. Kinsey claims: "It was her avowed intention to fatten me up, get me a decent haircut, and a spouse" (281). When Rosie proposes that Kinsey needs someone to look after her, Kinsey ironically suggests a visiting nurse, which shows that Kinsey does not consider a man a necessity in her life (cf. 281–282). While Rosie emphasizes traditional expectations for female appearance and a woman's lifestyle, Kinsey reveals such notions as socially constructed.

Henry, her landlord, also cares about Kinsey. She values his presence and describes him as "handsome in the manner of a fine antique, handcrafted and well-constructed, exhibiting a polish that suggests close to nine decades of loving use." Kinsey specifies: "Henry has always been loyal, outspoken, kind, and generous. He's protective of me in ways that feel strange but are welcome, nonetheless" (34). Hence, Kinsey usually appreciates and follows Henry's advice, for example, when he tells her to report certain findings to the police (cf. 198).

When he advises Kinsey to leave the case alone because, in his opinion, it is police business and she might have to neglect the law with her investigations, however, Kinsey is upset. She dislikes that Henry domineers over her. As a consequence, Kinsey acts in a stubborn and resistant manner, and she replies: "This is exactly who I am: a liar and a thief. You want to know something else? I don't feel bad about it. I'm completely unrepentant. More than that. I like it. It makes me feel alive" (168).

Likewise, Kinsey explains that she partly identifies with the shady biker Duffy:

> As crude as he was with his racist comments, with his tortured grammar, and his attitude toward crime, I understood his yearning. How liberating it was when you defied authority, flouted convention, ignoring ordinary standards of moral decency. I knew my own ambivalence. On the one hand, I was a true law-and-order type, prissy in my judgment, outraged at those who violated the doctrines of honesty and fair play. On the other hand, I'd been known to lie through my teeth, eavesdrop, pick locks, or simply break into people's houses, where I snooped through their possessions and took what suited me. It wasn't nice, but I savored every single minute of my bad girl behavior. Later, I'd feel guilty, but still I couldn't resist. I was split down the middle, my good angel sitting on one shoulder, Lucifer perched on the other. (322)

Kinsey possesses nonconformist tendencies, and she enjoys breaking the rules. Her feeling of guilt and the term "bad girl" show that she knows that such behavior is not adequate, especially for a woman. Even more, Kinsey savors resisting such traditional expectations of flawlessness and good behavior, and she concludes: "If the bad guys don't play by the rules, why should the good guys have to?" (323).

Like Marlowe, Kinsey's sense of justice prevents her from severely falling on the wrong side of the law. Moreover, her unlawful acts are only for the purpose of investigating. As she tries to find Mickey in the beginning of the novel, for example, Kinsey goes through a dog door opening to get into a house (cf. 23). She admits that this is not routine behavior for a private eye, and she knows that her action is trespass and that she would be subject to arrest if she was caught (cf. 24).

In such situations, Kinsey is more excited than her male forerunners. She describes: "My heart was thumping so loud it sounded like a clothes dryer spinning a pair of wet tennis shoes. I could see my left breast vibrating against the front of my coveralls. I couldn't swear to this, but I think I may have wee-weed ever so slightly in my underpants" (25–26). Kinsey does not mind putting herself in uncomfortable situations for investigating, and the resulting thrill and excitement seem to be aspects that Kinsey loves about her job.

She also begs for information or entry, and takes on a needy role, if necessary. When Kinsey wants to enter the Honky Tonk for investigating although it is about to close, she begs, puts her knees together, clasps her hands like a child at prayer, and so she is allowed in by the doorman. She concludes: "It's perplexing to realize how far you can get with men by pulling girlish shit" (214). Kinsey outwits the bouncer by playing with childish and feminine charms because she rightly guesses that he will fall for that. Inside the bar, however, Kinsey would need to squeeze into a small space that is full of spiders. In that situation, she reaches her limits, rejects, and finds another way (cf. 217), which makes her lifelike.

In general, throughout the investigation, it is obvious that the case at hand is difficult for Kinsey because she is emotionally involved. She admits: "The emotional roller coaster of the past few days had generated an odd mood – weariness masquerading as depression. Whatever the source, I was feeling raw" (164). Kinsey is also seriously concerned about her physical integrity at times. Before she flies to Louisville, for example, she knows that this trip could turn out dangerous and she clears up her office, in case, as she says, that she will not make it back (cf. 292).

Despite her emotional entanglement and such fears, Kinsey works in her usual professional manner. She is always determined, works at every hour, and drives long distances if it seems gainful (cf. 140). Her thorough knowledge of Mickey's habits and preferences helps her investigate. When she tries to make out his space, for example, Kinsey guesses that he has rented something plain. Indeed, she finds the building, which is similar to the one he occupied when they first met. Moreover, Kinsey is aware that Mickey must have frequented the local restaurants when he was too lazy to cook, which makes her talk to the right people (cf. 112).

When she interviews them, Kinsey works in a thorough manner. She notes down insights quickly and in detail. She explains: "Later, it's the odd unrelated detail that sometimes makes the puzzle parts rearrange themselves like magic" (138). Apart from pieces of information, Kinsey lines up Mickey's items repeatedly and in various configurations as though a story could be made from a meaningful sequence of them. Thus, Kinsey is more systematic than early male hard-boiled detectives. She complements their way of investigating in the criminal world with rational approaches that are reminiscent of early English detectives. Still, Kinsey prefers to investigate practically and she sometimes cannot bring herself to theoretical work (cf. 288).

Kinsey especially likes inspecting places. When she waits in the hall of Dixie's house, for example, she envisions how she would operate: "I did a one-eighty turn so I could scrutinize the place like a burglar-in-training, a little game I play. I noted entrances and exits, wondering about the possibility of a wall safe. If I were bugging the place, where would I tuck the surveillance equipment?" (64). Kinsey does not only investigate a case in her imagination, but she tracks dangerous people all alone. As Kinsey has learned that the reputedly dangerous biker Duffy might have shot Mickey, she goes after him in her own straight away, although Jonah tells her not do so. Kinsey concludes: "I wasn't going to wait until Monday. How ridiculous. Duffy could be long gone; I couldn't take the risk" (241).

At the end of the novel, Kinsey takes a significant risk by speaking to Mark on her own. As she realizes that he might be willing to shoot her, she stays calm and wonders if the bullet would hit her before she heard the sound of the shot (cf. 351). Finally, Duffy comes to helps her and runs Mark over with a tractor. Kinsey observes in a distanced manner and in precise language: "Mark's neatly severed head thumped into the bucket like a cantaloupe" (353). She is strong and tenacious although, in this case, she needs a man who rescues her. Hence, she is not portrayed as invincible, but again, Kinsey appears in a realistic manner.

5.5.2.2 Her Failed Marriage

Kinsey's authentic humanity, as mentioned above, is also underlined by her emotionalism. It is obvious throughout the novel that Kinsey loves Mickey, although she claims that she does not want to reconnect with him, but rather abolish her memories because they parted on bad terms. She affirms that she forgot him: "I'd put the man in a box and dropped him to the bottom of my emotional ocean, where he'd languished ever since" (29).

Kinsey recollects that she married Mickey after nine months, at the age of twenty-one. He had been a police officer for sixteen years and when she joined the department, Kinsey was dazzled by the image he projected, "seasoned, gruff, cynical, wise" (47). Looking back, Kinsey explains that she was not only infatuated with his attitude and his headstrong character, but also full of admiration for his striving to enjoy life to the full.

Kinsey remembers that Mickey was a hedonist and that with him, she felt very alive: "I remembered experiencing a nearly giddy relief at his gluttony, his love of intoxication, his appetite for sex" (164). He offered her "a tacit permission to explore [her] lustiness, unawakened until then" (165). In addition, Mickey embodied nonconformity. For example, he gave Kinsey a gun as a wedding present and she was thrilled with the gift. She explains that she saw it as an indication that he considered her as a colleague, which is a status that only few women in those days were accorded. Now, Kinsey wonders what man gives his bride a semiautomatic firearm on their wedding night, but back then, she felt accepted (cf. 33–34). While being a detective and carrying a gun now feels natural for Kinsey, she strived for acceptance back then.

Soon after the marriage, Kinsey realized that Mickey was out of control, but she did not want to recognize the truth about him: "I saw him as an idol, so I accepted his version of events even when common sense suggested he was slanting the facts" (47). Kinsey remembers that she thought of herself as mature back then, but now she considers her behavior foolish and unenlightened, and she states that her judgment and perception were flawed (cf. 310). Likewise, when she

5.5 Sue Grafton

remembers how often they were at the Honky Tonk at the time, Kinsey realizes that it was an enormous waste of time, but she concludes that it was their way of avoiding each other, and bypassing the real work of marriage, which is intimacy (cf. 246).

Mickey increasingly operated outside the standards of most other police officers and he was the object of complaints. Kinsey explains that it was the era in which law enforcement began to change and the image of the tough police officer was replaced by the appearance of restraint (cf. 45). Mickey did not fit into this new image. In 1971, he resigned from his job because of arising conflicts and he was accused of burglary. He was also under investigation for voluntary manslaughter after a bar dispute and asked Kinsey to lie for him and to give him an alibi for that particular night.

Kinsey, however, already had fixed ideas of what was acceptable and what was not. Because he had mistreated the law and tried to drag her into it, Kinsey immediately left and filed for divorce because, as she explains, Mickey had violated her sense of honor (cf. 29). Thus, her feelings of justice and self-esteem, characteristics that she still shows, made her end the relationship.

In the years following the divorce, Kinsey's anger decreased, and she neither wanted to see Mickey, nor did she wish him ill (cf. 49). She only heard that he was doing personal security, "a once dedicated cop demoted to working night shift in an imitation cop's uniform" (49). Kinsey herself enjoyed her freedom and took the opportunity of uncommitted sex. This was no longer unusual for women at the time, as she pictures:

> In the late sixties, early seventies, sex was casual, recreational, indiscriminate, and uncommitted. Women had been liberated by the advent of the birth control pill, and dope had erased any further prohibitions. This was the era of love-ins, psychedelics, dropouts, war protest, body paint, assassinations, LSD, and rumors of kids so stoned their eyeballs got fried because they stared at the sun too long. (45)

As Kinsey first walks into the Honky Tonk after years, she recalls her behavior when she was "single and hunting:"

> Given my current state of enlightenment, I wouldn't dream of circulating through the bar scene—barhopping, we called it—but I did in those days. In the sixties and seventies, that's what you did for recreation. That's how you met guys. That's how you got laid. What Women's Liberation 'liberated' was our attitude toward sex. Where we once used sex for barter, now we gave it away. I marvel at the prostitutes we must have put out of business, doling out sexual 'favors' in the name of personal freedom. What were we thinking? All we ended up with were bar bums afflicted with pubic vermin. (172)

Kinsey clarifies what the Liberation Movement offered for women—promiscuity. Although she condemns it from her current perspective, one has to consider that it gave women the chance to decide upon their own bodies. Kinsey is now resting in herself and she is satisfied without a partner, but this might be due to her gradual awareness that sexual intercourse is not necessarily connected to a relationship and that both are not absolutely vital to a fulfilled life. Hence, the freedom of the time has allowed Kinsey, and other women, to balance what is fulfilling for them personally and to choose their individual lifestyles.

Despite her contentment with her life, one can see that Kinsey is emotionally affected by this past marriage. When she learns that Mickey has had an affair with Dixie, she has to swallow her outrage, dismissing it as unproductive (cf. 58). She describes: "Even fourteen years later, I felt humiliated and incensed. I closed my eyes, detaching myself emotionally as though at the scene of a homicide" (59). The fact that Kinsey has to force herself into rational thinking shows how wounded her pride is. She explains: "What was at stake was my integrity, whatever sense of honor I possessed. I know my limitations. I know the occasional lapses I'm capable of, but a transgression of this magnitude was impossible to ignore" (61).

Despite her anger, Kinsey knows that she was an accomplice to his downfall. She wonders if she was wrong to jump at conclusions about Mickey quickly back then just because it suited her and at a certain point, she was disenchanted with him anyway. She also feels bad about assuming that he was guilty without wanting to hear his side of it (cf. 85). Her conclusion is to talk to him, to apologize, and to help Mickey financially, if necessary, because she is sick about the part she played in his slide from grace (cf. 87).

When the police tell Kinsey that Mickey became the victim of a shooting and is on life support, she is shocked and, although the officer is still talking, she suffers a temporary hearing loss and has to concentrate in order not to hyperventilate (cf. 92). Kinsey explains she cannot believe that anything bad could ever happen to this apparently invincible man (cf. 93), which still shows some admiration for his strength. Kinsey plans to visit Mickey in hospital: "I'd fancied a moment by Mickey's bed, some feeling of redemption, the chance to make amends" (104).

Mickey is now almost fifty-three, the same age as Robert Dietz. Sitting next to Mickey, Kinsey wonders if her involvement with Robert has been an unwitting attempt to replace Mickey (cf. 108). Moreover, she adds: "I didn't understand that I sought in him the qualities I lacked or hadn't yet developed. I'd have denied to the last breath that I was looking for a father figure, but of course I was" (109). Concerning her age being twenty-one and Mickey's being thirty-six at the time, looking for a father figure seems plausible, especially if one bears in mind that Kinsey does not have a father.

Kinsey explains that she finds it embarrassing to recall love once it is gone, but she remembers "all the passion and romanticism, the sentimentality and sexual excess" (109). Kinsey even experiences a sexual shiver when she thinks of a kiss with Mickey (cf. 118–119). This is proof of the strong feelings she has once had for that man. In the end of the novel, Mickey dies. Kinsey is with him and she gracefully thinks of everything he taught her and of all the good memories of their marriage: "My life was the richer for his having been part of it. Whatever his flaws, whatever his failings, his redemption was something he'd earned in the end." With her cheek pressed against his hand, she is with him until the last breath (cf. 355). After Mickey's death, Kinsey sells his guns and she inherits money that she donates, hoping that Mickey would have liked that because he often donated money to charities himself (cf. 355). Hence, despite the humiliation, Kinsey is able to forgive Mickey, and she treats him and his will in a respectful manner.

In retrospect, this marriage helped Kinsey develop and become independent. The fact that she admired Mickey for his willfulness and unconventionality shows that those were character traits that she did not have, or rather, which she was not allowed to show. As a child, Kinsey was "autonomous, defiant, and as hard as a nut" (32), but then she was pressured to change in order to be a gentle young woman. Looking back, Kinsey admires the resilient child she was, and her refusal to conform. These are qualities that she rediscovered in Mickey, and over the years, Kinsey dared to return to these character traits, showing that defined characteristics for girls and boys, as well as women and men, are performative and reduce individuality (cf. 32).

Kinsey has turned from a modest young wife who sought to be accepted by her strong-willed husband into a self-assured woman who filed for divorce because her moral values were violated. Although she still cherishes the love her first husband gave her, Kinsey carries on with her life and she eventually chooses the lifestyle that suits her. Although she acknowledges that being autonomous can bear potential for conflicts in society, being true to herself makes her content and she recommends following one's own ideals instead of trying to fulfill society's outdated expectations.

5.5.2.3 Further Troubled and Unequal Relations

Having deliberately decided how she wants to live, Kinsey is interested in the different ways of life of women, in the past as well as today. As she looks at the yearbook of the 1960s, she detects that, unlike in modern days, most of the girls were dressed in dark colors and wore their hair short in order to be discreet (cf.

313). When she recognizes one of the girls, who got married and is a wealthy woman now, she concludes: "In those days, a rich husband was the obvious means by which a woman could elevate her social standing and improve her prospects" (316).

Nowadays, women are not necessarily dependent on men, but they can be the dominant partners, as the following example shows. Camilla Robb, Jonah's wife, is reminiscent of the *femmes fatales*. She has been together with Jonah since Junior high school, but in the course of the years, they separated many times. Kinsey describes how Camilla plays Jonah like a yo-yo, kicking him out and taking him back again, or leaving him alone for long periods, during which he cannot even see his two daughters.

During one of their longer separations, Kinsey became involved with Jonah, but she soon understood that he would never be independent from Camilla and thus, Kinsey broke up, which shows that, in contrast to him, she has self-respect. The two of them have reverted to friends, but Camilla is still jealous, although she is pregnant by someone else, "of course," as Kinsey comments (cf. 220). This man, however, abandoned her, and Jonah took her back (cf. 221). After Jonah has told her about the news, Kinsey concludes: "[H]e sounded pretty cheerful for a guy whose nuts were being slammed in a car door" (222). Grafton portrays a good-natured male character who lacks self-respect and a female character who takes advantage of this.

A similar female character is Dixie Hightower. Her disdain for men evokes antipathies in Kinsey, as well as the fact that her ex-husband betrayed her with Dixie. Kinsey starts a dispute and she enjoys the chance to free herself from her annoyance:

> I don't often go up against other women in verbal combat. Such clashes are strange, but not without a certain prurient attraction. I thought of all the male-fantasy movies where women fight like alley cats, pulling at each other's hair while they roll around on the floor. I'd never had much occasion, but maybe that would change. I could feel myself getting in touch with my 'inner' mean streak. (66–67)

Kinsey adopts a male fantasy of animalistic women and turns it into her own. She starts the verbal fight and adjusts her language to her anger: "I had no idea you were balling my beloved husband. You want to talk about that?" (69). Dixie is baffled by the statement and apologizes, but then, she criticizes that Kinsey is not familiar enough with men to see through their bad intentions. Dixie thinks that there is no romance with men: "They want to get in your panties and let it go at that" (70). She does not even want to call her past relationship with Mickey an affair, but rather sexual addiction, "a mutual service we performed" (70).

Like Kinsey, Dixie is very realistic and can differentiate between love and sex, but she goes one step further. Dixie seems angry with men in general while Kinsey believes in harmonious relationships between women and men. Thus, she does not accept Dixie's reply and she clearly shows that, to her, wedding vows mean something and that it is not acceptable if a woman sleeps with a married man. Dixie then again lays the blame on Mickey (cf. 71).

As a result, Kinsey closes her eyes and feels like "lift[ing] her front chair legs and flip her backward, just for the satisfaction of hearing her head thud against the stone floor" (72). Given the brevity of the marriage, Kinsey assumes Mickey had been faithful. She summarizes the new information as follows: "Guilty of infidelity, innocent of manslaughter" (77). Thus, infidelity to Kinsey is a major offense that she mentions along with homicide. Nevertheless, Kinsey does not blame the man alone, but she perceives women of being as capable as men, for good or ill. This also shows when Kinsey is shown the place where Mickey was shot. As the man talks about the criminal as "he," Kinsey inserts "she," and he smiles (cf. 160). Kinsey again emphasizes defined characteristics for women and men as constructed.

In the following novels, Kinsey continues to investigate in her usual manner. In *"P,"* she has to rent a new office space while she juggles the jobs that dysfunctional families offer her (cf. *"P" Is for Peril*). In *"R,"* Kinsey starts a pleasant, but insignificant affair with longtime friend and police officer Cheney Phillips. She remains friends with him after their split (cf. *"R" Is for Ricochet*).

Moreover, Grafton varies her narration. In *"S,"* Kinsey's first-person reportage is interrupted by retrospects from the past (cf. *"S" Is for Silence*). *"T"* offers shifts to the narrating voice of the killer at times (cf. *"T" Is for Trespass*), and in *"U,"* Grafton moves the narrative between the past and present, changing points of view, and building multiple subplots (cf. *"U" Is for Undertow*). The last novel of the alphabet series, *"Y" Is for Yesterday*, published in 2017, follows two timelines, and it will be discussed in detail in order to trace further developments in Kinsey's character and gender portrayals.

5.5.3 *"Y" Is for Yesterday*

5.5.3.1 The Imperturbable Detective

The novel is set in 1989 and Kinsey has just finished a job when Lauren and Hollis McCabe call her and ask her for help. Their son, Fritz, has recently completed a 10-year sentence in a youth prison for kidnapping and murdering a female classmate, Sloan Stevens. Since he has reached the age of 25, the state is forced to let him go. Now, he is being blackmailed and the extortionist demands $25,000 to keep an old video, which shows Fritz and some friends seducing Iris Lehmann, an underage girl, a secret. The novel alternates between 1989 and 1979, when Fritz killed the girl.

In 1979, Fritz and his friends, who went to a fancy, private college prep high school, were involved in a scandal. Two students were given a stolen copy of the proficiency test and used the answers to improve their scores. It turned out that freshman Iris had stolen the test. Someone sent a note to the school naming the two students, Troy Rademaker and Poppy Earl, who were then suspended. Therefore, the students and their friends victimized Iris on a video tape. Sloan was said to have revealed the names and the group condemned her. In order to threaten the boys, she stole the video tape and after a party, more by accident than on purpose, Fritz killed her, accompanied by his friends Troy and Bayard Montgomery and instigated by Austin Brown, who supposedly fled when Fritz confessed the murder.

Kinsey, whose investigation is disturbed by the fact that an old tormentor, Ned Lowe, is still after her and breaks into her office and home, detects that Iris and her fiancé Joey Seay are the blackmailers. She finds Fritz dead in the area where they killed Sloan back then, and she discovers a second victim, namely Austin. Kinsey concludes that Austin did not flee back then, but that Bayard killed him because he had threatened to call his homophobic father and tell him that Bayard was homosexual. Bayard also killed Fritz to avoid being exposed in Austin's murder because Fritz had found the body. Bayard is arrested as he is about to leave the country, but the authorities do not declare him guilty because they do not seem to have enough evidence.

By the time the novel is set, Kinsey is thirty-nine years old, and her life has not changed profoundly from the last novel. She still lives in her small studio apartment and describes herself as single and content, being cranky-minded to hear people discuss her lifestyle because she does not consider this status anything special (cf. *"Y" Is for Yesterday* 13). As in the previously discussed novel, Kinsey loves to do what she likes without having to explain herself to anyone, for example, when having buttered popcorn and Diet Pepsi for dinner (cf. 46). Rather than a domestic woman, Kinsey is a dedicated detective who uses her kitchen table to clean her gun instead of having meals (cf. 317). For food and company, she goes to Rosie's, her friend's tavern, three or four times a week (cf. 19).

Kinsey further appreciates to spend time with her landlord Henry and she even misses him when she does not see him for a while (cf. 317). However, she dislikes the fact that Henry has invited a homeless woman, Pearl White, to move in with him because Kinsey considers her an unkempt moocher. Later in the novel, Henry takes up Lucky, Pearl's homeless friend, and Kinsey charges them both with taking advantage of Henry. She specifies that she has little sympathy for such people because her aunt taught her not to ask for anything of others since she hated dependence and advocated self-sufficiency (cf. 45–46). Likewise, Kinsey's virtues in life are independence, discipline, and determination in the occupational as well as in the private sphere.

Concerning the murder case, Kinsey is as rational as usual. When she initially watches Iris's sexual abuse on tape, for example, she manages to show no emotional reaction: "As horrific as the tape was, it would be unprofessional to express repulsion or disapproval" (36). Despite this unsettling material, Kinsey is determined to solve the case on her own: "The little terrier in my nature was busy chasing after the problem, throwing dirt up behind me as I dug my little hole. There was a rat down there somewhere and I would have it for my very own" (47).

In order to reach her goal, Kinsey complements her investigations with systematic work. After each interview, she takes notes thoroughly, and she organizes them well, making three different piles for the sexual abuse, the cheating scandal, and the shooting (cf. 239). Still, she prefers investigating in practice and her scrutinizing manner puts her on the right track. Kinsey realizes that the account of Iris's physical abuse is just an arranged story because the people involved all use the same words to describe the incident (cf. 239). Kinsey is annoyed by such dishonesty (cf. 242). She is willing to lie herself, for example, as she pretends to be a reporter to get some information about Austin (cf. 51), but she does so just in order to reveal the truth eventually.

For this purpose, and to satisfy her clients, Kinsey also endures conversations and actions that are tiresome. For example, Lauren wants Kinsey to talk to Fritz. Kinsey describes her annoyance: "I could feel myself rolling my eyes. I pictured myself in a verbal tussle with the kid, which would be a colossal waste of time. Then again, she'd written me a check for twenty-five hundred bucks, and so far I didn't feel I'd earned my keep" (84). When Fritz's mother later asks Kinsey to look through his room, Kinsey underlines that they are on their best behavior and that she is pretending to be agreeable although she knows that she is not going to find any evidence in the room (cf. 342). In the end, Kinsey meets the demands of her clients, and, like male hard-boiled detectives, she offers them adequate service in return for their money.

However, Kinsey cannot always pretend to be interested in the conversations, especially if the interviewee lacks intelligence. When she interrogates Poppy, who asks some naive questions, Kinsey reflects: "I knew I sounded outraged, judgmental, and condemnatory, but I couldn't help myself. I watched her and wondered why she wouldn't meet my eyes. Probably I was talking to her like the idiot she was." Although Kinsey knows that such behavior is not expedient, she cannot help but show her annoyance: "I knew I'd pressed her to the point of defensiveness, which is seldom productive" (164).

Such conversations put Kinsey under stress and hence, when Lauren supposedly fires her for accusing Troy of lying, Kinsey reacts in a relaxed manner: "So what if it was a weekend and I was unemployed? Worse things had happened." She explains in a straightforward way: "I could see the bright side of what might have seemed insulting at first blush. Lauren McCabe had turned out to be a pain in the ass. I was glad to be shed of her, and Hollis as well. Fritz was a first-class jerk and whatever became of him henceforth was no concern of mine" (259).

In the beginning of the novel, Kinsey is unbiased when she meets Lauren and Hollis, and she even feels appreciation for their lifestyle (cf. 29–30). However, as she gets to know them better, Kinsey detects that Lauren is self-absorbed (cf. 306) and Hollis is ruthless. When Kinsey interviews Fritz, who is moody, his father threatens to punch him in the face. Kinsey describes the situation: "I couldn't believe Hollis had threatened to deck his own kid in front of company. The threat made my nerves crackle, and the hair on my arms lift as though from static electricity. My heart gave an uncharacteristic thump in case I was next" (89). Kinsey describes the man as terrifying, which hints at the immense helplessness the boy must experience. In addition, this situation demonstrates another aspect of patriarchy than male predominance over women, namely power of the older over the younger man. This involves physical violence and aims at upholding the traditional order.

Apart from parental abuse, Kinsey discloses their marriage as unhappy. She observes that, when Lauren and Hollis meet, they exchange "one of those dutiful kisses that signify marital niceties, but not much else" (108). Their conversations are characterized by murmuring with a rising and falling tone to it that reminds Kinsey why she is so happy to be single (cf. 343). Even when they are told about the death of their son, they do not sit together or touch, and Kinsey realizes that she is looking at the end of a marriage. She concludes that money and status do not render people happy or immune to such a loss (cf. 402–403).

In the following, it turns out that Lauren did not intend to fire Kinsey, who demands an apology for Lauren's emotional outbreak before she agrees to continue working on the case (cf. 311). This shows that Kinsey has become more demanding. Toward dominant men, she still acts with unagitated certainty. When Hollis mocks Kinsey by calling her "Sherlock," and by asking if she has found any secret messages written in invisible ink, she reminds him that she can do without the sarcasm (cf. 345).

While mature Kinsey does not let herself in for a discussion of such statements because she generally feels on an equal footing, the younger Iris is more resolute. When Bayard hears that Kinsey is a "girl detective" and laughs, Iris replies that she would appreciate if he entered the twentieth century (cf. 141). Just like her parents, she is committed to the notion of equality between the sexes and fights remaining injustices (cf. 4).

In return for supporting her, Kinsey helps Iris understand that what the boys did to her back then was not fun, but rape, and thus a crime (cf. 70). And indeed, toward Joey, her future husband, Iris admits that she still suffers from that experience (cf. 82), and later on she attends a support group for victims of rape and sexual assault (cf. 441). Kinsey is more experienced and makes Iris put her theoretical ideas about equality into practice and fight patriarchal violence toward women.

In the end, Iris confesses her deeds without consulting Joey, which shows that she has developed and gained some independence in the relationship. Her honesty pays off because since their plan was not brought to an end, they do not have to serve any jail time (cf. 481). Bayard, whom Kinsey convicts all alone (cf. 473), is not sentenced in the end, which makes Kinsey suspect that he must have paid much money and criticize the corrupt jurisdiction again (cf. 483).

When it comes to talking to Margaret Seay, Sloan's mother, Kinsey is not as determined, but rather sensitive. Kinsey does not know how to speak to a woman who has just lost her only child. Moreover, she fears that she cannot promote justice for Sloan when she was hired for something else (cf. 174). In the end, Kinsey decides to postpone the interview and goes to bed "feeling cowardly, but relieved" about her decision (cf. 175).

When she speaks to the mother of the dead girl later in the novel, Kinsey acts in a caring and empathetic manner. Initially, she considers thoroughly how much she is allowed to tell without the client's permission, but in the end, she neglects the rules and decides that, if she asks Margaret to trust her, she has to give something away as well (cf. 222). As a consequence, Margaret confides to Kinsey that she would like to see Fritz dead, but Kinsey advises her: "You'd find that tougher than you think. Guilt makes your hands shake. It makes the blood drain out of your head. Suddenly, you're not as cool and composed as you thought you'd be. I've been on both sides of the law and you don't want to go down that road" (225). Kinsey appears wise and experienced and acts as a counselor for Margaret.

In summary, Kinsey has become more mature in the course of the novels. She is now an experienced woman at ease with herself, who supports other people, and especially women, who are less experienced or vulnerable. Kinsey has become more self-confident and strong-willed. More than ever, she cherishes skills, discipline, and determination in others. When people do not live up to these ideals, Kinsey is less cautious than before, but she can become annoyed and impatient. She tries to satisfy her clients, but she demands to be treated with respect.

Overall, in the last novel, Kinsey seems at peace with herself and with her single life. This lifestyle is the result of her experiences with men. As Grafton claims, Kinsey takes responsibility for the failed marriages (cf. *Letter to the Author* 3), and thus, she remains independent and does want to limit her freedom. While she admired Mickey, her first husband, for his strong character, she developed this quality herself after the divorce. Toward Charlie, the dominant police officer, Kinsey verbalizes her demands more and more clearly, but the relation is primarily sexual and Kinsey does not let Charlie get close. In the course of the novels, Kinsey is more and more unwilling to take risks. All her relationships are more physical than emotional, and she works better with the men on friendly or professional terms. Kinsey shows that women are no longer dependent on the other sex and do not necessarily orient their lives toward men, preferring to please themselves. Men, in the end, are not necessary for women's welfare and vice versa. Kinsey uncovers several relationships and marriages that are defective.

5.5.3.2 The Male Ripper

Despite Kinsey's skills and experience, there are situations that bring the detective to her limits. The year before the novel is set, she had an encounter with Ned, a serial killer of young women who fled before the police could arrest him. He almost succeeded in strangling Kinsey to death. Since then, she has been troubled, fearing that he might come back. Hence, Kinsey has applied for and been granted a permit to carry a concealed weapon (cf. *"Y" Is for Yesterday* 14). She expresses that she does not want to live like that, but she has to be sensible (cf. 281).

Being aware that a gun is not a guarantee for safety, Kinsey works on her strength and endurance. She goes to the gym and works out "in a room full of fitness nuts, most of them male, with the occasional kick-ass female" (15). Kinsey has always been exercising, but rather in order to stay fit. Now, the focus has changed to preparing herself for a potentially dangerous situation.

5.5 Sue Grafton

In addition, Kinsey does a ten-week program in women's self-defense in order to build up the resilience she lacks. She laments: "The odd but unremarkable truth about women is we've had the aggression bred right out of us. Many of us are constitutionally unable to handle any kind of confrontation without bursting into tears" (71). Kinsey criticizes the way of educating girls to be tender, which makes them weak. This hints at missing equality in terms of upbringing and criticizes that socially constructed gender roles are still present.

Kinsey proves tough during the lessons. For instance, when the women are asked to scream at the top of their lungs, she does a good job and stands in contrast to most of the others who just manage a squeak or are even afraid about hurting the potential offender's feelings (cf. 312). Although Kinsey sometimes does not feel like going to class, she is very disciplined and does so anyway: "It's all too easy to let these things slide. If I missed one class, I might as well kiss off the rest" (311). Kinsey works so hard that every muscle in her body aches, but her heart is at peace (cf. 317).

The women are taught how to avoid dangers, such as rape and physical assault at the hands of strangers and acquaintances. Kinsey learns that the majority of rapes are perpetrated by men the victims know, "a sad cause for reflection when embarking on the dating scene." She concludes: "I counted myself wise to confine my love life to cops and other law enforcement worthies to whom I could at least recite the relevant penal code" (312). Again, Kinsey hints at the fact that within her professional surroundings, she feels safe, also with respect to dating.

Despite all the precautions and her strong character, Kinsey still feels vulnerable and she is aware of the physical superiority of Ned. Consequently, she carries her gun even when she just walks over to Rosie's, and she checks the locks on all windows and doors before she leaves her apartment (cf. 98). Kinsey prefers to spend time at places with people around (cf. 15), and as soon as she is home alone, she is afraid (cf. 49). She even panics from time to time, but then her intellect mostly reasserts control (cf. 96). Kinsey did not show these character traits in the previous novels.

Nevertheless, Kinsey is brave and she tries to find Ned instead of hiding from him. She explains: "Ned was like a poisonous snake—better to keep in sight than to wonder where he might strike next" (206). Kinsey contacts Ned's second wife Phyllis Joplin and arranges a meeting to find out more about his whereabouts. Although Phyllis lives in a gated community, Kinsey finds her in the apartment injured after a careless neighbor let Ned inside. Ned wanted to find mementos from the young girls he had killed, and he thought that Phyllis might possess them (cf. 274). Kinsey knows that, in addition, Ned wanted her to find Phyllis because he had monitored their phone call, and she reports: "That's how his mind works. That way he has the pleasure of beating the shit out of her and putting me on notice at the same time" (274).

Soon after this encounter, Kinsey detects that Ned has not only tried to break into her office and tapped into her telephone line, but he has also been sleeping under her office floor for a week. She goes downstairs, finds his shelter, and plans to call officer Philip Cheney: "I had no fantasies about nailing him on my own. Forget a citizen's arrest. I know when I need help and this was clearly a situation that called for the big guns" (287). Again, Kinsey appears as modest, accepting that there are limits to her capability, and she is willing to call the police for help. Such behavior was unimaginable for male hard-boiled detectives because they considered themselves as physically superior to anyone and morally superior to the police.

Then, Kinsey overhears an animal, crawls into an opening, and finds and rescues Ed, the cat. She then calls Henry and plans to escape, but Ned returns before she can leave. Kinsey waits in the opening with her gun in hands. She describes: "I didn't want Ned to stick his head in the opening because if I was forced to shoot, my target would be the top of his skull, a fatal injury in most cases. Let's not even talk about the mess." As he approaches, she elaborates: "I was hyped. I focused on my breathing, clearing my mind of everything but the task at hand" (293). In dangerous situations, Kinsey is absolutely focused and professional, putting aside all her fears.

When Ned knows about Kinsey's presence, he warns her that he has a can of gasoline and can easily burn the place down. She realizes that, under these circumstances, she has to shoot him. Kinsey quickly figures out where he stands, at which angle she has to shoot, and, as intended, she hits his right thigh with the first shot. With the second shot, she does not want to hit him at all, but alarm the neighbors (cf. 295). As Ned escapes, he drops the lighter, and the liquid catches fire. Before the police and firefighters arrive, alarmed by Henry, Kinsey has already freed herself and put the fire out with her fire extinguisher (cf. 304). In contrast to her own perception, Kinsey is capable of fighting Ned on her own, thanks to her skills, her discipline to stay fit, and her calmness in serious situations.

After this attack, however, Kinsey is even more afraid of another encounter with Ned. She describes her fears: "At that point, my paranoia had leapt into the red zone. I spent twenty minutes daily on my hands and knees crawling around on my office floor, looking for listening devices" (305). Nevertheless, in the end, she is strong and she helps Ned's former wife Celeste Lowe, who is affected by her fear. Kinsey observes that life with Ned had deadened her and that she looks like a prisoner of war recently released from captivity (cf. 462).

Kinsey takes Celeste to the police station since she has the evidence of Ned's murders. Kinsey is aware of the fact that Ned might try to chase her, but she concludes: "Better me than her, I still had a score to settle with him in any event" (408). It seems that Kinsey is afraid when she is home alone, but as soon as she has to protect weaker clients, and especially women, her fighting spirit comes up.

Indeed, as Kinsey is back home, Ned again attacks her. Kinsey, not equipped with a weapon, gets help from Pearl, who sends her Rottweiler after him and who fights him violently. Kinsey assists her by using the dog's chain and Henry's shovel to stop Ned. Finally, Pearl sits on Ned and limits his breathing because this is what he did to his victims (cf. 478). Kinsey warns her that she is about to kill him, but Pearl finishes her task with the words: "You don't never want to mess with women, son. They will take you down" (479).

Pearl proves that, no matter how tough a man is, if he mistreats women, it might be his downfall. Ned can be seen as embodiment of patriarchy since he literally used to hush women by suffocating them. The conclusion of the novel can be interpreted as female victory over patriarchy, and it advocates women's physical, but also intellectual capability. Since Pearl pretends to have fallen unconscious on top of Ned, she is not held accountable (cf. 481). In addition, female solidarity is portrayed as a desirable goal. Although Kinsey disliked Pearl in the beginning, she is willing to reconsider her own stereotypes and she is grateful for having her as a neighbor in the end.

5.5.3.3 Various Lifestyles of Modern Women

Not every strong woman in the novel, however, has a good character. At Rosie's birthday party, Kinsey describes Camilla, who appears "like the evil fairy at Sleeping Beauty's christening" (245). Camilla walks over to Kinsey and suspects her of being pregnant by her husband Jonah because Camilla has found a bill by a gynecologist. Kinsey states that Camilla and Jonah lead an open marriage in theory, but that Jonah is not allowed to participate because the fling with her brought nothing but guilt and fear for him, which the current situation demonstrates again. Kinsey, who claims that she is not "loose" and only rarely has affairs (cf. 22–23), has not been sexually active for more than a year (cf. 248) and it turns out that her cousin Anna Dace is pregnant by Jonah (cf. 251).

Anna has frequent affairs, and she does not want to marry or have children, claiming that she has always looked in horror at her siblings and their families. Ellen, her sister, is happily married, but she is exhausted and does not seem to be full of maternal love. Her brother Ethan's marriage is not ideal, and although he is a good father, his career suffers (cf. 349). Hence, Anna views parenthood as "a fatal trap" for both women and men (cf. 316).

Kinsey, in contrast, claims that it has only been two weeks since Anna's pregnancy has been made known, and she already looks "Madonna-like, bathed in serenity" (460). Kinsey, although she herself does not have any children, is positive about parenthood, and she underlines that many people manage to balance family and job well. This goal of a harmony of the private and professional lives seems to be at least partly achieved in the novel. Kinsey's friend Vera Hess, for example, works and has five children, and Kinsey uses her as a role model for Anna (cf. 349).

Vera confesses that her life as a mother has changed profoundly. She explains that raising children is exhausting and that there is little time for herself. Moreover, she describes pregnancy as her "being as big as a house again with milk squirting out of [her] jugs" (352), but then again, she claims that she would like to raise another child and offers to adopt Anna's, in case she wants to go through the pregnancy and then decides not to keep it (cf. 352). Thus, although it is exhausting, she is overall positive about motherhood.

Anna, however, brings up the subject of abortion. Kinsey advocates that Jonah should be asked if he agrees with an abortion. Vera, in contrast, claims that men do not care about these things, and that the choice is Anna's. However, she is principally against abortion and tells Anna that she has also gone through all kinds of emotions and that eventually things will work out (cf. 353). At the end of the novel, Anna still does not know if she wants to keep the baby and she tries to convince Kinsey to take it, but the latter argues that she has her hands full with Killer, the dog, and Ed, the cat, and she claims that she is not exactly a maternal type (cf. 480).

The fact that abortion can be discussed openly and that there are different opinions prevailing is the result of the feminist movement, which advocates women's free decisions over their bodies. Likewise, women now have the open choice to either have children or dedicate themselves completely to their jobs.

5.6 Muller's and Grafton's Innovations Compared to Their Forerunners

5.6.1 Characteristics of the Female Detectives

Muller's and Grafton's novels basically adhere to Poe's conception of detective fiction. More than a century later, they present a modern, metropolitan setting and focus on the rational as well as intuitive problem-solving of their detectives, who are at the core of the works—with the difference that now they are female. In contrast to Golden Age writers, such as Christie, who created a female amateur protagonist that operated within a domestic sphere, Muller and Grafton have their professional detectives solve cases in the public sphere. There, they face barriers for women's independence, and, like Sayers and Allingham, and far beyond, they comment on inequalities on account of their sex. Moreover, they make love interest a subject of discussion, which was not the case in the Golden Age, but they do so in a realistic instead of a traditionally romantic manner.

The public sphere in which the female investigators operate is no longer noble, but the women navigate through realistically portrayed urban areas in the western USA, the places where also male hard-boiled detectives investigated. The women can only be successful in these corrupt surroundings because they are tough. Like their male predecessors, Sharon and Kinsey show some rough habits which are reminiscent of their male predecessors, but they are less pronounced. Their eating habits are rather poor, they drink alcohol, and they occasionally curse, which hints at the fact that women are now free to behave in any way they want. Noble reserve is no longer required.

Although they are not highbred, the women are educated, and they speak in this manner. If they use vulgar language from time to time, they do so deliberately, mostly in order to get some information from members of the lower class. Especially Sharon received a good education—she studied sociology, which represents women's newfound educational opportunities—and she educates herself further, for example, in antiques and arts.

Like their male forerunners, the women are modest in terms of their lifestyles. They both live in small flats (although Sharon later moves into a house), drive inexpensive cars, and wear comfortable clothes. They cherish function more than beauty, and they are self-confident and at ease with themselves. Still, in contrast to Spade and Marlowe, Sharon and Kinsey are not indifferent to their surroundings, but they reflect on their behavior and on their looks from time to time.

Nevertheless, they do not live up to societal expectations for women's appearance, but they remain individuals and make deliberate choices according to their preferences. Kinsey reveals that the feminine beauty myth, created by male demands, has been a prison for women and seems to have become a new male instrument for social control although other rights have long been achieved. With this, she is in line with Naomi Wolf's (*1962) central work of critical gender studies, *The Beauty Myth*, published in 1990. It reveals male expectations of female outer appearance and the resulting concern of women about their bodies as the last remaining patriarchal instrument of power in an otherwise emancipated society and hints at the financial and creative resources this takes up for women. Wolf criticizes that this is a massive backlash for feminist ideas and claims that the past feminine mystique of domesticity and motherhood has been replaced by the beauty myth and the consequential obsession with the outer appearance (cf. Funk 121–122).

Being highly aware of male preferences concerning female looks and behavior, Sharon and Kinsey sometimes act out their feminine charms in order to wrap men around their little fingers and get some information for the investigation. By skillfully performing the traditionally feminine role, they outwit men. Thereby, Sharon and Kinsey show that clearly defined gender images and behavior patterns are artificial and outdated, and that men who still believe in such ideas cannot be taken seriously.

Moreover, it is telling that such men mostly come from the criminal milieu. The women are willing to investigate in this underworld, and especially Kinsey likes taking on the role of the outlaw at times and feels liberated by defying authority, while Sharon rather despises crooked people. Still, the detectives set themselves apart from such people because, like Marlowe, they have a sense of morality. They do not mind lying for purposes of investigation, but they never betray clients for money or kill, apart from reasons of self-defense. Moreover, they feel morally responsible for generally fighting the corruption in the world. Thus, they investigate beyond their cases in order to reveal the truth and to restore order. In doing so, the female detectives also often operate in the upper class. Due to the lack of honorable values of its members, Sharon and Kinsey condemn most of them, just as Marlowe did.

The two women are common middle-class investigators who are dedicated to their work, and they are as capable as their male predecessors. They investigate in a rational manner, and especially Kinsey has strategic puzzle-solving qualities that are reminiscent of early English detectives, as well as a profound knowledge of her tools. More than with male hard-boiled detectives, the women's intelligence is in the focus, and they profit from their conversational skills and their knowledge of human nature, as well as from their intuition. In addition, the authors make their detectives more attentive, empathetic, and caring and show

5.6 Muller's and Grafton's Innovations Compared to Their Forerunners

the benefits of such traditionally feminine characteristics for investigating. Thus, the women are more complex characters than their male predecessors since they combine sensitive understanding with toughness.

The female detectives are brave in dangerous situations, and, if necessary, they even risk their lives. The rare acts of violence in the novels serve to demonstrate their physical as well as mental strength. The women are partly emotionally involved with the victims and even villains whom they fight nonetheless, once the villains have revealed their cruel intentions. In contrast to the traditional notion that women are overly emotive, the authors show that their detectives are indeed able to work in a rational and determined manner, even if they are personally entangled in a case.

Compared to the myth of the male detective hero, who is indestructible, however, the female investigators are indeed more emotional and vulnerable. They are not indifferent to death or danger, and they utter their concerns, stress, and fears. Although it is their major goal to solve the cases on their own, they admit that they are not always capable to do so. In such cases, they ask friends or the police for help. Sharon and Kinsey are on better terms with the police than male hard-boiled detectives used to be, most likely because these institutions have become more professional and trusted.

In a nutshell, the female investigators are modeled after male hard-boiled detectives, and they fulfill their jobs just as well, but Sharon and Kinsey are less heroic and more complex than Spade and Marlowe. They are more plausible in that they encounter problems, admit them, and seek help. Moreover, they are more physically vulnerable and less violent than their predecessors. Thus, they demonstrate that physical strength is not the most important aspect of being a good detective. They rather rely on their highly refined intuition and their empathy, which assist them in finally solving their cases.

Another means by which Muller and Grafton make their detectives authentic is their surroundings. Sharon and Kinsey are not complete loners, but they are given a social environment that consists of co-workers, family, and friends. Thus, the female authors refrain from the romanticized picture of a lone detective in a shabby office, but they portray the complex living environments of their investigators and take a great interest in their private lives and their states of mind.

Hammett and Chandler were not so much interested in the emotional states of their protagonists. Hammett, with his selective omniscience, only allowed the reader to witness Spade's emotions when his eyes widened. The female authors, like Chandler, make use of a first-person narration and reveal their protagonists' thoughts in detail. The detectives do not only describe certain actions and places in which they operate, but they draw conclusions from their surroundings and explain the reasons behind their acting. They also use more dialogue that their male predecessors and discuss certain topics with their social contacts.

Thus, the women integrate their female voices into the genre, and they reveal the psychology behind their actions. With this, the authors add a new dimension to the figure of the hard-boiled detective, and they reveal complex realities of female thinking and behavior, which become more important than the murder cases. This is also the reason why they write series. They give their characters a vita and offer the readers the opportunity to trace their developments, along with social changes.

Sharon and Kinsey develop from young employees in rather patriarchal institutions into responsible and self-determined freelancers. Thus, they have succeeded in a male-dominated sphere. They have also become more demanding in the course of time, for example, in their relation to clients and co-workers, and their social criticism has become more rigorous. In the later novels, Sharon and Kinsey are mature, and they do not only fight inequality for themselves, but they use their experience to instruct more vulnerable women to do so as well.

Stephen Knight adequately summarizes these features of the modern female detective:

> She is mature and experienced as well as inquisitive and skillful; she is wary of but not fully opposed to the police; she has sexual identity and also an extended connection with family and, especially, friends, both women and men; she has substantial empathy with victims of crime; she pursues her inquiries with courage, often being alarmed or physically hurt in the process; the crimes she confronts can be violent and distressing, and unlike the male private-eye tradition they derive mostly from a real combination of urban corruption and personal betrayals. She embodies an optimistic sense that crime can be contained and a better life enjoyed for women, even in the big bad city, even among the secrets and dangers of modern human interaction. (166–167)

The presentation of determined, skilled, and tough women who are equally considerate of others is an innovation, compared to the depiction of women in early male hard-boiled novels. Spade and Marlowe mostly encounter *femmes fatales* such as Hammett's Brigid O'Shaughnessy or Chandler's Carmen and Vivian Sternwood. They are pretty, but aimless, foolish, and in need of male guidance. Still, they know how to make use of their feminine charms in order to deceive the detectives and pose a threat to them.

Apart from deceptive women who are objects of sexual desire for the detectives in early male hard-boiled novels, there are women who are part of the gang

5.6 Muller's and Grafton's Innovations Compared to Their Forerunners 139

of criminals, for example, Chandler's Agnes Lozelle, or who are loyal but helpless, such as Mona Grant. The latter is portrayed in a neutral manner because she adheres to gender roles of the time. In any case, the male hard-boiled detectives despise them all. In this male conception, men are stereotyped as heroes, and they downgrade women. This can also be seen in their conversations. Men are the dominant conversation partners and speak to the women, whose speech is trivial and ineffective, in a rather blunt way.

Male-dominated conversations only take place between the female detectives and the police in Muller's and Grafton's early novels, which shows that there were still patriarchal structures in law enforcement in the early 1980s, more than 15 years after women legally had the right to professionally enter the police forces. The women find their abilities challenged based on their sex, but due to their skills, intelligence, and determination, they convince the male police officers of their capabilities by and by. Although these men primarily resist integrating women into the force, the female detectives embody a new consciousness and work alongside men in a professional manner. Thus, they challenge remaining injustices, even in a male-dominated institution, which proves to be hard, but a great success.

Hence, Sharon and Kinsey dismiss the traditional female roles as seducer, criminal or dependent woman, which were present in Hammett's and Chandler's works. Still, they play with their feminine charms to deceive patriarchal men from time to time, showing that a clearly defined female identity is obsolete. Moreover, they reveal the connection of the female sex with a prescribed lifestyle as constructed. Sharon and Kinsey are not dependent on men, and they detach the longing for a permanent relationship, domesticity, and motherhood from the female sex, suggesting that every individual is free to choose how to live.

Sharon and Kinsey embody the image of the New Woman that was achieved by second-wave feminists. In the initial novels, they are introduced as being single, childless, independent, and self-reliant, and they feel complete without men, although they like to have good men around. The fact that Muller and Grafton construct their protagonists in this way without social disrepute shows that those trends, which had arisen in the 1960s, were implemented into the minds of people by the 1980s. The only commitment for Sharon and Kinsey is their self-realization.

The protagonists offer a new consciousness and contentment that cannot be repressed anymore. The women do not seem to consider being single a loss of security, as many women in the 1970s still did. Especially Kinsey has experienced that bad relationships are obstacles to happiness. In contrast to Spade and

Marlowe, however, Muller's and Grafton's female detectives are not artificially destined to be lonely and they have long-term connections.

Their choices of men show that the women develop in the course of the novels, which follows current trends in society. While they both try to impress dominant police officers in the beginning, they learn that such unequal relationships are not fulfilling, and they look for partners who treat them equally and respectfully. Still, the women do not strive for permanent commitment. Sharon, although her relationship with her partner Hy is rewarding, does not plan to marry, but Hy is the one who longs for a fixed relationship. Thus, the connection of the female sex with the desire for marriage is denied. As Sharon finally agrees to marry Hy, she demonstrates that matrimony no longer means subordination for a woman, but they have a trusting and equal marriage in which both partners feel comfortable.

Kinsey is not willing to share her life with a man eventually. She acts uncompromisingly and pragmatically, and she never really trusts her partners. Her affairs are primarily sexual, which mirrors that women are now free to embrace their sexual freedom. Her explicit observations of men's bodies are reminiscent of the male detectives' carnal descriptions of women in the hard-boiled novels of Hammett and Chandler. The fact that Grafton undertakes a role reversal and that it is now a woman who describes the other sex in this manner reflects that, from the 1980s onwards, women have been increasingly outspoken and have expressed their sexual desires. Grafton, with Kinsey, presents an entirely independent female protagonist who is not interested in permanent commitment.

5.6.2 Various Lifestyles and Qualities of Female and Male Characters

Apart from independent professional detectives, Muller and Grafton offer a variety of female characters with different lifestyles and characteristics, depending on their individual ambitions. Some women are freedom-loving, single, childless, and working, such as Muller's Cara Ingalls and Grafton's Dixie Hightower. Others are working mothers, for instance, Grafton's Vera Hess, or pregnant women considering abortion, such as Kinsey's cousin Anna Dace. The novels show that female identification is not tied to roles such as the domestic wife or mother any longer. Women now have all the opportunities to choose from. Hence, de Beauvoir's assessment from the 20th century which states that women do not have the chance to create meaningful lives of their own is no longer valid.

In terms of character traits, the authors also present a wide range of women. Many women are amicable and thoughtful, such as Sharon's friends Paula Mercer,

5.6 Muller's and Grafton's Innovations Compared to Their Forerunners

Adah Joshlyn, and Daphne Ashford, and Kinsey's friend Rosie. Others are inhumane and careless, for example, Muller's Cara Ingalls, or dominant and deceiving, such as Grafton's Camilla Robb and Dixie Hightower.

Likewise, Muller's and Grafton's novels offer a variety of different men. Some of them are caring, such as Muller's Hy Ripinsky and Hank Zahn, as well as Grafton's Henry Pitts. Grafton's Charlie Scorsoni and Daniel Wade are dominant and reckless, others are selfish and pushy, such as Muller's Oliver van Osten and Ben Harmon, and Ned is a brutal killer. The offenders in the novels are mostly male, and they are often conservative patriarchs who feel downgraded by strong women and react to the new social order in an overly dominant manner. The fact that they are convicted at the end of the novels suggests a triumph over outdated world views and a better life for women.

In contrast to men who subdue women, some male characters are submissive toward strong women, most importantly Grafton's Jonah Robb. The fact that he is a police officer proves that the police business has changed. While male hard-boiled authors described the officers as being dominant, tough, and corrupt, the female writers portray dominant and crooked officers (such as Grafton's Charlie Scorsoni), skilled and professional ones (Grafton's Robert Dietz and Con Dolan), as well as weak and good-natured ones. Thereby, Muller and Grafton present multi-faceted men in the police and alter the stereotypical and one-sided depiction of its members.

In sum, the female authors avoid traditional gender stereotypes and show that women as well as men may be both good and evil, and that they may choose their lifestyles and jobs freely, according to their wishes. Thereby, they emphasize that precisely attributed characteristics and life plans for both sexes are socially and culturally constructed and performative. As a result, female hard-boiled detective novels become places of negotiating a new order of the sexes and different constructions of what it means to be female and male. Muller and Grafton integrate gender awareness into a traditionally male-dominated genre, and they show that it is compatible with modern attitudes.

In doing so, they do not portray their female detectives as being radical or hostile toward men, because Sharon and Kinsey do not perceive themselves as victims, but they celebrate female independence, self-respect, and authentic, individual identities. As a result, they strive for harmony instead of war between the sexes and cooperate with men for their own good. Such behavior is characteristic of liberal third-wave feminism, in which the female authors have matured. When they introduced their professional detectives around 1980, the highly political and active second-wave feminist movement had lost momentum because major legal achievements had been made and women had gained a new consciousness. Thus, liberal feminist ideas became widespread and women concentrated on dialogue in every area of life.

Sharon and Kinsey can be seen as literary pioneers of this triumphant and non-activist third-wave feminism, having its peak in the 1990s, because they employ individual approaches to fighting remaining gender injustice. Their acts of resistance are rather personal than political. Sharon explicitly criticizes radical groups of both women and men that aim at smearing the reputations of the other sex. She also sets herself apart from women who are angry with men, and shows that men respond more positively to less radical women who demand one step at a time instead of a complete reversal of gender roles. Thus, Muller portrays aggressive feminism as unproductive.

Therefore, as Elliott rightly claims, Muller cannot be called a feminist in the political sense. She did not actively take part in the feminist movement. Her protagonist has a feminist mindfulness, but she rather responds to issues of gender as an American woman (cf. 15). This approach has also been criticized. Klein points out that "[Sharon] has little to say about her consciousness of women's position in society except as men exasperate her with patronizing remarks" (cf. *The Woman Detective* 209). Klein's description of Sharon as "having feminist inclinations without explicitly defining [herself] that way" (202) is therefore adequate, but not less progressive.

Grafton wrote in the same tradition, and she has similarly been criticized by feminists for violating their principles by adhering to the genre conventions of male hard-boiled fiction and thus, supposedly supporting patriarchal constructions (cf. Walton 111). Grafton, however, explained her choice as a conscious decision:

> I don't consider myself a feminist author. I'm a huge fan of strong women and I support equal pay for equal work, but I've parted company with the current generation of feminists, who seem angry with men, who see the world in terms of patriarchal conspiracies designed to keep women down, who feel victimized no matter how many counter-examples one might point out. I'm apolitical. I'm not mad at anybody. I have no axe to grind. I'm not pushing a point of view. I don't believe a detective novel should serve as propaganda, which is a distortion of the truth in any event. (*Letter to the Author* 1)

Grafton was not angry with men, and so she avoided stereotypical portrayals of either sex. She stated: "I don't want to create a world in which women appear to be superior or more intelligent. I admire women who are fearless and accomplished. I admire the women who go about their business without reference to the politics of gender. I admire many men for the same reasons" (3). Grafton accentuated individualism in her works, and, similarly to Sharon's, Kinsey's actions are rather personal reactions to remaining sexism.

5.6.3 Social Concerns Beyond Gender

Apart from gender issues, Sharon and Kinsey respond to various other social concerns, and in the course of their series, they do so increasingly. While their first novels were published around 1980, the ones last discussed in this study both date from 2017. Over this time period, achievements of the feminist movement led to increased gender equality and so, gender issues lost urgency in the course of the years. This gave the authors the chance to explore further concerns in American society.

Kinsey mainly comments on topics concerning sex, gender, and sexual orientation. For example, she deals with female ageism (cf. *"A" Is for Alibi* 83), and she discusses female concerns such as abortion rights (cf. *"Y" Is for Yesterday* 353) and the double burden of work and family (cf. 349). Moreover, Kinsey uncovers domestic abuse, (cf. 89), rape, and sexual assault (cf. 70). Furthermore, she clearly criticizes homophobia, since this attitude leads to a murder in *"Y" Is for Yesterday*. Kinsey also hints at more global social issues such as dysfunctional families (cf. 402–403), class divisions, and superficial upper class life (cf. *"O" Is for Outlaw* 63–67; 228–234), as well as corrupt social structures (cf. 483).

Muller's novels explore broader social issues, and they especially focus on the wellbeing of, and the successful interaction between members of society. For example, Sharon criticizes racial hatred in her city (cf. *The Color of Fear* 165), and she hints at the clash of cultures when Hy is called to a hostage situation in France in which Syrians are involved (cf. 170). Moreover, she laments excessive consumerism in society (cf. 132), and she indicates the serious impact of the growing digitization and electronic devices on people's lives at the expense of personal relationships (cf. 121). In addition, Sharon is concerned about the widespread possession of firearms, which she views as a major threat in American society (cf. 115). Elliott rightly calls Sharon a "touchstone" for realities and concerns in changing American society (cf. 13).

Conclusion 6

In sum, the present study shows that the genre of detective fiction can serve as a vehicle to explore social issues at different times. The characters of the detectives and the social surroundings in which they operate reflect every shift in society—this includes modifications in the perception of gender roles and gender relations.

Originally, the detectives were naturally male, and being an investigator was long considered unimaginable for a woman. In Poe's early detective stories, women were primarily victims, and they appeared either as servants or as domestic wives and mothers in Doyle's tales. Especially from the 1920s onwards, women called attention to themselves, and some of the English detective novels of the Golden Age presented female protagonists. However, authors usually did not depict their female characters as being overly progressive, as the example of the domestic amateur spinster Miss Marple shows.

Authors of the American hard-boiled tradition from the 1920s to the 1940s actually intended to present a more masculine type of detective than Agatha Christie's Poirot and Dorothy L. Sayers's Wimsey, whom they considered not hard enough. Thus, Hammett and Chandler portrayed their male protagonists as masculine, tough, and they asserted their strength. Conversely, they reduced the female characters to their sexual attractiveness, emphasized their immoral conduct, and their dependence on male guidance. Although women were standing up for their rights in real life at that time, the male authors preserved the traditional social order of the sexes in their fiction and marginalized women.

This negative depiction of women in literature changed with the increasing valorization of the female sex in the course of the second wave of the feminist movement. Muller's and Grafton's professional female detectives, created around 1980, differ significantly from Hammett's and Chandler's female characters. They

© The Author(s), under exclusive license to Springer-Verlag GmbH, DE, part of Springer Nature 2024
S. Bernhard, *Gender Identity and Gender Relations Redefined*,
https://doi.org/10.1007/978-3-662-69867-9_6

are modeled after the male investigators in that they are independent and successful in their work, but they are not stereotyped. The women are complex and authentic characters in a homelike social surrounding, who add conversational skills, intuition, and empathy to the tough detective figure. Moreover, they are less violent and more vulnerable, and they reveal problems they face during their investigations in a society whose power structures still partly exclude them.

As a consequence, Muller and Grafton did indeed reinvent the American hard-boiled formula of their male forerunners to a significant extent, especially concerning its gender perceptions. They did not just alter the sex of the stereotyped male hard-boiled protagonists, but they integrated and revalued traditionally feminine characteristics and created credible, sociable detectives. These women assert female autonomy and present the female state of mind, including women's worldviews, attitudes, and problems.

Thus, Muller's and Grafton's style of writing corresponds to Marty S. Knepper's definition of a women's literature that supports gender equality:

> Feminist writing shows as a norm and not as freaks, women capable of intelligence, moral responsibility, competence and independent action; reveals the economic, social, political and psychological problems women face as part of a patriarchal society; explores female consciousness and female perception of the world; creates women who have psychological complexity and reject sexist stereotypes. . . .
>
> It values female bonding, awareness of women without continual reference to or affiliation with men, and the self-knowledge which prompts women to independent judgment on both public and personal issues. (399)

What is more, Muller and Grafton portray their male characters in a complex and authentic manner. They do not debase men, just as male writers used to do with women, but the authors redefine archaic conventions and assumptions about gender in general. Their works emphasize that both women and men may have positive as well as negative characteristics. Muller and Grafton do no longer accredit such attributes to the sex, but to individual traits. Moreover, both sexes now have the opportunity to lead a variety of different lifestyles, and to choose from various jobs. Many former gender limitations have been eliminated and ideally, every human can seek self-fulfillment according to her or his preferences, ambitions, and skills. In sum, their works reflect modern notions from liberal and pluralist thinking, and gendered identity has dissolved into individual identity.

In this way, Muller and Grafton emphasize gender's performative nature and are in line with Butler's ideas as well as the constructivist perception of gender. Muller's and Grafton's works illustrate that traditional notions of femininity

6 Conclusion

and masculinity are indeed socially and culturally constructed and validated in everyday life, and that they change according to their temporal contexts. Thus, the supposed link between sex and gender, and distinguishing characteristics, lifestyles, and work areas for women and men, have turned out to be outdated.

This approach allows Muller and Grafton to challenge the hard-boiled formula and its conventions of gender without erasing its characteristics. They problematize male hard-boiled toughness by showing that the traditional identification of strength and success with masculinity is outdated. Since courage depends on individual ambition, the subgenre opens up to include women as successful detectives. Thereby, the authors redefine the status of women in society and authority, and they legitimate their presence in these spheres. In doing so, the authors do not undermine the genre and write one-sided female fantasies, which would bring them to the edge of parody (cf. Klein, *The Woman Detective* 174), but they manage the difficult task to combine a traditional formula with a modern gender awareness.

Consequently, Muller and Grafton are in the feminist tradition since they resist unequal treatment of women and want to improve their participation in the social, political, and economic spheres of life, but, having matured within third-wave feminism, they are not active feminists. Considering the central themes of Muller's and Grafton's works, they focus on the goals of liberal third-wave feminism such as gender equality in business and the reduction of the double burden of employment and domestic responsibilities. Their works, especially the later ones, also explore the concern of intersectionality, namely that different aspects of a person's social identity, such as gender, age, class, and race, combine and create discrimination.

Likewise, Muller's and Grafton's protagonists are sensitive to how people who use gender categories judge, and they face sexist comments with confidence and defend their values, but they do not embody the image of grim, aggressive, and antagonistic women. The protagonists show that today, standing up for gender equality does not involve hatred of the other sex, but they offer a positive attitude to life and emphasize the satisfaction of self-realization. Their approach is individual rather than systematic.

The conclusion of this study, namely that Muller and Grafton redefine male hard-boiled ideologies concerning gender identity and gender relations in their works, can be related to the main views of scholarly discussion in the field of American female hard-boiled detective fiction. My findings disagree with Klein's claim from 1988 that, due to the conservativeness of the subgenre, the effects of placing a woman at its center are far from radical and that the ideology embedded in this genre overcomes the feminist counter-ideology (cf. *The Woman Detective*

209). Klein underlines "the primacy of the conventional private-eye fictional formula over the feminist ideology which falsely seems to signal a change in the genre." She even claims that female hard-boiled works "demonstrate a triumph of the genre over feminist ideology in much the same way that patriarchal/sexist ideology triumphs over the genre in most of the preceding novels" (221).

The authors tolerate the system of the genre in order to be able to reform it from within, which allows them to be successful. Aggressively rejecting conventions and downgrading men has not been expedient, as the decline of radical feminism shows. The female detectives do indeed change male ideologies by avoiding stereotyped characteristics for women and men. In the end, the fact that they manage to change male perspectives on women's abilities in a male-dominated sphere makes their success even greater.

Concerning Klein's claim that characteristics of the male formula prevail in the female novels, the findings of this study agree with Reddy's ideas, which were also published in 1988, but offer a perspective that sharply differs from Klein. Reddy adequately postulates that the only traditional characteristics of the formula in the female novels concern the surface, such as the detectives' profession, lifestyle, their tough talk, and their attitude toward the police (cf. 120). Apart from that, according to Reddy, the female authors have altered many features of the hard-boiled novels, such as the detective's isolation and connectedness, the attitude toward violence, the sense of justice and, above all, the sense of self. Thereby, Reddy claims, female writers have created a counter tradition in detective fiction, namely a female literary tradition with a modern female self-conception, by displacing the traditionally male consciousness and offering a woman-centered worldview (cf. 148–149). Thus, female hard-boiled detective novels "participate in the larger feminist project of redefining and redistributing power" (cf. 149).

Muller and Grafton do indeed offer novels that portray modern women with a new self-conception. Therefore, the works redirect social and economic participation and power to include women, which is the utmost goal of any feminist conviction. What is more, the works (especially the later ones) explicitly present a modified male identity. They also reveal traditionally defined and generalized characteristics for men, such as power and ambition, as performative, just like prescribed working areas.

Having explored and compared Muller's and Grafton's approaches in selected works, this study is not exhaustive. It would be desirable if also Muller's future works became subjects of discussion in order to trace Sharon's ultimate personal development. Furthermore, Sara Paretsky's feminist approach could be contrasted

6 Conclusion

to Muller and Grafton in order to specify the extent of gender reversal, the treatment of men, and the compatibility of political feminism with the hard-boiled formula.

In addition to the previously mentioned authors, Linda Barnes (*1949), Janet Evanovich (*1943), and Nevada Barr (*1952) present independent female private eyes, and their approaches could be analyzed in a similar way, as demonstrated in this study, in order to trace how they create their female protagonists as well as further female and male characters. Moreover, since homosexual detectives have occurred in recent decades, created for instance by Katherine V. Forrest (*1939), Barbara Wilson (*1950), and Laurie King (*1952), scholarly research could analyze if a different sexual orientation leads to any other changes concerning the presentation of both sexes. Finally, it would be interesting to see if there is any nonbinary gender identity among fictional detectives and whether genderfluidity can be implemented into a genre which traditionally relies on gender binary.

Considering the further development of women within the genre of detective fiction in general, apart from the female private eye novel, which has been the most visible of all subgenres since the 1980s, many female authors have made use of the police procedural in recent decades. While Muller and Grafton reveal gender-related ills inherent in police institutions rather from the outside, police procedurals show how these systems resist the integration of women from within. It would be desirable if existing gender perceptions were further analyzed in this particular subgenre.

The phenomenon of female investigators is not limited to the medium of the book. Especially since the 1970s, women have increasingly been protagonists in television series and movies. To name some examples, prominent are the beautiful and courageous female investigators in *Charlie's Angels* and the intelligent and successful protagonists in *Wonder Woman* and *The Bionic Woman*. In the 1980s, it was not only young and single women who worked as detectives anymore, but there were all sorts of female investigators, including married or divorced ones, mothers, and elderly women. In addition, women of color appeared, although most often as minor characters, for instance, in *Miami Vice*.

In the 1990s and 2000s, women were increasingly presented as important characters in police procedurals such as *Law & Order: Criminal Intent* and *CSI: Miami*, although the protagonists were mostly male. *Rizzoli & Isles*, in 2010, finally presented two professional and skilled female crime solvers as protagonists (cf. Romanko 5–14). Such television series and movies, which are partly based on literary sources, are of high significance in mainstream entertainment culture. In the context of transmediality, they could be analyzed, applying the same criteria as to literary works in this study. It would be interesting to explore the question of whether there is a difference in gender awareness between the two media. The current heated discussion about a woman, or a person of color, as the new James Bond (cf. Owoseje), for example, shows that the representation of women and ethnic minorities as agents on television is still not unquestioned and that literature is one step ahead in this context.

In fiction, detectives from different sexes and sexual orientations, as shown above, can be heroes. Moreover, detective fiction is also used by ethnic writers, for example Tony Hillerman (1925–2008), Harry Kemelman (1908–1996), and Walter Mosley (*1952), in order to portray successful detectives. This trend is not limited to detective fiction. In recent decades, several, especially female, authors have explored gender, sexual orientation, ethnicity, religion, race, class, and history. The current focus on intersectionality has additionally encouraged the exploration of the relationship between these attributes. Successful authors like Adrienne Rich (1929–2012), Toni Morrison (1931–2019), Alice Walker (*1944), Rita Dove (*1952), Sandra Cisneros (*1954), Amy Tan (*1952), and Louise Erdrich (*1954) prove that there is room for the recognition of formerly underrepresented and marginalized groups.

Adrienne Rich, who began writing in the 1950s, did not only experiment with content, but also with style —especially in her poetry —and her works prove her evolving feminist radicalism. In her later works in the 1970s, she finally embraced lesbianism as a form of activism to demand equality for women in the personal as well as professional spheres. Her thoughts on feminism were progressive and revolutionary at the time, and she constantly called for social change in her six-decade career (cf. Martin and Williams 165–167). She is also considered one of the pioneers of LGBT (Lesbian, Gay, Bisexual, and Transgender) rights and history.

LGBT groups brought about a cultural shift in the United States because they fought and won legal battles to include various sexual orientations in local, federal, and state laws. In 2015, the *Obergefell v. Hodges* decision of the Supreme Court of the United States guaranteed same-sex couples the fundamental right to marry and recognized marriages of same-sex couples on the same terms and conditions as marriages of opposite-sex couples (cf. 195). This has fundamentally changed people's views on gay rights for the better.

Since the 1970s, African-American women have increasingly made major contributions to American literature. They do not only present the devastating effects of racism and slavery, but they also show the strength, solidarity, and spirituality in African-American communities. These writers won some of the prestigious literary awards and prizes. Alice Walker, for example, got the Pulitzer Prize, America's National Book Award, for her work *The Color Purple* in 1983. Toni

6 Conclusion

Morrison got the Pulitzer Prize for *Beloved* in 1988, and she was awarded the Nobel Prize in Literature in 1993 (cf. Fox). Rita Dove was named United States Poet Laureate in 1993 and held the office until 1995 (cf. Martin and Williams 182).

In addition to African-American literature, American Latina literature became popular at around the same time. Chicana writer Sandra Cisneros's first novel *The House on Mango Street* in 1984 was a success, preparing the ground for authors with other Latin American heritages who also explore women's identities in various culturally specific contexts across the Americas (cf. 185–186).

Moreover, Asian-American authors entered mainstream literature, for example Amy Tan with her works *The Joy Luck Club* in 1989 and *The Kitchen God's Wife* in 1991. Asian-American writers primarily explore the challenge of assimilating to the current culture while maintaining their traditional cultural values. Such conflicts often show in cross-generational contexts (cf. 187–188).

Lastly, Ojibwe writer Louise Erdrich attracted attention to the long tradition of literature by Native American women writers with her work *Love Medicine* in 1984. She explores the roles of women in Native American communities and their relations to the United States. Several Native scholars have explored similar themes to this day, and Louise Erdrich won the Pulitzer Prize for her novel *The Night Watchman* in 2021 (cf. 188–189).

In sum, in recent decades, there has been a whole range of American women's literature that presents female and feminist perspectives, which have become inseparable from queer and multicultural ones. American women writers are less and less limited by national borders, but literature today has a transnational quality. The authors mentioned above introduce readers to various regions and offer different cultural and ethnic contexts of America's rich and varied history. Thus, they present the diverse collective American identity, and they create a comprehensive fictional picture of human existence in which movement and connections of nations and peoples around the world are indispensable.

All this goes to show that there is now an unprecedented number of successful female American authors with various backgrounds and lifestyles, and they participate in a literary tradition that once misrepresented them. Women now write texts in great numbers about any topic in any form, and they cover all kinds of genres, as well as every important American literary and cultural movement. In the past decade, eight out of ten of the best-selling books in the United States were written by women (cf. Lapidos), which proves that women writers and their works have changed the traditional social order of the sexes in mainstream fiction. Women's literature is highly visible in the American literary canon, and it is subject of scholarly discussion.

Elaine Showalter, in the introduction to her history of American women writers, adequately summarizes that women's writing developed from a feminine period, in which female authors imitated existing traditions, through a feminist stage, during which writers protested against these traditions, to a female phase, in which women discovered their voices and developed aesthetically (cf. xvii).

The literary feminist movement corresponds with the political one. What Showalter calls "feminist" covers ideals of first- and second-wave feminism and the "female phase" is equivalent to third- and fourth-wave feminism. While women fought for equality in real life, they simultaneously expressed their viewpoints and implemented their new freedoms in literature to make their formerly ignored identities visible. Thus, literary progress has cultural and political value. Through literature, the perception of women has changed in readers' minds, at universities, and in professional life.

Despite all progress, current instances of sexual[1] and racial[2] discrimination show that gender and racial equality, as well as mutual respect in general — and concerning diverse sexes, sexual orientations, races, cultural and religious values, and lifestyles—should still not be taken for granted and remain ideals worth fighting for. In our ever-changing world, literature is and will continue to be a major space for public discussion of social trends and challenges, especially with the expansion of the literary marketplace by digital technologies and digital publishing media. Such technological change has revolutionized the production, distribution, and consumption of literature and it has facilitated the output, interaction, and public perception of writers who tend to be marginalized by publishing houses. Thus, in the future, there will be ever more opportunities for authors of all kinds to present their works to a global public and to find complete expression.

Since within detective fiction the readership is accustomed to exploring serious public discourse, it can be assumed that this popular genre will continue to play a major role in giving expression to former socially disadvantaged groups.

---

[1] The #MeToo Movement, which was initiated on social media in 2006 by American activist Tarana Burke, has demonstrated how many women, especially young and colored ones, are sexually assaulted, primarily in the workplace (cf. Synder and Lopez). In addition, Femen, a radical feminist activist group that was founded in Ukraine in 2008, calls attention to the fact that male power structures, which do not necessarily harm women physically, may influence them in a mental way nonetheless. (cf. Funk 107–109).

[2] Incidents of racially motivated police violence created the Black Lives Matter movement in the United States in 2013. The political movement became highly topical again after the death of George Floyd, an American citizen of African-American origin, in May 2020, which triggered demonstrations across the globe (cf. "Black Lives Matter").

6 Conclusion

Different as all the future investigators and their crimes may be, they will certainly all share the aim of improving or even saving the world. In the end, their noble ambitions and heroic actions will be much more important than their origins or lifestyles. Hence, detective fiction can be seen as an equalizer because people from different classes, gender, and ethnic groups can be heroes, at least in fiction. Hope remains that this sense of equality and aim to strive for it will continue to be adopted into real life.

Works Cited

1. Primary Sources

Allingham, Margery. *The Fashion in Shrouds*. 1938. London: Ipso, 2016.
Chandler, Raymond. *The Big Sleep*. *The Big Sleep and Other Novels*. 1939.London: Penguin, 2000. 1–164.
Christie, Agatha. *The Body in the Library*. 1942. New York: Pocket, 1970.
Conan Doyle, Arthur. "A Scandal in Bohemia." *The Adventures of Sherlock Holmes*. 1891. London: Macmillan, 2016. 7–38.
Cross, Amanda. *In the Last Analysis*. 1964. New York: Ballantine, 2001.
Grafton, Sue. *"A" Is for Alibi*. Three Complete Novels: *"A" Is for Alibi, "B" Is for Burglar, "C" Is for Corpse*. 1982. New York: Wings, 1999. 1–279.
Grafton, Sue. *"D" Is for Deadbeat*. London: Pan Macmillan, 1987.
Grafton, Sue. *"E" Is for Evidence*. New York: St. Martin's Press, 1988.
Grafton, Sue. *"G" Is for Gumshoe*. New York: St. Martin's Press, 1990.
Grafton, Sue. *"H" Is for Homicide*. New York: St. Martin's Press, 1991.
Grafton, Sue. *"I" Is for Innocent*. New York: St. Martin's Press, 1992.
Grafton, Sue. *"M" Is for Malice*. New York: St. Martin's Press, 1996.
Grafton, Sue. *"O" Is for Outlaw*. New York: St. Martin's Press, 1999.
Grafton, Sue. *"P" Is for Peril*. New York: Putnam's Sons, 2001.
Grafton, Sue. *"R" Is for Ricochet*. New York: Putnam's Sons, 2004.
Grafton, Sue. *"S" Is for Silence*. New York: Berkley, 2005.
Grafton, Sue. *"T" Is for Trespass*. New York: Putnam's Sons, 2007.
Grafton, Sue. *"U" Is for Undertow*. New York: Putnam's Sons, 2009.
Grafton, Sue. *"Y" Is for Yesterday*. London: Pan Macmillan, 2017.
Hammett, Dashiell. *Red Harvest*. London: Orion, 1929.
Hammett, Dashiell. *The Maltese Falcon*. 1930. London: Orion, 2005.
Muller, Marcia. *Edwin of the Iron Shoes*. 1977. New York: Mysterious Press, 1993.
Muller, Marcia. *A Wild and Lonely Place*. 1995. New York: Warner, 1996.
Muller, Marcia. *Coming Back*. New York: Little, Brown and Company, 2010.
Muller, Marcia. *Games to Keep the Dark Away*. New York: Warner, 1984.
Muller, Marcia. *Where Echoes Live*. 1991. New York: Warner, 1992.
Muller, Marcia. *Someone Always Knows*. New York: Grand Central Publishing. 2016.

Muller, Marcia. *The Color of Fear.* New York: Grand Central Publishing, 2017.
Muller, Marcia. *The Dangerous Hour.* New York: Warner, 2004.
Muller, Marcia. *The Ever-Running Man.* New York: Warner, 2007.
Muller, Marcia. *Till the Butchers Cut Him Down.* New York: Warner, 1994.
Muller, Marcia. *Wolf in the Shadows.* New York: Warner, 1993.
Paretsky, Sara. *Indemnity Only.* London: Penguin, 1982.
Poe, Edgar Allan. "The Murders in the Rue Morgue." *Selected Tales. Edgar Allan Poe.* 1841. London: Penguin, 1994. 118–153.
Poe, Edgar Allan. "The Purloined Letter." *Selected Tales. Edgar Allan Poe.* 1844. London: Penguin, 1994. 337–356.
Sayers, Dorothy L. *Busman's Honeymoon.* New York: Harper, 1937.
Sayers, Dorothy L. *Gaudy Night.* 1935. New York: Harper, 1995.

2. Secondary Sources

Allyn, David. *Make Love, Not War: The Sexual Revolution: An Unfettered History.* New York: Routledge, 2001.
Anderson, Karen. *Wartime Women: Sex Roles, Family Relations, and the Status of Women during World War II.* Westport: Greenwood, 1981.
Baker, Robert, and Michael T. Nietzel. *Private Eyes. One Hundred and One Knights: A Survey of American Detective Fiction 1922–1984.* Bowling Green, Ohio: Bowling Green State University Press, 1985.
Binyon, T.J. *Murder Will Out: The Detective in Fiction.* Oxford: Oxford University Press, 1989.
"Black Lives Matter." *Encyclopedia Britannica Online.* Encyclopedia Britannica. 09 February 2021 <https://www.britannica.com/event/shooting-of-Trayvon-Martin>.
Bloom, Harold. *The Western Canon: The Books and School of the Ages.* New York: Harcourt Brace & Company, 1994.
Bouchier, David. *The Feminist Challenge: The Movement for Women's Liberation in Britain and the USA.* New York: Schocken, 1983.
Bradford Wilcox, William. "The Evolution of Divorce." 2009. *National Affairs* 43 (2020): 81–94.
Cassuto, Leonard. *Hard-Boiled Sentimentality: The Secret History of American CrimeStories.* New York: Columbia University Press, 2009.
Cawelti, John G. *Adventure, Mystery, and Romance: Formula Stories as Art and Popular Culture.* Chicago: University of Chicago Press, 1997.
Cawelti, John G. "Canonization, Modern Literature, and the Detective Story." *Theory and Practice of Classic Detective Fiction.* Ed. Jerome H. Delameter and Ruth Prigozy. Westport: Greenwood, 1997. 5–17.
Center for American Women and Politics "2018 Election Night Tally." 2018. *Center for American Women and Politics.* 04 June 2020 <http://cawp.rutgers.edu/2018-election-night-tally>.
Chamberlain, Prudence. *The Feminist Fourth Wave: Affective Temporality.* Cham: Springer, 2017.

Works Cited

Chandler, Raymond. *Raymond Chandler Speaking.* Ed. Dorothy Gardiner and Kathrine Sorley Walker. Boston: Houghton Mifflin, 1962.
Chandler, Raymond. "The Simple Art of Murder." *The Atlantic Monthly* December 1944: 53–59.
Collins, Gail. *When Everything Changed. The Amazing Journey of American Women from 1960 to the Present.* New York: Little, Brown and Company, 2009.
Committee for Economic Development. "Fulfilling the Promise: How More Women on Corporate Boards Would Make America and American Companies More Competitive." Washington, 2012. *Committee for Economic Development.* 04 December 2018 <http://www.fwa.org/pdf/CED_WomenAdvancementonCorporateBoards.pdf.>.
Craig, Patricia, and Mary Cadogan. *The Lady Investigates: Women Detectives and Spies in Fiction.* Oxford: Oxford University Press, 1986.
Davis, Jack E. *The Civil Rights Movement.* Malden: Blackwell, 2001.
Davis, Jenny L., et al. "Opposites Attract. Retheorizing Binaries in Language, Gender, and Sexuality." *Queer Excursions. Retheorizing Binaries in Language, Gender, and Sexuality.* New York: Oxford University Press, 2014. 1–12.
Delamater, Jerome H., and Ruth Prigozy. *Theory and Practice of Classic Detective Fiction.* Westport: Greenwood Press, 1997.
Doyle, Martin. "Agatha Christie: Genius or Hack? Crime Writers Pass Judgment and Pick Favourites". *The Irish Times.* 16 September, 2015.
Durham, Philip. *Down These Mean Streets a Man Must Go: Raymond Chandler's Knight.* Chapel Hill: University of North Carolina Press, 1963.
"Elaine Showalter." *Encyclopedia Britannica Online.* Encyclopedia Britannica. 03 April 2022. <https://www.britannica.com/topic/Brandeis-University>.
Elliott, Winter S. "Changing the World. One Detective at a Time: The Feminist Ethos of Marcia Muller and Sharon McCone." *Marcia Muller and the Female Private Eye.* Ed. Alexander N. Howe and Christine A. Jackson. Jefferson: McFarland, 2008. 13–26.
Fitzgibbon, Russell H. *The Agatha Christie Companion.* Bowling Green: Bowling Green University Press, 1980.
Fox, Margalit. "Toni Morrison, Towering Novelist of the Black Experience, Dies at 88." *The New York Times.* 06 August 2019. *The New York Times on the Web.* 05 October 2021 <https://www.nytimes.com/2019/08/06/books/toni-morrison-dead.html>.
Friedan, Betty. *The Feminine Mystique.* 1963. McKeesport: W. W. Norton & Company, 2013.
Funk, Wolfgang. *Gender Studies.* Paderborn: Wilhelm Fink, 2018.
Grafton, Sue. *Letter to the Author.* 30 August 2010.
Grafton, Sue. "A Conversation with Sue Grafton 1996." *Sue Grafton Website.* 1996. 12 December 2010 <https://web.archive.org/web/20061231203224/http://www.suegrafton.com/interview.htm>.
Grosz, Elisabeth. *Space, Time, and Perversion. Essays on the Politics of Bodies.* New York: Routledge, 1995.
Hamilton, Cynthia S. *Western and Hard-Boiled Detective Fiction in America: From High Noon to Midnight.* Basingstoke: Macmillan, 1987.
Hartman, Susan M. *The Home-Front and Beyond: American Women in the 1940s.* Boston: Twayne, 1982.
Haycraft, Howard. *Murder for Pleasure: The Life and Times of the Detective Story.* 1939. New York: Appleton, 1941.

Heilbrun, Carolyn. "Keynote Address: Gender and Detective Fiction." *The Sleuth and the Scholar: Origins, Evolution, and Current Trends in Detective Fiction*. Ed. Barbara A. Rader and Howard G. Zettler. Westport: Greenwood Press, 1988. 1–8.

Hofstede, Geert. *Masculinity and Femininity: The Taboo Dimension of National Cultures*. Thousand Oakes: Sage, 1998.

Hornung, Alfred, editor. "Kriminalliteratur." *Lexikon Amerikanische Literatur*. Mannheim: Meyers Lexikonverlag, 1992. 181–183.

Horsley, Lee. *The Noir Thriller*. Houndmills: Palgrave MacMillan, 2001.

Howe, Alexander N. "Introduction. Re-Reading Marcia Muller—Gender, Genre, and the Trauma of Interpretation." *Marcia Muller and the Female Private Eye*. Ed. Alexander N. Howe and Christiane A. Jackson. Jefferson, NC: McFarland, 2008. 1–12.

Humm, Maggie. "Feminist Detective Fiction." *Twentieth Century Suspense*. Ed. Clive Bloom. London: Macmillan, 1990. 237–354.

Iannello, Kathleen P. "Women's Leadership and Third-Wave Feminism." *Gender and Women's Leadership: A Reference Handbook*. Ed. Karen O'Connor. New York: Sage, 2010. 70–77.

Jackson, Christine A. *Myth and Ritual in Women's Detective Fiction*. Jefferson, NC: McFarland, 2002.

Klein, Kathleen Gregory. *The Woman Detective: Gender and Genre*. Urbana: University of Illinois Press, 1988.

Klein, Kathleen Gregory, editor. "Women Times Women Times Women." *Women Times Three: Writers, Detectives, Readers*. Bowling Green, OH: Bowling Green State University Press, 1995. 3–13.

Knepper, Marty S. "Agatha Christie, Feminist." *The Armchair Detective* 16.4 (1983): 389–406.

Knight Stephen. *Crime Fiction: 1800–2000*. New York: Palgrave Macmillan, 2004.

Kramer, Cheris. "Perceptions of Female and Male Speech." *Language and Speech* 20 (1977): 151–161.

Lapidos, Juliet. "There Is a Culture Industry That Gives Its Top Prizes to Women: The Big Literary Awards This Year Have Been Positively Dominated by Female Writers." *The Atlantic*. 14 January 2020. The Atlantic on the Web. 05 October 2021 <https://www.theatlantic.com/ideas/archive/2020/01/where-women-make-blockbusters/604867/>.

Lauzen, Martha M. "The Celluloid Ceiling: Behind-the-Scenes Employment of Women on the Top 100, 250, and 500 Films of 2017." San Diego, 2018. *Center for the Study of Women in Television and Film*. 04 June 2020 <https://womenintvfilm.sdsu.edu/wp-content/uploads/2018/01/2017_Celluloid_Ceiling_Report.pdf.>.

Leonardi, Susan J. "Murders Academic: Women Professors and the Crimes of Gender." *Feminism in Women's Detective Fiction*. Ed. Glenwood Irons. Toronto: University of Toronto Press, 1995. 112–127.

Lindsay, Elizabeth Blakesley. *Great Women Mystery Writers*. 2nd ed. Westport, CT: Greenwood, 2007.

MacShane, Frank. *The Life of Raymond Chandler*. New York: Dutton, 1976.

Martin, Susan Ehrlich, and Nancy C. Jurik. *Doing Justice, Doing Gender*. Thousand Oaks: Sage, 1996.

Martin, Wendy, and Sharone Williams. *The Routledge Introduction to American Women Writers*. London: Routledge, 2016.

McCann, Sean. "The Hard-Boiled Novel." *The Cambridge Companion to American Crime Fiction*. Ed. Catherine Ross Nickerson. Cambridge: Cambridge University Press, 2010. 42–58.

Messner, Michael A. "The Limits of the 'Male Sex Role': An Analysis of the Men's Liberation and Men's Rights Movement's Discourse." *Gender and Society* 12.3 (1998): 255–276.

Mizejewski, Linda. *Hardboiled & High Heeled: The Woman Detective in Popular Culture*. New York: Routledge, 2004.

Muller, Marcia. "Marcia Muller: 'The Time was Ripe.'" *Publisher's Weekly* 241. 32 (1994): 361–362.

Nickerson, Catherine Ross. "Women Writers Before 1960." *The Cambridge Companion to American Crime Fiction*. Ed. Catherine Ross Nickerson. Cambridge: Cambridge University Press, 2010. 29–42.

Oakley, Ann. *Woman's Work: The Housewife, Past and Present*. New York: Pantheon, 1974.

Owoseje, Toyin. "Female 007 Ruled Out by James Bond Producer." *CNN*. 16 January 2020. *CNN on The Web*. 09 February 2021 <https://edition.cnn.com/2020/01/16/entertainment/james-bond-female-broccoli-intl-scli/index.html>.

Panek, LeRoy Lad. *An Introduction to the Detective Story*. Bowling Green, OH: Bowling Green State University Press, 1987.

Prchal, Timothy R. "An Ideal Helpmate: The Detective Character as (Fictional) Object and Ideal Imago." *Theory and Practice of Classic Detective Fiction*. Ed. Jerome H. Delameter and Ruth Prigozy. Westport: Greenwood, 1997. 29–39.

Priestman, Martin. *Detective Fiction and Literature: The Figure on the Carpet*. Basingstoke: Macmillan, 1990.

Prüfer, Jan-Christoph. *Hardboiled Hollywood: Traces of American Heroism and Cultural Change in the Portrayals of the Detective Hero in* The Maltese Falcon *and* The Big Sleep. Saarbrücken: VDM Verlag Dr. Müller, 2007.

Rachman, Stephen. "Poe and the Origins of Detective Fiction." *The Cambridge Companion to American Crime Fiction*. Ed. Catherine Ross Nickerson. Cambridge: Cambridge University Press, 2010. 17–28.

Reddy, Maureen T. *Sisters in Crime: Feminism and the Crime Novel*. New York: Continuum, 1988.

Reger, Jo. *Everywhere & Nowhere: Contemporary Feminism in the United States*. Oxford: Oxford University Press, 2012.

Richards, Linda. "Interview with Sara Paretsky." *January Magazine*. 2001. 15 December 2020 <https://januarymagazine.com/profiles/paretsky.html>.

Roberts, Jeanne Addison. "Feminist Murder: Amanda Cross Reinvents Womanhood." *Feminism in Women's Detective Fiction*. Ed. Glenwood Irons. Toronto: University of Toronto Press, 1995. 94–112.

Romanko, Karen A. *Television's Female Spies and Crimefighters*. Jefferson, NC: McFarland, 2016.

Sayers, Dorothy L. Introduction. *Great Short Stories of Detection, Mystery and Horror: Part I: Detection and Mystery*. London: The Camelot Press, 1949. 9–47.

Scaggs John. *Crime Fiction*. New York: Routledge, 2005.

Schmidt, Jochen. *Gangster, Opfer, Detektive: Eine Typengeschichte des Kriminalromans*. Berlin: Ullstein, 1989.

Schwab, et al. "The Global Gender Gap Report 2017." 2017. *World Economic Forum*. 04 June 2020 <http://www3.weforum.org/docs/WEF_GGGR_2017.pdf>.
Sherrill, Andrew. "Women in Management. Female Managers' Representation, Characteristics, and Pay." 2010. *United States Government Accountability Office*. 06 June 2020 <https://www.gao.gov/assets/130/125312.pdf>.
Showalter, Elaine. *A Jury of Her Peers: American Women Writers from Anne Bradstreet to Annie Proulx*. New York: Knopf, 2009.
Shuker-Haines, Timothy, and Martha M. Umphrey. "Gender (De)Mystified: Resistance and Recuperation in Hard-Boiled Female Detective Fiction." *The Detective in American Fiction, Film, and Television*. Ed. Jerome H. Delameter and Ruth Prigozy. Westport: Greenwood, 1998. 71–83.
Siebald, Manfred. *Dorothy L. Sayers: Leben. Werk. Gedanken*. 1989. Schwarzenfeld: Neufeld Verlag, 2017.
Slotkin, Richard. "The Hard-Boiled Detective Story: From the Open Range to the Mean Streets." *The Sleuth and the Scholar: Origins, Evolution, and Current Trends in Detective Fiction*. Ed. Barbara A. Rader and Howard G. Zettler. Westport: Greenwood, 1988. 91–100.
Suerbaum, Ulrich. *Krimi: Eine Analyse der Gattung*. Stuttgart: Reclam, 1984.
Stewart, Victoria. *Crime Writing in Interwar Britain: Fact and Fiction in the Golden Age*. Cambridge: Cambridge University Press, 2017.
Symons, Julian. *Bloody Murder: From the Detective Story to the Crime Novel: A History*. London: Faber & Faber, 1972.
Synder, Chris, and Linette Lopez. "Tarana Burke on Why She Created the #MeToo Movement — and Where It's Headed." *Business Insider: businessinsider.com*. 13 December 2017. *Business Insider on the Web*. 09 February 2021 <https://www.businessinsider.com/how-the-metoo-movement-started-where-its-headed-tarana-burke-time-person-of-year-women-2017-12?r=DE&IR=T>
"Table 318.30. Bachelor's, Master's, and Doctor's Degrees Conferred by Postsecondary Institutions, by Sex of Student and Discipline: 2015–16." 2016. *National Center for Education Statistics*. 04 June 2020 <https://nces.ed.gov/programs/digest/d17/tables/dt17_318.30.asp?current=yes>.
Taylor, Bruce. "'G' is for (Sue) Grafton." *The Armchair Detective 22.1* (1989): 4–13.
U.S. Bureau of Labor Statistics "Labor Force Statistics from the Current Population Survey: Employment Status of Civilian Noninstitutional Population by Age, Sex, and Race." 2020. *U.S. Bureau of Labor Statistics*. 04 June 2020 <http://www.bls.gov/cps/cpsaat03.htm>.
Van Dine, S.S. "Twenty Rules for Writing Detective Stories." Online Posting. 13 January 2013. Gaslight.mtroyal.ca. 12 November 2020 <https://web.archive.org/web/20130113070900/http://gaslight.mtroyal.ca/vandine.htm>.
Walters, Margaret. *Feminism. A Very Short Introduction*. New York: Oxford University Press, 2005.
Walton, Priscilly L. "'E' Is for En/Gendering Readings: Sue Grafton's Kinsey Millhone." *Women Times Three: Writers, Detectives, Readers*. Ed. Kathleen Gregory Klein. Bowling Green, OH: Bowling Green State University Press, 1995. 101–115.

Warner, Judith, et al. "The Women's Leadership Gap. Women's Leadership by the Numbers." 2018. *Center for American Progress.* 04. June 2020 <https://www.americanprogress.org/issues/women/reports/2018/11/20/461273/womens-leadership-gap-2/>.

Welton, Benjamin. "Dean of Detective Fiction's Decalogue: An Appreciation for Monsignor Ronald Knox." (2014). *The Imaginative Conservative.* 08 April 2020. <http://www.theimaginativeconservative.org/2014/04/dean-detective-fictions-decalogue-appreciation-monsignor-ronald-knox.html>.

White, Kevin. *Sexual Liberation or Sexual License? The American Revolt against Victorianism.* Chicago: Dee, 2000.

Whitney, Phyllis A. "Gothic Mysteries." *Morde, Meister und Mysterien: Die Geschichte des Kriminalromans.* Ed. John Ball. Berlin: Ullstein, 1988. 164–170.

Winks, Robin W. Foreword. *The Sleuth and the Scholar: Origins, Evolution, and Current Trends in Detective Fiction.* Ed. Barbara A. Rader; Howard G. Zettler. Westport: Greenwood Press, 1988. ix–xiii.

Zarya, Valentina. "The Share of Female CEOs in the Fortune 500 Dropped by 25% in 2018." *Fortune.* 21 May 2018. 04 June 2020 <https://fortune.com/2018/05/21/women-fortune-500-2018/>.

Printed in the United States
by Baker & Taylor Publisher Services